I Must Be Dreaming

I Must Be Dreaming

Louise Laughlin

ISBN: 978-0-9815814-3-9
Library of Congress Control Number: 2009932056

Written by Louise Laughlin
Edited and produced by Pamela R. Goodfellow
Book Design: The Printed Page

Back Cover Photo: karamayphotography.com
Stained glass art on back cover by Larry Laughlin

Gahan Wilson cartoon reproduced by Special Permission of *Playboy* magazine. Copyright © by *Playboy*.

The text is set in 12 point Granjon and 11.5 point Cambria on 15 point leading.

Dedication

Whoever said that "Home is where the story begins" struck a familiar note with me. This book is dedicated to my husband, Larry. No matter where we are; together or apart, he is my home.

Acknowledgments

I have always wondered why authors dedicated a page or two of acknowledgements in their books. As a reader, I didn't much care, but felt obliged to peruse the words of thanks as a courtesy. Now, that I've completed the four-year journey of writing this book, I understand. One doesn't get this accomplished alone.

First, I owe thanks to Howard Brooks, who put the idea in my head that Larry's antics were worth sharing with the multitudes. The years we spent in Georgia were often in the company of Howard and his wife, Gloria. Each time Larry would pull one of his stunts, though unintentional, Howard would comment, "There's one for the book."

Five years after we left Georgia and moved back to Arizona, my friend, Francene Adcock, who had taken some creative writing classes in college, started a support group, Creator's Conclave, where we learned about authorship. She told me of a conversation seminar, which I attended. I learned in the seminar that the most important part of writing a book was getting it down on paper. The instructor encouraged the class to have acquaintances read our work and provide us honest feedback. He warned that if our readers were close friends, that the feedback would be biased. I wrote with a fury. When I had about seventy thousand words on anecdotal stories about Larry written, I gave my work to Colleen Ullinger, who was a neighbor I had met where our cabin is located in Forest Lakes, Arizona and to Eric Wiebusch, the account manager at the Residence Inn where I was a regular when I traveled on business to Denver. I didn't know either of them well, but discovered each had an interest and/or a background in creative writing. Their willingness and dedication to reading my very rough draft encouraged me to continue.

It was at a publishing seminar of Paul McNeese that I heard about and met Dr. Pamela Goodfellow. I picked up one of her fliers that advertised her classes on writing the character-based novel. Her instruction and method of critique refined my skills. Granted, I had to rewrite the entire book, but it was worth the effort. She and I shared a similar experience of having watched the men we loved suffer from esophageal cancer. This created a bond of trust and friendship between us. Her developmental editing led to her becoming my producer in the publication of this memoir. I owe a debt of gratitude to her direction and teaching. Thanks, Pam. I could not have finished without you.

I would be remiss if I didn't thank my children, Jason and Jacob for becoming such admirable, supportive and loving young men. I am so proud of you both. Their wives, Jean and Nikki appreciate me as a mother-in-law or at least they tell me that and I believe them. I adore my grandchildren; Madison, Chloe and Dylan and pray for the next grandchild that's destined to show up sooner or later. In the meantime, Bailey and Max, my granddogs have demonstrated their love for me and have never bitten me. I hope you all enjoy reading the honest, sometimes heartbreaking, often hysterical journey of our lives.

Foreword

Esophageal cancer has increased by nearly five hundred percent each year and it annually strikes about sixteen thousand victims, fourteen thousand fatally. Seventy percent of its victims are men. It is two times deadlier than melanoma. I think the reason for the high mortality rate is that most people who get it don't know they have it until it's too late. It can be masked as throat burn, coughing or acid reflux, but the significance is ignored by sufferers and often by physicians.

Researchers believe that obesity, which has increased in the United States, is a strong factor. Alcohol and smoking may be other causes. Untreated, Barrett's Esophagus is considered to be a precursor to cancer. It is caused by gastro esophageal reflux disease (GERD) where contents of the stomach damage the cells lining the lower esophagus. One of the dangers of Barrett's is that some people have no symptoms. There is no relationship between the severity of heartburn to Barrett's, but chronic heartburn is integral in the development of Barrett's.

My husband contributed his acid reflux to heartburn. When his consumption of antacids reached the stage where he popped handfuls versus one or two, he sought medical advice. Larry had an endoscopy, a diagnostic scope procedure, which revealed the valve at the bottom of his esophagus that is supposed to keep acid from creeping up from his stomach had deteriorated. To prevent the reflux, he had a procedure called a tri-fundoplication, where his surgeon took some of his stomach and created a new valve. He was provided an antacid prescription and told he should be fine. Within a year he began having severe chest pains, which prompted visits to the emergency room. A heart attack was ruled out, but another endoscopy revealed he had Barrett's Esophagus.

He carried a few extra pounds of weight, but was not obese. He also drank alcohol, but did not abuse it. He didn't smoke, although he had in his early twenties for a couple of years, but he did chew tobacco. Another thing he did was drink diet soda throughout his workday. The combination of the carbonation on his already damaged digestive system and the aspartame in it are suspect as a cause of his condition.

He was required to have semi-annual endoscopies. Each time a biopsy of his throat was taken from the lining and the polyps that grew. The frequency of this procedure may have saved his life.

Chapter One

Larry was born on January 12, 1946 making him a member of the first class of baby boomers. His birthplace was the small steel town of Massillon, Ohio where fathers labored long hours and mothers stayed home with their children. Newborn boys received a football from the city hospital in the hope that they would grow up to be athletes, and play for the famous Massillon Tiger football team. They had historically had one of the best high school football programs in the United States. Its teams had won numerous state titles and several national titles. Success on the team was seen as these little ones' tickets out of town and away from the sweat and drudgery of the steel mill.

Larry was destined to play football. By the time he was in the sixth grade, he played on a school team. He began maturing in the seventh grade evidenced by the dark facial hairs that had sprouted on his face, which he proudly shaved. Typical for boys of his Irish Catholic heritage, he attended Catholic grade school, which provided him with a disciplined learning environment. Each day began with mass. Larry was soon inspired, both spiritually and

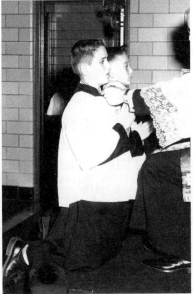

Larry and Joey; altar boys

emotionally, to serve his church as an altar boy. This required that he learn some Latin and the ritual of the mass. It was an honor to achieve this goal. He followed all direction provided to him without question.

One of the perks of his altar boy status was special recognition from the priests. He was one of a few neighborhood boys whom the associate pastor of the church favored and took on long, extended vacations during the summer months. One such trip crossed the country to California. The priest promised it would be a great vacation. One of Larry's schoolmates was also invited. Though the trip itself was a selling point, the priest took time to describe the upcoming events.

"The three of us will take Route 30 out of town and head to Disneyland. We'll even stop at Yellowstone on the way. On the trip home, we'll take Route 66 and stop to see the Grand Canyon."

Larry thanked the priest and went right home. He was thrilled with his good luck invitation and was anxious to tell his parents. He yelled as he ran through the front door.

"Mom, Dad, you won't believe where I'm going."

It was a Saturday evening and Larry went into the kitchen where his mother, Helen, was preparing dinner. His dad, Whitey, had just entered the kitchen from the back door. He had been working in the yard.

"What's all the excitement?"

"Fr. Tony invited me to go on vacation. I'll be the first kid in my class to go to Disneyland. Maybe I'll be the first kid in my class to leave the state of Ohio. I can't wait. Can I go?"

His parents were pleased that Larry's diligence in school and church had earned him an opportunity for travel that they could not provide.

Larry, school picture the year he went to Disneyland

It was difficult enough to feed their brood of six. Vacations were generally out of the question. His mother nodded approval. His dad slapped him on the back in an "atta boy" gesture, which pleased Larry.

"Of course you can go. When do you leave?"

"We leave next Saturday. I'm going upstairs to pack."

That night when Larry was lying in bed still too excited to sleep, his mind wandered to more unpleasant thoughts. On a couple of occasions, Fr. Tony had fondled Larry while teaching him Latin. But, on the other hand, the priest had also bought him big bowls of ice cream and had taken all the boys camping. He hoped he was mistaken. Besides, Joey would also be on the trip. In 1956, young boys and girls didn't question the Church authority figures even if they thought the adult was wrong. Larry was no exception. He resolved he would be fine.

They were only on the road for a few days when the molestation began. Some nights they camped out, but when they stayed in a hotel, the boys took turns sleeping with the priest. This allowed one of them to claim a whole bed for himself. This was a real treat when one considers both boys were from large families and had never known the luxury of an unshared bed.

It began with light fondling. But, the anguish of knowing Larry's turn to sleep with the priest was rapidly approaching became a dread. He even hoped they would camp out more often. He could zip up his sleeping bag, which offered an element of security; or, so he thought. The night they stayed in Yellowstone, they were supposed to camp out, but because of fear of the bears and the hard rainfall, the priest decided they would sleep in the car. It wasn't too comfortable as he and Joey had to share the back seat.

In the middle of the night, Larry awoke suddenly to a sensation that he needed to urinate right away. When he opened his eyes, he saw that Fr. Tony's body was slung over the front seat and his face was between Larry's legs. Larry put his arm straight out toward the priest with his hand flat in a stop motion. Then he rolled over and covered himself up with his sleeping bag. The priest slunk back into the front seat. No words were spoken.

Often while riding the long miles in the quiet car, Larry wondered if the other boy was having the same terrible experience. Though he desperately wanted to talk to Joey about it, he remained quiet. Shame, embarrassment and the lonely feeling of helplessness not only overwhelmed him, but it also forced him to keep the dark, awful secret to himself. He never mustered the courage to ask Joey if it had happened to him.

There was nothing he could do about his situation. He had no money. He was hundreds of miles from home. His parents certainly didn't have the financial means to rescue him. Instead, Larry quietly dealt with the discomfort of his personal nightmare.

After they all arrived home, the priest continued his behavior. Larry tried to oppose the priest's unwelcome advances, but the priest persisted. One Friday night, a couple of years after the molestation began; Larry was at the rectory going over the Liturgy for Sunday morning's mass with Father Tony. Larry and the priest were sitting next to each other on the couch with a bible in their hands. Father Tony reached toward Larry and began to fondle him.

"Why don't you spend the night?"

Larry jumped up from the couch. "I can't. In fact I have to go home right now. My dad has some chores for me to do."

The priest stood up. "Let's go ask him. I'm certain he'll let you stay if I ask."

Larry knew that the priest was right. Whitey would be agreeable. Larry practically lived in the shadows of the church. His house was only the next street away. While Father Tony got into his car to drive around the block, Larry ran home cutting through the familiar grounds of the cemetery. As he dodged some headstones and tripped over others, he prayed for help.

When he reached his yard out of breath and panic stricken, he raced into the small house where he found his dad in the living room watching the Friday night fights. Larry shouted at his father in a pleading manner, talking as fast as he could.

"Dad, Father Tony is on his way here to ask if I can spend the night. Please, please tell him no. Tell him I have chores to do."

Whitey could see the fear in Larry's eyes. Larry could already hear the priest's car pulling into the driveway. He sat down on the heating vent on the living room floor and watched as his father opened the front door. Larry was filled with anxiety as he waited to listen in on the impending conversation. Father Tony came into the living room greeting Whitey with small talk. Larry wrapped his arms around himself and crossed his legs.

"Mr. Laughlin, I'm wondering if Larry could spend the night at the rectory. He and I could work on Sunday morning's mass."

In a firm manner, Whitey declined. "There's work left undone that Larry is responsible to complete tonight."

During the course of conversation, Father Tony asked more than once in his most persuasive manner, each time leaving Larry with the impression that Whitey would change his mind and agree. But, Whitey stood firm. Larry's fears were allayed. He let out a huge sigh of relief and realized he must have been holding his breath for most the conversation. The priest left disappointed, but sent his regards to the family. Whitey confronted Larry.

"What's all this fuss about?"

"Father Tony is a queer."

Whitey hung his head, turned around and walked out the door. They never spoke of that night again; although, Larry always felt his dad understood the real problem. He fantasized that Whitey would pop the priest in the face with his strong fist, but knew it wouldn't happen. It wasn't a topic he could discuss with his dad or anyone else.

Armed with the knowledge that his father had stood up for him at a critical time, Larry gained the confidence to protect himself. Thankfully, by the next year, Larry's physical size became a crucial factor in his defense. At a pivotal point when Father Tony approached him, Larry grabbed the priest by the front of the shirt.

"Stay away from me and don't you ever touch me."

Father Tony never bothered him again.

Larry never told anyone, family or friends, about his horrifying encounters. It was not an open topic of discussion in the fifties. After we had been married for ten years, he finally told me. Even then, more than twenty-two years after the molestation began, Larry cried hurtful tears. His body shook with grief, shame and humiliation. He never sought counseling except for confiding in me. I didn't think it was possible to love him more, but the trust he placed in me created an even closer bond. Though I had never met the priest, Larry's mother had given us a photograph of Larry in his cassock with Father Tony. When I look at it, I see a monster standing by an innocent little boy.

In 2001, when the world was becoming enlightened to the horrific childhoods so many boys endured, Larry decided to call the diocese of his neighborhood church and share his story with the Monsignor. Even then it took tremendous courage to relay what had happened. I offered my support to hold his hand as he relayed the information but he declined.

"I need to do this myself. I cannot allow that horrible man to hurt anyone else."

He dialed the number and asked for the Monsignor, who came to the phone immediately.

"Sir, forty-five years have passed, but my memory has not diminished. Please know that what I'm about to share with you is still difficult to discuss. However, I must tell you what my parish priest did to me beginning when I was ten years old."

Larry told the Monsignor about his experience. He knew Father Tony had dropped out of sight for a few years. In fact, Larry heard a rumor that he had been hospitalized in a mental institution. Though Larry didn't know if that part was true, he did know that Father Tony was active as a priest at the present time.

"I cannot bear the thought of what he might be doing to helpless boys. I want him stopped."

The Monsignor listened to Larry's story without interrupting.

"I'm terribly sorry to hear of these circumstances. Please know our diocese will take immediate action to investigate your claims. I'll call you back as soon as I can."

Larry was relieved that the Monsignor seemed to have believed him without question.

Within days, the Monsignor reported back to him.

"Larry, we appreciate your stepping forward. Subsequent to our conversation, the Bishop interviewed Father Tony and although he didn't specifically remember you, he did apologize for any harm he may have caused you. As a result of that interview, Father Tony has been stripped of all his priestly duties and confined to a retirement home. He will not have access to any children. We would like to offer you counseling if you think it would be of benefit to you."

Larry declined the Monsignor's offer.

"I don't want anything from the Church other than its commitment to prevent Fr. Tony from harming another young victim."

I remember silently wishing that Larry had accepted the counseling as I felt he could have benefited from it. But, in our discussions, he was vehemently opposed to it. He didn't feel he could bare his soul with all of the sordid details to a stranger.

For many years, Larry was estranged from his church. We attended mass on occasion, but made no special effort. I suggested we try another church, but his indoctrination in the Catholic Church would not allow his conscious to switch. We had returned as regular attendees in 2000, which I believe gave him the strength to address his childhood nightmares. The immediate action taken by the Monsignor confirmed he had made the right choice. I was proud of him for his courage to face his years of fear.

We heard through hometown friends that Fr. Tony died a few months later. I suspect his conscience got the best of him. Larry was comforted with the knowledge. I was glad for Larry as it brought finality to the issue.

Chapter Two

My childhood wasn't all bad. My Uncle Chuck influenced my sense of humor from the time I was six. His tall tales caught me off guard and I'd fall for his jokes every time. Once I thought about what he'd said to me, I'd realize he was teasing me. I acquired his style of communication with children and have used the same type of fantastic, unbelievable antics on my sons and my grandchildren since becoming an adult. Uncle Chuck had a positive outlook on life in spite of his confinement to a wheelchair. I enjoyed every visit with him. One hot and humid July day, he called me.

"Have you been outside sledding down the hill in your backyard?"

"Uncle Chuck, it's hot outside. There's no snow."

My uncle lived about eight miles on the other side of town from our family.

"Well, you better get your dad to get you over here quick. Della and Karen (his daughters) are outside right now sliding down the hill next to our house. It's snowing like crazy here."

I was all excited. "I'll come right over."

I hung up the phone and ran to find my mom. "Will you take me to Uncle Chuck's house? It's snowing over there and the girls are out sledding."

My mother grinned at me. "That Chuck is a kidder."

Then she continued with her work without really giving me a yes or no answer. With my shoulders drooping, my arms hanging straight down and my head bowed in disappointment, I went outside. I looked up at the bright sunshine and realized how ridiculous it sounded to be snowing across town. I laughed out loud, headed to my friend's house to play and thought that Uncle Chuck sure was funny and tricky.

Another time I remember being a victim of his joke was when my family visited him.

"Larry. See this new dog we have? He's the smartest dog in the world."

I was eager to see if he knew tricks already. "What makes him so smart, Uncle Chuck?"

"Well, yesterday, he pooped on the carpet. I rubbed his nose in that dodo and carried him upstairs and threw him out the window."

I was shocked that he'd throw a dog out a second story window. The fact that Uncle Chuck couldn't walk up the stairs didn't sink in. "Yikes. I don't understand why that makes him so smart."

"I'll tell you. A little while ago, he crapped in the same spot on the rug. He rubbed his own nose in it, ran up the stairs and jumped out the window on his own."

I was sure impressed with that dog.

I also loved any activity that was played outside. My brother, Kenny, and I would leave on Saturday morning and wouldn't come home until the streetlights came on, as was the rule for most of us in our generation. It never occurred to us that our mother might be worried. Rather, I think she appreciated not having us under foot.

One of the favorite games of the neighborhood boys was a BB gun fight in the church cemetery. We played on the back half of the church property, far enough from the rectory that the priests couldn't see us. It was a spiced up version of hide and seek or could be likened to a game of war. Our ages ranged from ten to twelve. We hid behind headstones and shot at each other when we saw movement. We knew if Father Reichlin, the church pastor, ever caught us, we'd be doing penance for years. We weren't deterred and never thought of it as dangerous. It was fun and exciting to hear the zing of a flying BB. It wasn't until I hit one of the guys right between his eyes that the games stopped. There was blood everywhere, but other than the BB lodged between his eyebrows, there was no permanent damage.

Often times, Father Reichlin recruited a few of us sixth and seventh grade boys to pull weeds and do general clean up in the cemetery. As we worked, Father would walk through the cemetery supervising us and inspecting the headstones. One time, he was so close to me that I could have reached out and touched him. I watched him out of the corner of my eyes as I pulled weeds. Father Reichlin felt a damaged edge of a headstone. He turned his head sideways and leaned forward as he slid his glasses up higher on his nose to get a closer look. He scratched his head. I heard him talk to himself under his breath.

"How are these headstones getting chipped?"

I couldn't believe he didn't know how, but then he had never caught us. I had been on my knees on the ground and had to lean forward with both hands in the grass as I stifled a snicker and pretended not to notice. As soon as he walked away, I straightened my body and waved at a fellow conspirator. I pointed to the headstone damage and then to Father. The boy collapsed on the ground in a fetal position as he laughed. Fear of getting caught in the act, made the regular summer evening game even more exciting. This may have been the catalyst for my enduring interest in extreme sports.

My friend, Johnny Simon and I were in the same classroom at school, although he was in the eighth grade and I was in the seventh. The church school was so small; it was typical to have two grades in one room. We were also both altar boys in our church. Good friends outside of school, we had built a hut in the woods in our neighborhood. On Fridays, we were always in a hurry to get started to make improvements on our weekend project.

During the season of Lent, it was expected for all of the grade school children to attend the Stations of the Cross ceremony at two o'clock every afternoon. There were fourteen plaques on the walls on either side of the church that depicted scenes from the day of the Crucifixion of Christ. The priest, the cross bearer and two altar boys each holding a candle would stand before a station while the priest recited the bible verses that described the action. He'd pray and the group would move to the next station. Neither Johnny nor I wanted to go. We preferred to work on our fort. There was a built in cloak closet on one wall of our classroom where we housed our winter boots and coats each day. We discussed our plan at recess. Our teacher, Sister Marie Celeste, lined up the students two by two in the classroom. We were the last pair. As the students filed out of the classroom, we took a step backward and sneaked into the closet and closed the door.

Sister locked the room and left. We crept back out of our hiding place and tiptoed over to the window. We saw the rest of our fellow students filing into the church, which was the next building across the playground from the building where we hid. When we had determined the coast was clear, we opened the window and shinnied down the water pipe on the outside of the building. We were only on the second floor so even if we fell, we figured we'd be okay.

We hurried out of the schoolyard and ran to the woods behind Johnny's house, which was a couple of blocks away. We worked the rest of the afternoon on our hut and then headed home when the sun began to set.

About six in the evening, our home phone rang. I answered it. I recognized the stern voice of my teacher.

"Is your mother home?"

I gritted my teeth and closed my eyes and thought to myself . . . she knows. But how?

"Yes, Sister, I'll get her."

I called my mother to come to the phone. She and Sister had a long conversation. While they talked, I watched the look change on my mother's face and knew I was toast. Her eyebrows furrowed and her mouth pursed. Mother hung up the phone, walked over to me, grabbed me by the ear and sat me down in a chair at the kitchen table.

"You are in big trouble. You skipped the Stations of the Cross today. Is that right?"

I nodded my head. Now, I was sweating. My dad wasn't going to like this. I knew I'd get spanked.

"Yes. How did Sister know?"

My mother wouldn't let me off that easy. "What were you doing?"

"We were in the woods working on our hut."

I swear my mother stifled a grin. She was good at that. Mother sat down at the table, folded her arms and looked directly at me.

"When your class arrived at the church, Father Reichlin was in the Sacristy. He stuck his head out the door and asked Sister where his altar boys were. She looked at her chart. You were supposed to carry the Crucifix in the procession and Johnny was supposed to carry one of the candles."

I closed my eyes. I was caught.

"Your father will handle this."

My dad whooped me that night. I could tell he wasn't angry, as the swats he rendered weren't too hard.

I knew that wouldn't be the end of it though, and I was right. The following Monday at school, Sister made Johnny and me stand bent over with our hands on our knees so that we faced the class. She spanked us. I watched my friend wince as he received his penance and braced myself. Her swing of the paddle was fiercer than my father's hand and stung my backside. We sure had fun playing at the fort, though.

When I was fourteen, some friends and I camped out a few miles from home one Saturday night. Our escapade started with cruising around town in Ray Fiechter's car, the only sixteen-year-old legal driver among us. We picked up some girlfriends for the ride. I talked Mary Lou Mayloth, a neighbor I'd known most of my life and two years older than I, into teaching me how to kiss. That fun ended when we took the girls home in time for their nine-thirty pm curfew.

We went back to our camp and drank the beer we had acquired from a stag party at the golf course where some of us caddied. It didn't take much to get us drunk. We told ghost stories and recalled special plays at football games. The conversation included girls we liked and our bravado. Someone in the ring around the campfire suggested we go for a little ride even though it was about two-thirty in the morning.

I jumped into the backseat of the car, a couple others joined me, but three boys jumped onto the hood of the car, including Ray, the owner, who sat in the middle. Dale volunteered to drive, but had to hang his head out the window to see the road. The ride was slow down the two-mile stretch of gravel road by the camp. As soon as we turned onto the blacktopped highway, the hood riders saw the headlights of an approaching car. That meant trouble.

"Cops."

The boys on the fender sides of the hood jumped off. But Ray leaped off the front. Dale, an inexperienced driver, not to mention being in an impaired condition, could not react fast enough and ran over him. He slammed on the brakes.

"Shit. I ran over Ray."

We scrambled out of the car to see if Ray was hurt. We discovered that his shoulder was pinned under the wheel. Another two inches forward and his head would have been crushed. While others hollered reactions and foolishness, not knowing what to do, I took action.

"We have to pull him out from under there. I'll move the car a little bit and try to get his shoulder free and his clothes untangled."

What I didn't know was that Ray's foot was also wedged in the framework of the car. My adrenalin was pumping. My primary driving experience at that point in my life was a tractor at the dairy farm where I worked during the summer. I jumped back in the car and threw the gear into reverse, but I stepped on the gas too hard. I dragged Ray about thirty feet. This caused most of Ray's clothes to be torn from his body, but at least he was no longer pinned under the car. We were horrified to see how bad Ray looked, but too stupid to take immediate corrective action.

There had been no real threat of getting caught as the car with the headlights turned down another road. We began to panic. We looked like the Keystone Cops as we bumped into each other concerned how to pick up Ray without causing more injury. We gently put him in the back seat of the car and drove the car back to camp. Billy retrieved a sleeping bag from the pile on the ground where we had dumped them when we arrived. We wrapped it around Ray and left him in the car. Young, dumb and scared, we sat by the fire to drink more beer for courage and conjure up a story to explain what had happened. For thirty minutes, we could hear Ray's moans come from the car. Billy finally walked over to check on him. He opened the door to peek in when Ray grabbed his sleeve.

"Take me home."

Billy jerked back at the unexpected motion from Ray.

"Okay, hang on. Hey you guys, he looks really bad."

We all went over to the car. He was right. Ray didn't look well. We decided we needed to clean him up before we took him anywhere. The only liquid we had was beer. We grabbed the corners of the sleeping bag, pulled him out of the car and poured beer on him.

"Stop. You're hurting me."

Ray's father had suffered a heart attack and had just returned home from the hospital. We knew we were in way over our heads, but didn't want to go there and scare his parents. Dale felt responsible for running over Ray.

"It's my fault. Let's take him to my house."

We all pitched in, grabbed our gear, and threw it in the trunk. We threw dirt on the fire to put it out and drove in to town to Dale's place.

Because we were afraid of the consequences, we wanted to leave Ray on the doorstep, but our better judgment overwhelmed us. Dale's family lived in an upstairs apartment. Dale raced up the stairs taking them two at a time. It was almost four in the morning when he woke his mother. She came down to the car, took one look at Ray, pushed us away, jumped in the car not one bit concerned that she was in her bathrobe and sped to the hospital. It was nice of Dale's mom to take care of Ray. We were all burdened with guilt. We feared the trouble we were in and hoped Ray would have a speedy recovery. Billy, Dale and I went to Billy's barn, climbed into the hay loft and prayed the rosary until we fell asleep.

The next day, I left town with my next older sister, Marlene, who was driving to Oklahoma to visit my eldest sister, Joann. Marlene had invited me to join them a few days earlier, but I wasn't interested until this episode happened. I knew I'd be in a better position to be far away when the incident hit the local paper. This would be big news in our little town. Since everyone was under age, I knew my name would not appear, but I was confident my parents would figure out I had been involved. I thought it better to let them cool off for a couple of weeks before I had to face them. As it turned out, for some reason, my mother and father never heard of our trouble. Fortunately, Ray's injuries were not life threatening; although, he did have a considerable number of stitches and a broken arm. There was a lesson to be learned in regard to drinking and driving, but I doubt any of us took heed, probably because we had escaped punishment. We were invincible. I never found out what Ray's parents did to him, but then I didn't try very hard. I wanted to pretend it had never happened.

What I loved to do the most was play football. I have always been competitive, even when I was young, but I understood the importance of teaming, sportsmanship and winning as I became older. My goal was to get a college scholarship. To do that, it was critical that I achieve high grades in school and play football well.

I decided to go to Central Catholic High School in Canton, Ohio. All of my older siblings had attended there. My brother, Tom, only stayed two years, but Joann and Marlene graduated from Central. The football coach was John McVay, a great, successful leader whom I admired and wanted to play for. The

CO-CAPTAINS
JIM GRYWALSKI   LARRY LAUGHLIN

private school offered a strict learning environment with smaller classes. The first half of my freshman year, I was able to take a school bus from Massillon to Canton, but then my parents built a new house five miles out in the country. There was no school bus or public transportation so I hitchhiked the fifteen miles to school for the next semester and all of my sophomore year. I often caught a ride about a mile from my house with a man who worked in Canton. He'd drop me off about a mile from school. It was worth it to play for McVay.

The summer before my junior year I heard that Coach McVay had accepted an opportunity to coach at Michigan State. Without him at Central, I decided to transfer to Washington High School in Massillon. It would cut ten miles off my commute each way.

The new coach came to my house to speak with my parents and me to coax me to stick with Central. As an added incentive, he told me he'd provide transportation to and from school, a serious consideration for the winter snow season. His promise lasted the first morning of the school year. Coach didn't even get me a ride home that day. I was disappointed with the broken promise and afraid to confront him for fear I would get benched, but it didn't hinder my dedication. I had more integrity than most of the adults I had encountered in my young life and was committed to my team. I chose to hitchhike the fifteen miles each way, every day. This became a dreaded chore after football practice; especially, when the temperature was low and the snowdrifts were high. My competitive spirit and determination kept me going even on those nights when I couldn't get a ride. I would walk along the street frozen from the cold and feel sorry for myself because I didn't have a dime to call home. I kept up that pace until I graduated and while I followed the coach's direction throughout the years, I always thought he was a jerk.

🐤🐤🐤

I excelled in both football and education and earned a scholarship to college. I wasn't perfect, but I was a strong-minded leader among my peers and I knew it. I was co-captain of the football team, a class officer and all around fun guy. To earn tuition, I worked in the cafeteria during the school year and painted the stadium steps in the summer. As Treasurer of the Student Body my senior year, I procured four school buses to transport students to an away basketball game. My buddies and I managed to get on one bus. We headed to a pool hall to have a few beers and play pool when we reached our destination. Most of us were of legal drinking age in the state of Ohio. The game didn't start for an hour after we had arrived. Unfortunately, we didn't keep track of the time and arrived at the basketball game when it was half over. A busload of kids arriving that late did not go unnoticed by school representatives. When we came back home, the prefect of discipline stood outside the school bus door and wrote down all of our names as we exited the bus.

Most of the students received a three-day suspension and forty-five days of after school detention. The principal had other plans for me and called me into his office.

"Larry, I consider you a role model as a leader in this school. In addition to the suspension and detention, you have been stripped of your class officer status, your co-captain football title, your position in the cafeteria and all extracurricular accomplishments."

I stormed out of his office and cursed under my breath. I was furious at being singled out from the crowd of guilty students.

I felt crucified. I went back to my desk, gathered up the stack of ledgers for my treasurer position and headed back to the office.

There was a nun, who sat at the receptionist's desk. She was on the telephone engaged in what seemed like a casual conversation. I tried to wait patiently for her to acknowledge me. I looked at my watch more than once worried I'd be late for the next class. I feared a tardy would bring more punishment. When she continued to ignore me, I reached over the high counter, dropped the books down on the desk and stomped away. The nun slammed down the phone receiver, rose from her seat and ran after me. She grabbed me and managed to push me against the wall in spite of our size difference. Because she was a nun, I didn't put up much resistance.

"Get your hands off me. I've done nothing to you."

I walked away.

"Don't you walk away from me. You'll regret it."

I left anyway and ignored her. I served my detention time and three-day suspension. My parents had no sympathy for my punishment even though the time off caused me to get zeroes for all of my tests and homework on those days and could have had a negative impact on my successful graduation and pending college scholarship. Their attitude was whatever punishment the school rendered I deserved, guilty or not.

The nun's influence on the leaders of the school resulted in another bazaar punishment that has haunted me for a lifetime. Instead of my picture posted on the front page of the class with the other class officers, they put my class picture in the W's where it was difficult to find. Jim Grywalski was my best buddy and co-conspirator in our terrible offense. His picture was in the L's, but he had been allowed to keep his titles.

The school's action has angered me for my entire life. I've managed to retaliate, however. I have abstained from pledging donations for the annual school fund drive. The only thing I've managed to change over the years was to get my named corrected from Lawrence to Larry. Every year my mother would change my name on my report card and send it back. But the nuns refused to accept my name as Larry because that was not a saint's name. This aggravated my mother, but she never protested beyond the passive actions she took changing my name. Now, the school addresses my mail to my rightful name, but I don't send them money. They were wrong.

🐛🐛🐛

My only other disappointment from my high school days was that my father never attended one game to watch me play football. Dad had played in Massillon in the mid 1920s, which were the leather helmet days. One of his teammates was Paul Brown, a legend in professional football. Because of my dad's achievements, I thought he'd be anxious to come to a game. He worked a night shift in the steel mill and couldn't take off. I accepted that it wasn't an option for him, but I never told him or anyone else for that matter until years later that it bothered me. After my father died, my brother-in-law, Roy, and I were having a conversation about football and he told me how proud Dad was of me.

"Your dad listened to every game while he worked at the mill. Whitey told me he was glued to the radio as he listened to the play by play of the announcer with the radio blaring over the din of the steel furnace. He was frustrated that he could not be there in person."

I felt a twinge in my gut when he told me about my dad. I would have loved to have known that he was with me in spirit while I played. My father was not a demonstrative man and a little bit of love and emotion would have gone a long way with me. Had I known this at the time, it may have influenced decisions I made in college. I always thought no one cared what I did as long as I didn't get in trouble. I made up for the lack of attention from my parents by becoming a clown, prankster, and storyteller. My friends liked it and it made me feel good to entertain them.

I was recruited to play football at Arizona State University for Coach Frank Kush. I was flown to Arizona for a familiarization weekend to see the school and learn about the football program. When I left Ohio, it was snowing so I was wearing heavy corduroy pants, a sweater and a Navy pea coat. When I arrived, the coaches greeted me dressed in shorts and short-sleeved shirts. Springtime there was radically different. During the flight, the attendants had served food, but I had declined, as I had no money. I had never flown before and didn't know it was included in my airfare. I was hungry when we landed, so Coach Kush and Coach Tamburo took me for lunch at Bill Johnson's BBQ near the airport. They told me about the football program while I ate.

"So, Larry, do you think you'd like to play football for Arizona State?"

I gazed outside and realized I was squinting at the bright sunlight that filtered through the windows.

"Coach, I don't think I even need to see the school. Sign me up."

The coaches took me to the school, though, to seal the deal and showed me the campus and stadium. It solidified my decision. That night, they took me to Pinnacle Peak for a steak dinner. The only steak I had ever had, up to that moment, was round steak. There were six kids in our family; too many for my parents to afford a better cut of meat. In 1964, Pinnacle Peak seemed miles out in the desert. We drove from Tempe down Scottsdale Road. The road north of Camelback Road was gravel. I didn't have a solid trust of adults and could not imagine where they were taking me. My patience was rewarded, however, when I took the first bite of my steak. I have never tasted better. The food was so memorable that in the years since, Louise and I have taken friends and family, who have visited us in Arizona to the same place for a steak dinner.

🐤🐤🐤

Larry — football at ASU

I came back to Arizona in August for pre-season training and to begin my new life in college. I was a bit homesick by Thanksgiving, but I adjusted. It seemed to take no time at all to store away the bad memories of my childhood and the last semester of high school. In my sophomore year, I met a freshman girl and fell in love. I was so serious about this girl that I took her home to meet my parents at Christmas time. We even discussed marriage.

One evening toward the end of summer before I had to report for pre-season practice, I asked my girlfriend to go out.

"I can't go. I'm sorry. I have a school project I have to work on."

I didn't think much about it. I met up with Stan, a guy my girlfriend had gone to high school with and introduced to me. My good football buddies had not yet arrived for the school year. Stan wanted to stop by the dorm to talk to his girlfriend for a few minutes before we went to play pool.

I waited in the car. As we were leaving, I spotted my girlfriend walking across the street with a young man. I was furious.

"She lied to me."

She had books in her hand, but she had failed to tell me about her study partner. Stan knew who the guy was.

"Don't get so upset. He's one of our high school friends."

I knew better. That guy had been her boyfriend in high school.

"I want to talk to him."

Stan agreed to drive me so we followed him all the way to Goodyear. It was just thirty-five miles away, but in 1967, there was no freeway and it seemed like a hundred. I fumed the entire way, which caused my imagination to run wild. When we caught up to him, I screamed at him. I don't even know what I said, but I had to get the rage out of my system. Stan shrugged his shoulders when the guy looked to him for help. The whole scene only lasted about ten minutes, and then I nudged Stan.

"Let's go back to the dorm."

I never touched the guy, but I knew I had frightened him. I had scared myself a little to think I could become so angry.

My girlfriend was furious with my behavior. I was equally upset with her misleading excuse for not going out with me. It was another occasion where someone whom I cared for had betrayed me. We never talked through the situation, as she would not listen to my side of the story. She assumed I had done more than scream. This traumatic scenario haunted me. When the team went to Camp Tontazona for training, I couldn't concentrate on football. All of my thoughts were with the unfinished business with my girlfriend. The second day of practice, one of my teammates was kicked off the team for lack of performance. Because of my preoccupation with my girlfriend, it was the excuse I needed to quit. I walked off the field and headed for the highway. A younger player, Jimmy Kane, who I had helped to recruit, followed me. I got into an altercation with him.

"Go back. You can't walk out on your scholarship."

"I'm coming with you, Lock."

Lock, short for Laughlin, was a nickname I'd had a long time, but only my close friends ever called me that. I knew I had to try to convince Jimmy to stick with the program even if I was making a mistake.

"No you're not."

He wouldn't go back so we hitchhiked the hundred miles back to Tempe. The next day, Jimmy returned to camp, but I slipped out of sight. I wanted to be alone. In spite of the reasons I left camp, I didn't call my girlfriend. In fact, I avoided her. I found a job, a room to rent and walked away from my scholarship and college life. I had sense enough to convince my friend he should stay with the team, but not enough to recognize my irrational behavior. My decision to leave the team that day has haunted me all my life. I feel now that walking out on my scholarship let down my team, my coach, my family and myself.

Chapter Three

spent the summer of 1967 working in a restaurant that my aunt managed in California. I had split up with my boyfriend of two months and even though it was a short relationship, I had been smitten. I thought the change of scenery would be exactly what I needed in order to move on. I loved my aunt and her family, but I was bored a good deal of the time I was away from home. I went on a few dates with a couple of the men at work, but they were just friends; not love interests.

When I returned in late September, I went back to work at our family's pizza parlor in Scottsdale, Arizona. That's when I met Larry. My brother had hired him while I was gone. The Pizza Pub was one of three part-time jobs Larry held after he left college. Generally, once the dinner rush hour was over, only two people worked the rest of the night. Larry was my co-worker on my first shift after I came home. Larry worked the bar during the dinner hour. After everyone else had gone home, he gave me directions as if he were my supervisor.

"Louise, you work the bar for the rest of the shift and I'll take the pizza kitchen. That way, you can clean the back kitchen."

My reaction was not pleasant as I resented him giving me orders even though the jobs were equal. The fact that I didn't mind tending bar or washing the pots in the big kitchen in the back was beside the point. My first impression of Larry was that he was too bossy and aggressive. While he didn't know I had worked in the Pub for months before going to California; he should have known I didn't need instructions since my parents owned the restaurant.

"I've worked here longer than you have. I know the routine. I should delegate the work."

Larry walked back to the prep area in the pizza kitchen and muttered something under his breath as he went. I'm quite certain it was something like "bitch." I agree it was a little bitchy, but at least he knew where I stood.

The next shift we worked together, Larry tried to impress me with his bullshit stories.

"Did you know that our family owns Jones and Laughlin Steel Corporation?"

"Really? Why don't you have a car if your father is so prosperous?"

It insulted me that he'd fabricate a story like that and expect me to believe it. Besides he told me he was from Ohio and when I asked him where this steel mill was, he told me it was in Pennsylvania. His behavior did not have the effect on me that he had expected. Instead of my being impressed, I thought he was a liar. If I knew then what I know now, I would have realized it was the Uncle Chuck effect, harmless, but incredible. Instead of being mad or insulted, I should have laughed and played along.

Jack told me Larry was formerly a football player at Arizona State University. I thought that explained why he was so full of himself. I couldn't stand the thought that Larry would assume I'd be attracted to him because he was a jock, even if he was handsome. I knew I could be gullible; therefore was guarded when he told me his stories. After I had declined his several invitations for a date, he sent me a single rose. The card read, "Smile today or your flower will die." I couldn't wipe the grin off my face. I enjoyed the attention because it felt sincere.

When I was a little girl, my mother used to compare me to the cartoon character, Ferdinand the Bull because all I ever wanted to do was smell flowers. I was playful, but mellow and I never caused trouble. I had a great imagination and believed in fairy tales. Cinderella was my favorite.

As I grew older, I dreamed about Prince Charming. Although faceless, I knew my prince was handsome, strong and had a great sense of humor. Though I didn't recognize Larry as my Prince Charming immediately, I soon experienced an awakening.

I was in the back room of the Pizza Pub one evening shooting pool with my friend, Carol Masterton. I spotted Larry coming in the front door with a girl.

"Here comes that new guy. He's such a braggart."

Larry brought his date to the back room and introduced her to Carol and me. He put his quarter on the table to be next in line for a game. The whole time we played, Larry entertained all of us with his antics. When our game was over, Carol and I sat down at a table across the room. Carol liked him as she thought he was cute and fun.

"Why are you hesitant? Go out with him. He seems like a fun guy."

I had recently started dating an old boyfriend with whom I had developed an on-again, off-again romance over four years, but there was something about Larry that particular night that changed my opinion of him. Perhaps it was the flower he'd sent. I sensed there was much more to him than he had allowed me to see. Maybe the bravado was a screen. I was finally tempted to find out.

Larry and his date left, but an hour later he came back to the Pub. Carol and I were still shooting pool. I was pleasantly surprised to see him come back.

"I borrowed my friend's car. Do you want to go out now?"

Carol nudged me.

"Go."

I took Larry's hand. "I'll go, but just for awhile. I have to work a day shift tomorrow."

To this day, Larry claims he was persistent in asking me out because Jack didn't like the guy I had been dating and had paid Larry ten dollars to take me out. Whenever he tells that story, I always add that my brother then paid me fifteen dollars to go. No one will ever know the truth. Jack won't tell. Larry won't tell and neither will I.

❧ ❧ ❧

We went out on a few after work casual dates, but our first official date was for the Homecoming Game at ASU. Larry told me to get dressed up, as he wanted to surprise me with a special evening. I wore my favorite green velvet dress. Larry brought me a beautiful gold mum corsage. It was the perfect final touch. Since Larry was also decked out in his finest, I felt certain that we would go to the

Larry and Louise ready for the ASU Homecoming game

homecoming dance after the game, which would have been a special treat.

Larry had purchased an old Model A Ford that sometimes started without being pushed. But not that night. So Larry pushed the car while I popped the clutch until it started. Off we went to the game. After the game, I was filled with anticipation and thoughts about the dance. Instead, we went to the Oxbow Tavern, which was a smoky bar with one pool table. Larry and I sat in the back room around a huge table with several football players. The Oxbow was the favorite hangout of the team at that time. All they talked about the entire evening was the football game.

"What a game."

"Did you see that hit at the end of the third quarter?"

"How about that touchdown"

"That was the best block I'd ever seen."

I didn't participate in the conversation—not at all. While this was not how I had envisioned our date would turn out, it wasn't all that bad. It occurred to me as I listened that the game tickets and corsage were the extent of Larry's budget. I realized he was showing me off to his buddies, which was fine with me. I concentrated on the fact that here I was, the lone female sitting among several Arizona State football stars. I looked around the table. These guys were handsome hunks. I wondered if they brought their dates to this place very often. I bet they thought it was strange, me all dressed up and sitting there drinking beer with them.

They were polite to me and accepted me as part of the group. I was Larry's date; therefore, their friend. I drank my beer and enjoyed the view. I watched Larry interact with them and swelled with pride. Even though, he was no longer a player, it was evident he was still a member of their clan. It wasn't until years later that he confided that it was one of the biggest mistakes in his life to quit the team. I had a different opinion.

"I think it was the best decision you've made because you probably wouldn't have met me if you hadn't quit."

When one considers the many years we have been married, he had no argument and he knew it.

"You're the best thing that's ever happened to me."

He had the right answer to my observation.

What drew me to Larry was his sense of humor and animation when he told stories. His looks, however, had a flaw. My best friend since I was fourteen, Linda Brady, often teased me because the first thing I'd notice about a potential date was his smile and teeth. Larry had a great smile, but he flunked the nice teeth requirement. He was missing three of his front teeth; one of the hazards of being an aggressive football player. Consequently, he had an upper dental plate. To be funny, he would remove the partial and perform his Jackie Gleason's Joe, the bartender's visitor, Crazy Guggenheim impression. The patron, Guggenheim would ask for a beer and stare at Gleason.

"I'm not doing nuttin'. I was just standing here."

When Larry was included in our family gatherings, my young nephews delighted watching this routine and requested it to be repeated often. I liked how patient he was with the boys and how happy he was to accommodate them. His personality surpassed his flaw; not to mention he had potential as a future dad.

෯ ෯ ෯

As I became more acquainted with Larry, my infatuation with him grew to love. Like Larry, I had also had a love interest before we met. Marriage had been a consideration for me in that relationship. However, Larry demonstrated so much caring and love for me in the short time I'd known him that I broke up with my former boyfriend two months after I met Larry. During the two-week Christmas/ New Year's Eve Holidays, I went to my home state of Michigan to be an attendant in two of my cousins' weddings. I believe my absence solidified our feelings for one another. Larry had bumped into his old college sweetheart while Christmas shopping when I was away. It had been the first time he'd seen her since the previous summer before he went to football camp. At first, the memory of her filled him with conflicting emotions. The Christmas before, he had taken her home to meet his family because he had considered asking her to marry him. At this point, however, he felt indifferent. He met her that week for a date, but afterward, he never called her again. To him, his former long-term relationship was over. When I returned home, I had Larry's undivided attention.

While I was gone, Larry worked my one-day shift for me at the Pizza Pub. There were two local National Guards men, who usually stopped by once a week after work to have a beer or two. As usual, they came in, but Larry was tending bar, not I. One of the guys perused the room and had a puzzled look on his face.

"Where's that blonde who usually works here?"

32

Larry stopped washing beer mugs and made eye contact with the speaker.

"Why do you need to know?"

The weekend warrior leaned over the bar to make his conversation more personal.

"I'd really like to do her."

Larry reached over the bar, grabbed the guy by the neck of the shirt, nearly lifting him clear off the floor, and punched him square in the nose.

"That's my wife."

Jack rushed over from the pizza kitchen and broke up the impending confrontation. He took Larry aside.

"It's not a good idea to punch the customers. In fact, it's terrible for business."

The customer decided he might actually have deserved the punch and didn't complain. He paid for his beer and left. After I returned to Arizona from Michigan, Larry told me the story. I only heard one word . . .

"Wife? You called me your wife?"

I felt good about this. I had hoped we were both on the same track. He squirmed a bit as if he was uncomfortable with the conversation all of a sudden.

"Well, girlfriend wouldn't have been strong enough."

I logged the event into the Rolodex in my brain for future consideration.

🍑 🍑 🍑

We worked four night shifts a week together. As Larry had suggested the first night I met him, I tended bar and washed the kitchen dishes while Larry made pizzas and cleaned the prep area in the pizza kitchen. The routine worked.

Larry was renowned among us Pizza Pub workers as the best sauce maker. We used a fifteen-gallon container for all of the ingredients. The spices were particularly hard to mix in evenly when using a long handled spoon. Frustrated with the process, Larry called me into the kitchen one day.

"Check this out. I fixed the spice mixing problem."

Larry put his whole bare arm in the container and stirred.

"My mother would freak out if she saw you stirring that sauce with your hairy arm."

The word spread quickly among the workers. They thought it was hysterical. Our new name for the Pizza Pub sauce was the pube lube.

We both had Wednesday nights off and had the same routine each week. One of Larry's three jobs was coaching a youth football team at Our Lady of Mount Carmel Catholic School in Tempe, AZ. I babysat my nephews, Jimmy and Michael during the day. The four of us would go to the school for football practice. The boys and I watched as Larry worked. When Larry finished, we'd take the boys home, head to the take out chicken restaurant and go to Larry's place to eat and watch the weekly TV movie. We acted like an old married couple and it felt comfortable.

One of those nights, we fell asleep on the living room floor as we watched the movie. I woke up at six o'clock in the morning. I was frantic. I was twenty-one years old, but had moved back to my parents' house at my dad's request. Other than temporary moves home when I was in between apartments, I hadn't lived with my family since I was seventeen. My dad was a man of few words, but he loved me.

"You'll be out of the house and married soon. I'd like you to move home until you do."

I was happy to be home with no restrictions. I was respectful, however, of their house rules, which didn't include spending the night at my boyfriend's house. I also had my dad's truck. I raced the few miles home. When I entered the house, the kitchen light above the stove was still on for me. I tiptoed over to the stove to turn the light off. I was about to push the button when a quiet, low voice spoke from the next room.

"You can leave it on. I've been waiting for you so I could go to work."

I walked into the dark living room.

"Oh, Dad, I'm sorry. I fell asleep at Larry's house watching the movie."

I felt badly that my father was disappointed in me, but I knew he'd forgive me. I had never let him down before. I also knew he wouldn't tell my mother. It would be our secret. That afternoon, I was at the Pub tending bar. My dad stopped in for a beer. I apologized to him again. He stood close to me at the end of the bar.

"It's okay. You're grown up now, but don't do it again while you live under my roof. I was worried about you."

I gave him a hug and assured him the behavior wouldn't be repeated. I also knew that he liked Larry a lot and would be quick to forgive. He went into the back room to play a game of pool with my brother, whose shift had just ended. I knew Larry would stop by after he finished work at his third job; loading trucks for a meat packing company. The windows in the pub were dark gold opaque and rippled. While I could not actually see through them, I recognized the outline of Larry's Model A car pulling into the parking lot. I ran out the front door and told him that my father was inside.

"He's not happy about last night, but if you tell him you're sorry, he'll forgive you. He's in the back room shooting pool with Jack."

I went in the front door, but Larry waited a few minutes and headed in through the side door. I walked in from the other direction in time to see Larry standing in the doorway. He called out to my dad by his nickname.

"Hey Buster, I want to . . ."

That's all he got out of his mouth before my father raised his pool cue above his head and started running toward the back door.

"You . . . you kept my daughter out all night."

Larry did an about face and ran across the parking lot. My dad stopped at the doorway and buckled over in laughter. When Larry thought there was a safe distance between them, he turned around to see where my dad was. Dad waved him back.

"It's okay. I'm kidding you."

Larry walked back real slowly to make certain Dad wasn't angry. When he reached the door, Dad put his arm around Larry's shoulders.

"Come on . . . I'll buy you a beer. To make certain we understand each other, though. Don't let it happen again."

Larry shook Dad's hand. "No sir. You can count on me."

They played a game of pool and my dad won. Somehow I knew he would.

ಶ ಶ ಶ

Because Larry had dropped out of school, the draft board caught up with him. Ultimately, he received his draft notice in March 1968. Viet Nam had heated up and no one was exempt except full time students. While this was no surprise, we had hoped no one would notice his college hours had dropped below the minimum required for full time status. The only draftees who avoided induction were designated as 4F such as Larry's younger brother, Kenny, whose eye had been shot out in a gun accident when he was a senior in high school.

There were thousands of men being drafted for a war we knew little about. It was over there, not here. The news coverage on Viet Nam was minimal in the early spring of 1968. Certainly, we didn't know of the enormous number of casualties. The now famous protests happened later that year. Besides, I was such a Pollyanna that I didn't consider he could be killed. Rather, I just knew I'd miss him while he was away. Although Larry was not excited about being drafted, he felt a duty to serve his country. He depended on the decisions of the government, in spite of his lack of trust of his elders caused by the broken promises of his youth. He continued his obedient behavior as many of us in our generation did. We felt no entitlements; rather, gratitude for what had been given to us by our parents and others. Further, we didn't question the decisions the leaders of our country made. Larry and I both felt they wouldn't send young men to fight in an unnecessary war. We avoided discussions about his impending absence. Instead, we lived for the moment.

Mary Durand, one of Larry's friends who was also from Ohio, lived in an apartment near the college. It was our gathering place no matter what the reason. People would drop by unannounced. We were all drawn to her. She was generous and kind and never seemed to mind her apartment being invaded by unexpected guests. Everyone loved and respected her. She had transferred to ASU from St. Mary's College by Notre Dame. The convent atmosphere at that school never matched her lively personality. She had a way with words; many of which were unrefined. She cared for and loved all of her friends and welcomed me as if we had known each other for years. Mary's beauty shone from within.

"Let's have a going away party for the Lock."

Mary invited the guests, prepared for the party and made a big poster.

"Everyone needs to sign it. We'll hang it on the wall for Larry to see when he comes in the door."

Only Mary could come up with a poster that read God is 1A too.

When we arrived, Larry was thrilled at the acknowledgement his friends demonstrated with their attendance and the party decorations. We didn't, however, recognize the special meaning in the poster words that night. At our young college age, we thought we were indestructible. As the years passed, we discovered through God's protection, that He was, indeed, 1A in our life.

Larry and Louise — going away party

Larry was called in for his active duty physical exam. The doctor had Larry stand on the scale.

"Son, I'm sending you home. You're two pounds overweight. The Army can't take you."

He came by my house on his way home to tell me the news.

"The doctor sent me home. I think he had also been drafted and I suspect he was trying to keep me from going to Viet Nam."

Unfortunately, the draft board had another opinion. Larry got another draft notice a couple of weeks later. So much for the hope they'd forget about him.

Our college friends threw another going away party. I suspect this was not really an inconvenience, rather, a good reason to have some fun. Larry followed the same routine and reported for his physical exam. He jumped on the scale.

"I'm sorry to tell you that you are still overweight by two pounds. I can't pass you."

Larry left with a slight smile on his face and renewed bounce in his step. When he received his third draft notice and attended his third going away party, the trip to the enlistment center ended differently.

"Doc, I'm never going to lose those two pounds because my friends keep throwing me parties the night before my physical. You have to take me this time. My friends are getting tired of the drill. Besides, I'm ready to serve my country."

On the day of his induction, I drove Larry to the Army center. All of a sudden, reality hit me and I started crying. I noticed Larry's eyes had misted as he looked at me before he opened the door of the car.

"I want you to move on and start dating other men again."

I shook my head no. "I don't want to date anyone else. I love you."

He stared down toward the floorboard and was quiet a moment. He inhaled a deep breath and as he exhaled, he looked directly at me.

"I may not survive and I don't want you to be sad. If I do live and you're still available in two years, we can renew our relationship then."

My eyes filled and I couldn't stop the tears from cascading down my face. He kissed me goodbye and left. As I watched him walk away from me, I thought it might be the last time I would ever see him.

Within three months after meeting him I knew I wanted to marry him. All he had to do was ask, but he didn't. My heart was breaking. Carol Masterton, my friend who had encouraged me to date Larry, lived a few blocks from the induction center. I drove right there because I didn't think I could see to drive home. I stayed at her apartment all day crying. I secretly hoped Larry would call me there to tell me he had changed his mind and ask me to wait for him. I didn't hear from him. My sobs became uncontrollable and caused me to become physically sick. I lay on the couch until I finally fell asleep. The rest helped me to calm down. When I awoke,

I drove home. I felt like Scarlett O'Hara. I'd think about all of this another day.

ॐ ॐ ॐ

Larry was sent to Ft. Lewis, Washington for his basic training. It rained every day for six weeks. The rigorous training included learning how to shoot an M16, defending one's self with a bayonet, strengthening the body with exercise and lots of running in the rain. In addition, an outbreak of spinal meningitis on the post forced all trainees and staff to be quarantined to their barracks, except for training. During this long, dreary period, Larry became very lonesome. He wrote me often.

"I miss you more than I could have imagined."

This was endearing to me. I wrote him back and told him of my activities. I even sent him a care package of homemade chocolate chip cookies and Hershey bars. Even though I did go out on an occasional date as he had requested, my heart belonged to Larry. Mostly, I went to the drive-in movies with Linda Brady; a routine we'd begun in high school. We'd bring our own snacks and sodas so we could wear our flannel nightgowns under our trench coats. We had to have the coats in case we had to go to the bathroom. Otherwise, our attire was our own little secret. I think Larry tired of reading about my escapades. Even though, he was the one who had encouraged me to go out and have fun, he didn't want to hear about it. One night, he snuck away from the barracks and called me.

"Louise, I've changed my mind. I can't stand the thought of you dating anyone else. Will you wait for me?"

I couldn't have been happier to hear those words. "Of course, I will."

Larry wouldn't have risked asking me to commit to him unless he was serious about us as a couple with a future. I felt the same about him and was content to be his exclusively.

40

ತ್ರ ತ್ರ ತ್ರ

After basic training was over, he was scheduled to attend AIT (advanced infantry training) at Fort Sill in Lawton, Oklahoma. There he learned how to fire all artillery weaponry such as the 102, 105, 8 inch, 155 and 175 Howitzers. In addition, there was classroom instruction on judging coordinates, map reading, fire direction control, munitions, laying the battery on all six guns and forward observation; all critical elements in war. As the Infantry is known as the Queen of Battle, Artillery is known as the King of Battle and Larry was taught to know the King very well. Following AIT, Larry went to NCO (Non-Commissioned Officer) Academy where on successful completion he was promoted to Sergeant in charge of a Howitzer section. From start to finish, he was in training for nine months.

In peacetime, it took years to reach the rank of Sergeant. Because of the brevity of the training and speed of the promotion, soldiers called the graduates "shake and bake sergeants." In this emergency situation, young soldiers, like Larry were prepared to lead men into battle and understand the gravity of their leadership. They would be responsible for lives other than their own. The infantry troops the artillery would be supporting were those under direct fire. The speed with which Larry's section could react would make a significant difference in saving lives. At the end of this instruction, Larry was Viet Nam bound.

Larry became more informed about the conflict overseas as he mingled with soldiers who had been to Viet Nam in the months he spent at Ft. Sill. The men, who had returned spoke freely about how they felt about the war.

"The people in South Viet Nam do not want industrialization or democracy. They just want to have their little hooch and a bowl of rice."

This, of course, concerned Larry because he knew he was going there. The conversations planted doubt in his mind on whether or not placing his life on the line was justified. Larry didn't share anything he had heard with me. Rather, he shielded me so that I would not be alarmed. As I look back on those days, I am grateful for his protection. It helped me to cope with his absence more easily.

Since Larry hadn't seen his family for a couple of years, he applied for and received two weeks leave in between training units. He called to tell me.

"I'm going home to Ohio to see my parents in August. Will you meet me there?"

I was thrilled that he wanted me to meet his family. I hadn't seen Larry since he had been inducted three months earlier. Our letters and an occasional telephone call had been our only communication. To see him in person was a big motivation.

"I'll do my best to figure out a way to get there."

I knew I couldn't afford to fly, but I had a car. If I could manage to get a job and stay the summer, it would be a reasonable solution. I called our friend, Mary, who had thrown the parties for Larry and who was home in Salem, Ohio for the summer. She was from a large family, who were primarily college age or better.

"Larry is going to Massillon, on leave this summer. He'd like for me to meet his family so that we can become acquainted. Any chance I could stay with you so that I could see him on his leave."

There was no hesitation from Mary.

"Absolutely, we'll have a blast. In fact, I bet my mother can help you get some sort of job at the hospital. You can stay as long you want."

Mary's mother was happy to oblige and did get me a job in the billing department for the summer at the local hospital where she was the Nurse Administrator. This helped pay for my drive to Ohio in addition to allowing plenty of opportunity to visit with Larry's parents, sixty miles away, on the weekends. Perfect. Before I left, I shared a portion of one of Larry's letters with my mother.

"Mom, I want you to read this to see if you think Larry wants to marry me. He hasn't said it in those specific words, but why else would he want me to go to Ohio?"

My mom was thoughtful in her response.

"The way I read this is that he loves you. Meeting his parents is the first step toward a future together."

"So, you think I should go?"

"I think it would be fine. You haven't seen him in a while. This would be a good opportunity to see if you're still as serious about him."

Both of my parents loved Larry. He had already become an integral member of our family.

My next challenge was the drive from Arizona to Ohio by myself. One of the regulars at the Pizza Pub, a Viet Nam Vet named Terry, was from Illinois. All I really knew about him was that he had lost his sight in one eye in Viet Nam. He seemed nice enough. When he heard I planned to drive to Ohio, Terry offered to split the gas expenses and driving if he could hitch a ride home. He seemed excited to have the opportunity to get back to family.

"We could drive straight through to Illinois by taking turns sleeping while the other person drives."

I agreed with one exception. It was the end of June and Larry wouldn't be in Ohio until August when he would be on leave from training.

"I want to stop and see Larry in Oklahoma on the way. Do you mind stopping there and paying for your own hotel room for two nights?"

Terry had hoped to drive straight through, but it was still a cheaper deal for him than flying. We shook on it.

The first stop was Lawton, Oklahoma. It seemed to take forever, as I was anxious to see Larry. Terry and I didn't have much in common so we drove in silence most of the time. Though somewhat boring, it was better than driving alone. We arrived on

Friday evening. Terry went his way and I went mine. I didn't see him again until late Sunday afternoon.

Larry had to work Saturday morning, but had the afternoon and all day Sunday off. The only time we ventured out of the hotel room was for food. It was more fun to watch television and spend the short time together alone. On Sunday afternoon, before Terry and I were scheduled to leave, Larry and I drove to a desolate spot on the base. I had already checked out of the hotel and Larry wanted to talk privately with me. Based on the love he had professed in his letters and the great weekend we'd just had, I thought Larry was going to pop the question. Nope. It was quite the opposite.

"I love you, Louise, but I'm going to Viet Nam. I hope you'll wait for me. I'm excited about seeing you again on my leave. But, we need to wait to get married. If I get killed, I don't want you to be a widow."

Sheesh. Two "buts." The truth always comes after the "but." I could barely respond because my throat was constricting. I wondered if I had set myself up for disappointment by expecting too much. There was something in his eyes that betrayed what he spoke. I didn't think he believed his own words about marriage. I wanted to be his wife now, not put it off for a couple of years. I had always been a patient person, but this would be difficult.

"I'll wait."

What I really think I had agreed to was waiting until he changed his mind. I dropped him off at his barracks. We kissed goodbye. I drove back to the hotel, picked up Terry and we headed for Illinois. Terry had to drive at first because I was still crying. I slept for a little while then took my turn at the wheel. When we arrived at Terry's aunt's house, I was exhausted. My only other cross-country experience in a car was when I was fourteen years old and my dad had done all the driving. I had hoped Terry's aunt might extend an invitation to me to spend the night. Instead, she offered me the use of their bathroom to freshen up. An hour later, at two o'clock in the afternoon, I was on the road again by myself. I wasn't as frightened to go on alone; as I was fearful I wasn't rested enough for the trip. I figured it was only two states away. I didn't realize it was about four hundred and fifty miles to Larry's parents' house.

I had convinced myself it wouldn't take too long. However, a couple of hours later, I felt myself getting drowsy. When my head nodded in a jerk like fashion, I pulled off the road, slept for thirty minutes and then drove on. I entertained myself by singing songs as loud as I could from the musicals Oklahoma and South Pacific. I knew most of the words because my mother and I would put those records on the stereo and play them while we cleaned house on Saturday mornings. It was the only good thing about the weekly chore.

I also mused about the only time I had spoken to Larry's mother. I had called her from Arizona to ask if I could stop at their house to meet them on my way to Mary's house in Salem. As we began our conversation, my eleven-year-old sister Laura's chicken jumped on my head.

"Someone get this chicken off my head."

Larry's mother, Helen, started laughing.

"Did you just say chicken? Why on earth do you have a chicken in your house?"

I was mortified but I managed to explain the unusual pet. "My little sister, Laura, was the lucky kid who got to bring the class project home. It's getting too big to keep it in its box."

His mother seemed intrigued to meet me. Other than the chicken incident, I didn't know why. I was a little nervous about meeting them, but I was so tired, all I cared about was whether or not, they'd offer to let me stay the night. They didn't disappoint me.

When I arrived at Larry's parents' home at ten-thirty that night, the family was on the front porch waiting for me. They told me a few years later; they couldn't wait to see this girlfriend who was willing to drive across the country to see their son. His mother stood and smiled at me.

Matching beards

"Welcome to our home. You are much more attractive than the picture Larry sent."

Larry had warned me that the only picture she had seen of me was one taken on a day when Larry and I found a full-face, fake beard. Larry had a natural full beard so I had donned the fake one and had a friend take our picture. We were sitting on the ground with our arms and legs wrapped around each other like a pretzel. The fake beard even matched my hair color. We looked like twins.

"You look much better without the beard."

At first I was upset with Larry for doing that, but as it turned out, it broke the ice. We sat on the porch and talked for a short while when Larry's mother acknowledged I must be tired.

"We have an extra bed, if you'd like to spend the night."

"I'm exhausted. Thank you."

I grabbed my overnight case out of the car and followed Helen to the room that Larry and his brother had shared when they were both living at home. I was overcome with emotion from my long drive and my first encounter with his parents. They were as nice and as welcoming as Larry had promised they would be. I was asleep within thirty seconds of my head hitting the pillow.

On weekends, I stayed with Larry's parents; a great setup for getting to know each other. I became part of the family right away. Larry's mother and I would sit at the kitchen table every Saturday morning and talk. I drank my tea while Helen drank her weak instant coffee. She would boil water, dip her teaspoon half way into the cup of hot water and then dip it into the instant coffee. Then she'd add a powered creamer to the cup and mix it with the dipped spoon. I was mesmerized watching her. I knew my parents hated instant coffee. It wasn't robust enough for them.

"Do you ever drink regular coffee?"

"No, I just want some of the flavor of coffee. This is enough for me."

The rest of our conversation comprised of me telling her about myself. I told her why my family had moved from Michigan to Arizona when I was fourteen, how Larry and I had met and how many siblings I had. Every now and then, she would interject some anecdotal story about Larry, which I really enjoyed hearing. She also shared that the other girl he had brought home when he was in college spent an hour in the bathroom before she would come to breakfast. What a contrast. I had on my nightgown and robe and hadn't even brushed my teeth or combed my hair. Helen liked my casual style.

"I feel more comfortable with you. I like to relax a bit before I get dressed."

I was grateful I didn't have to put on airs. Yippee. I had scored a point with Larry's mother. She had a salt of the earth personality and I loved it. I knew our relationship would grow over the years after he and I married.

During the weekdays, Mary and I hung out. We ate dinner together in the evenings, after we each returned home from work. One night, however, was an exception to our mundane routine. There was a Wednesday night tradition of bar hopping all over Salem, for young adults. Mary and I decided to scope out the fun. It was the one time in my life where Larry's instructions on shooting pool served me well. I learned quickly that in Salem, the boys played while the girls gabbed. I didn't see one female at a pool table. When we entered a bar that wasn't crowded, I suggested to Mary, who was agreeable, that we get a beer and migrate to the poolroom.

"I'm putting my quarter on the table. I want to play."

Placing money on the felt at the end of the table was the way to challenge the winners. The boys at the table laughed and jabbed each other with their elbows and looked at me as if I were nuts.

"Do you really think you can beat us?"

"Watch me play and you'll find out."

It was a rather a ballsy or should I say a "steel ovary" statement, as I was not as confident as I sounded. The winners were respectful of the rules of the game, however, and when it was our turn to play, I broke. The boys each took a shot, but only dropped in one ball apiece. Mary did the same. Then it was my turn again. Each time I took my stance to shoot at a ball, I could hear low murmurs from the guys. I was certain they expected me to miss. One by one, I dropped the balls in the pockets until I ran the table and won the game of eight ball. The young men, who were the spectators, were stunned. They yelled responses.

"Did you see that? Where'd she come from? Wow!"

I stifled a grin and looked at them as if this was an everyday occurrence for me. The boys we had played were furious at their loss, but one of them was impressed with my skill.

"That was some good playing."

I said a simple thanks and then walked over and stood beside Mary. The other one threw his pool cue on the table.

"I don't believe it. I quit."

Mary and I gave each other a high five. The room continued to buzz with comments about the girls who had beaten the boys at the game. The males who had watched, scattered to the corners of the room, fearful they were next in line to be humiliated. I held up my hand.

"Thanks for letting us play, fellas, but we have to leave. We have no time for another game."

Mary looked quizzically at me as I gulped down my beer and grabbed my purse.

Mary Durand and Louise—pool sharks

"Let's go."

Outside, Mary grabbed my arm and stopped me. "Why did we leave? You were on a roll."

"I wanted to quit while I was ahead. I've never done that before. Better to leave them wondering where that pool shark came from."

I was right. I've never done it again. Fact is, these days, forty years later, if I hit one ball in the pocket without scratching, I'm happy. I did take time to thank Larry for teaching me and he was proud of my accomplishment that night.

About three weeks before Larry's leave in August 1968, Larry called me at his parents' house.

"So, you want to get married while I'm on leave?"

That was the extent of his romantic proposal. It wasn't Prince Charming, sweep me onto a horse and ride into the sunset like, but it sufficed.

"Sure."

Helen and I were at the kitchen table engaged in our Saturday morning ritual. I covered the mouthpiece of the telephone. "Larry asked me to marry him."

After Larry and I hung up from our conversation, I faced Helen with a big smile on my face. Helen was smiling too, but she had some things to say.

"I know that makes you happy, but you should wait. You're much too young."

"I'm twenty-two years old and so is Larry. This is exactly what I hoped would happen if I came to Ohio. I'm happy."

By now, I knew Helen well enough to know that she was kidding me. She knew our decision was final. All of a sudden she had this serious expression on her face.

"If he makes you work, feed him TV dinners."

I chuckled. "I couldn't do that."

The corners of her eyes began to crinkle as her smile broadened.

"Okay. Then never hand over your paycheck."

Her final tidbit of advice was to consider not having children until we were in our forties.

"Forties? We'd be too old then."

Now she was laughing out loud.

"That's my point."

I appreciated her wit. Helen Laughlin was a sage ahead of her time. I would be a rich woman, today, had I heeded her suggestions.

❦ ❦ ❦

When they heard the news, Larry's family, especially his sister-in-law, Charlene, pitched in to plan a wedding for us. She helped me plan a church ceremony with all the trimmings. I took private lessons in Catholicism in the three weeks that followed to prepare for a wedding in the church where Larry and his family attended. The priest agreed that if I wasn't ready to be a Catholic, he'd make arrangements with a protestant minister to help perform the ceremony. My final decision was to become Catholic so my baptism into the church was at our dress rehearsal. My first communion was at our wedding. At first, my mother thought I was making a hasty decision about changing religions, but in the end, it was my decision, not hers. She respected my right to choose. My parents thought the world of Larry and were happy we were getting married even if it would be a Catholic ceremony.

Laura Walters, Mary Durand, Louise, Larry, Ken Laughlin, Jim Berarducci

I was on a tight financial and time budget. Charlene borrowed a wedding dress from a co-worker who was my same size. My parents sent me some money, which I used for flowers and announcements. Since there was no time to go shopping together for wedding rings, I purchased those too. Larry's parents graciously offered to host a small reception since my parents had to fly from Arizona to Ohio for the occasion. Larry's older sisters brought food to the reception. They were, and still are, great cooks.

My parents and younger siblings, Laura and Charlie flew to Louisville, Kentucky and then drove with my Aunt Pat and Uncle Jack Spickard to Ohio. Many of my extended family from Michigan drove down to Massillon including the two cousins whose weddings I had attended nine months earlier. Both of them were nearly seven months pregnant, but made the trip anyway. I was touched by the love they had for me. In fact, I was overwhelmed at the number of other family members, including both of my grandmothers, some aunts, uncles and cousins, who made the trip. I nearly had as many guests as Larry did despite the short notice. My summer roommate, Mary, was my maid of honor or in Mary's words, "the best lady" and my sister, Laura, was a bridesmaid. Larry's brother Kenny, was his best man and a close high school friend, Jim Berarducci was a groomsman.

We were married at St. Barbara's Church in Massillon, Ohio on August 24, 1968. In addition to it being his family's church, it was also where Larry had attended grade school. The temperature on our wedding day was well over ninety degrees, as was the humidity. The air felt thick and difficult to breathe.

"Charlene, I'm so hot. Do you think we could take the long linens sleeves off this dress and just leave the lace overlay?"

We weren't certain so I took the dress off and Charlene inspected it.

"I think I can do it, but we don't have much time."

She gently pulled the threads leaving only the short sleeves. It looked as though it had been made that way. I put the dress back on and we left. We arrived at the church a couple of minutes late. The guests were a little anxious, but not as much as Larry. He told me later, he was concerned I had changed my mind. My dad smiled at me as he walked me down the aisle. He always had a calming effect on me, which at that particular moment I appreciated.

As Larry and I knelt at the altar, I looked at him and could see how miserably hot he was. His head was dripping with sweat. My own forehead and scalp were so damp that every time I bowed my head to pray, my veil would slide forward. I was afraid it would fall off. There was no air conditioning in the church. These days, Larry will occasionally tell people that it was the most miserable day of his life. I have to clarify his statement and provide the weather report. He is such a tease.

At one point in the ceremony, Mary swayed as though she was going to faint. She leaned against me.

"Get me out of here. I'm going to puke."

The priest stepped down and helped her to the sacristy. Once behind closed doors, he gave her a shot of whiskey. He thought it was her nerves. To the congregation, he was discreet and subtle. One would think this was a regular occurrence. He returned to the altar. As we continued with the ceremony, we could hear her retching in the background. We knew she suffered as much from a hangover from our small rehearsal dinner the night before as she did the heat. It caused us to giggle, but laughter was a big part of our relationship. It was an appropriate setting for us.

To complicate matters, my little brother Charlie, had developed an ear infection from the long flight. My mother had to take him outside, as he was also sick. The only thing I thought would be worse than my maid of honor throwing up in the Sacristy was if my younger brother had barfed in the front row. The remainder of the wedding went relatively well. I was thrilled to be Larry's wife. That was the beginning of the Larry and Louise Show; a nomenclature we would earn in later years.

ॐ ॐ ॐ

Two days later, we headed to Oklahoma to begin our lives together. We had little money, no place to live, and there was no on-post housing available for married servicemen. We searched the papers for apartments as soon as we arrived in Lawton. We found nothing we could afford and decided to drive up and down the streets of Lawton to look for rental signs. After what seemed like hours of fruitless searching, Larry spotted a tiny sign in someone's front yard. We stopped to inquire. He spoke to the little eighty-three year old lady, who came to the door.

"My wife and I would like to look at the apartment you have for rent."

The old lady looked toward the car. She held her hand over her eyes to shield them from the glare of the sun. She tried to get a good look at me, but I was too far outside her range of sight.

"Is she white?"

Larry was taken by surprise.

"Well, yes."

"How long will you be here?"

Larry explained he was still in the NCO Academy.

"I should ship out for Viet Nam next March."

"Okay. Meet me out back and I'll show it to you."

It was a small upstairs apartment, with a living room, kitchen, one bedroom and a bathroom, with a door so swollen from the humidity that we couldn't close it until the following winter when the humidity lessened. But, it was cheap and it was furnished. We took it and moved in the same day. We thought the landlady was a bit strange, but we didn't have much money and felt she was harmless.

Larry had to report in for duty the next day so I was home alone until I found a job. There were tenants who lived below us, but for some reason I was too shy to introduce myself. When Larry came home at night, I would report on the day's activities.

"That lady downstairs moves her furniture every day. I can feel the house shake when she does it. Do you think she's bored?"

On Larry's first day off, I heard furniture move. "See, there she goes again."

Larry started laughing.

"The movement you feel is artillery shells detonating out on the practice range fifteen miles from here."

"Oh my goodness. That's scary."

He took me by the hand and guided—well, dragged—me downstairs and introduced us both to the neighbors. We were good friends with Johnny and Barbara for the rest of our time there. Unfortunately, we lost touch with them a few years later.

Our landlady, Mrs. Head, was a hoot. She was about five feet tall and maybe weighed eighty pounds, but she was fierce. She was a southern Baptist. Not long after we moved in, she discovered Larry and I were Catholics.

"I knew there was something not right about you two even though you seemed nice enough."

In spite of our close quarters and meager income, our apartment became the weekend party place for all of our new friends. None of us had much money so we played cards and drank beer or spirits. The only snacks we could afford were peanuts. Alcohol was one of the cheaper things that could be purchased at the commissary. One Sunday morning after a rowdy Saturday evening game of Michigan rummy, we walked outside to find our empty bottles lying end to end across the yard. We had discarded them in the trashcan, but Mrs. Head had retrieved and displayed them in the yard. She noticed us staring at her display and came outside from her house.

"I don't want you drinking on my property. Alcohol is the work of the devil."

We didn't want to lose our apartment so were quick to agree.

"Yes ma'am."

For all future card parties, we sent our empties home with our guests.

On weekend days, Larry and I would go for a walk enjoying the fall weather. Larry would jog sometimes and sing.

"I want to be an Airborne Ranger; I want to live a life of danger."

He didn't mean it. It was just a marching song. He wanted to be as safe as possible. We were already talking about starting a family when he returned home after his tour of duty.

ॐ ॐ ॐ

We left Oklahoma in late February 1969. Larry had a month's leave so we took a circuitous route home to Arizona that included going back to Ohio to visit his family and up to Michigan to visit my grandmothers and other family. We drove to Iowa to visit Ron and Sandy Clarstrom, who we had met in Oklahoma. Larry and Ron were in the same artillery unit and Sandy was pregnant with their first child.

While we were still in Lawton, the four of us went to Oklahoma City one Saturday to see the Cowboy Museum. Since Larry drove,

Ron and Sandy sat in the back seat. Sandy giggled and whispered to Ron. I turned around.

"What's so funny?"

"The baby is kicking."

Always interested in something he's never experienced Larry spoke up.

"Can I feel?"

Not a bit embarrassed; rather, anxious to share, Sandy was agreeable.

"Sure, go ahead."

Larry reached his right arm over the front seat and stretched to reach Sandy's belly. His eyes got really big.

"Oh no, I think I stuck my thumb in the baby's mouth."

"That's my belly button, you fool."

The time we spent together in Oklahoma was always fun. When they invited us to come to Iowa on our way home, we agreed. We had a great time with them and their families in their hometown. We didn't want it to end. We invited the Clarstroms to come to Arizona where Larry and Ron could ship out to Viet Nam together and then we continued our drive south to Arizona. When we reached a town near Pueblo, CO, we stopped to visit friends of Larry's. They were very hospitable and invited us to stay at their father's studio. It was luxurious. It was the first time I'd seen a bathroom decorated in black with gold water fixtures. The shower was big enough for ten people. The whole place was beautiful. Never having had a real honeymoon, we took full advantage of our surroundings.

Ron and Sandy flew to Arizona the week after we arrived. We showed them as much of Arizona as we could in the short time they had to visit. On the last night before Larry and Ron's departure, we were at a loss of what to do. We were rather subdued. One of Larry's college friends, Bill Schammel called Larry.

"Why don't we go shoot shuffleboard at the Pueblo Bar?"

It was as good as anything else we could think of so we agreed. Bill met us at the Pub.

"Let's go, guys."

Sandy and I got up to go with our husbands. Bill did a double take as he saw us.

"You aren't going to take your wives to that dive of a bar, are you?"

Larry stopped.

"Bill, this is our last night at home. We aren't leaving them home."

Bill shrugged his shoulders. Being single, he didn't grasp the concept of marriage and commitments, but didn't argue. Bill was not only single but shallow and we all exchanged glances at his behavior. We left together and headed to the bar. On the way, Sandy asked me what I thought about Bill.

"He's okay. He's a bit selfish, but he means well. I ignore him."

We had a good time shooting pool and shuffleboard. It took the edge off the impending goodbye. As the night came to an end, however, Bill had some closing remarks for me. I had gained some weight, as had Larry, since we married. Bill had concerns.

"I hope you're going to lose some weight while he's gone. You're getting a bit chubby."

I was devastated that he'd have the audacity to say that to me; especially, after I had defended him earlier. Larry stood on the other side of me. I turned to him for support. Before I could say anything, he put his arm around me.

"You have put on some pounds."

Now, I was furious.

"So have you."

Larry knew his words had stung me. I was madder at him for agreeing with Bill than I was about what he said. I thought he'd punch Bill in the arm and tell him to mind his own business. Bill and Larry went to the bar to buy another pitcher of beer, which at that time cost $1.25. Larry had no money and Bill only had one dollar. He tore the dollar bill in half. He put one half in his pocket and handed the other half to Larry.

"Here, take this to Viet Nam with you. When you return, I'll have it framed."

Larry bowed his head so that his chin nearly touched his chest. I watched as his torso expanded from the deep breath he had taken. He exhaled slowly and looked back up at Bill.

"Thanks, man."

I knew Bill's gesture toward Larry was genuine. He wanted to get his buddy back from the war. I thought it was a kind moment, but that didn't let Larry off the hook on the mean comment Bill had made to me. We didn't talk on the way home. When we reached the privacy of our room, he apologized for not sticking up for me. I couldn't stay mad at him, as there was no time to reconcile before he had to leave the next day. So, I filed my anger away and forgave him.

The next day, our husbands donned their dress greens and we took them to the airport. It was a tearful farewell. Sandy flew home to Iowa the same day. The next Monday, I went job hunting. It took me the whole year he was gone, but I lost the weight I had gained. Larry, on the other hand, lost his in the first three weeks from the toil sweat and stress of his situation.

Chapter Four

I t was the end of March 1969. Many of my fellow NCO Academy classmates flew to Viet Nam on the same flight as I out of San Francisco, California. The flight included stops in Anchorage, Alaska and Tokyo, Japan before we arrived in Tan Son Nhat Airport in Saigon. I looked out the window and saw bomb craters everywhere. I thought we were alighting on the moon. In order to avoid ground fire, the captain descended quickly from a high altitude with a short approach to the runway. It was the fastest landing I had ever experienced. My apprehension about coming here was heightened by the sights. My training transpired in a pretend war scenario. This was real.

We were all dressed in our fatigues and carried our duffle bags and M-16 Rifles off the plane. I didn't know what to expect on the outside, but was ready to low crawl into battle or the terminal, whichever came first. As it turned out, our deplaning was much the same as it would have been at Phoenix, Arizona Sky Harbor International Airport in the summer except for the unbearable humidity. Our uniforms were soaked before we got to our transport. As we walked down the stairs of the plane the air smelled of filth, gunpowder and death. The next three hundred and sixty-four days could not tick by fast enough for me, but I kept telling myself that my country needed me or else I wouldn't be here.

Before I boarded a five ton truck that would take us to the base, I saw an airline tug pull a flat baggage cart toward the plane. It took a moment before I realized what I was observing.

"Those are body bags."

Then I looked closely at the driver and recognized him from basic training in Ft. Lewis, Washington last year. I told my buddies about Berryhill.

"That soldier might be the funniest man I've ever met. He kept all of us trainees in stitches. He had no respect for authority. Must be why he came directly to Viet Nam instead of to advanced training."

I yelled to him to get his attention.

"Berryhill, it's Larry Laughlin. Remember me?"

Berryhill turned toward me and stared. He eyes had a dull, vacant look to them, far from the former twinkle I remembered. He looked as if he'd been through hell. The laughter was gone from his voice when he responded with lifeless emotion.

"Good luck. You'll need it. Remember, it don't mean nothin'."

Then he walked away and finished his gruesome task of the loading the body bags in the cargo hold of the plane. I couldn't imagine all that must have happened to him to take away his joy. I hoped I would have a different experience.

This postcard came soon after Larry left.

"Hi Babe,

I'm here at last. My God, what a horrible place to send any man. It's hot. I guess we're getting into the monsoons. It's dirty to say the least. It's also very dangerous. There's bombing all night long. I don't have a permanent address yet. Maybe we will this afternoon. I miss you already; only 364 days to go."

I didn't know how I would endure the next year without him. I felt so alone in spite of my family being nearby. I dreaded the isolation I knew Larry would feel.

I was assigned to the 101st Airborne Airmobile Battalion. Ron and others from my class sympathized with me. I had been given the worst duty of us all. The 101 was a strike force as opposed to a defensive unit. The airborne ranger song I sang while I jogged on lazy Sunday afternoons with Louise came true. This was a dangerous assignment. I was a chief of section on a 155 Howitzer. The Army would drop my men and our big gun into some of the most active danger zones in all of Viet Nam; namely, the A Shau Valley near the DMZ. Before my classmates and I were separated, we went through jungle training to get us conditioned to the weather and environment.

A second postcard arrived two days later.

> *"We received our assignments today. This is where Ron and I split up as I've been assigned to the 101st Airborne, Airmobile unit. That means they'll drop this big 155 howitzer and me on a hilltop to shoot at the Viet Cong. The good news is that I won't ever be close to the enemy so I won't be engaged hand-to-hand combat. I'll be safe."*

I was so relieved for his safety. I was reminded of what he was taught in training; the purpose of a bayonet is to kill. I hoped he never had to use that skill.

I'd only been in Viet Nam for a few days when I had to spend one night as Sergeant of the guard on the perimeter. I thought it was basically safe given we were still near Saigon, but without knowing what to expect I was still scared. The day before I departed for Camp Eagle in the north, another seasoned sergeant and I were assigned to patrol an area along a creek not far from our base camp. We, and a squad of men, were taken by truck to the site and given a map, which indicated a stretch of ground about three miles long. The sergeant, who had been through this drill, explained we would move through the area as quickly and quietly as possible. We would call for a lift off at the other end and go back to the base to drink beer. He confided in me in a more thorough manner.

"The opposite side of this creek is supposed to be friendly so we can't shoot there. Let's hope we don't see anything."

A half hour later, we were on the receiving end of small arms fire from the friendly side of the creek. The RTO (Radio Telegraph Operator) was hit badly. I don't know if he survived. Another man was injured, but not as severely. The worst part was the delayed response to our request to return fire.

"Request denied. That is friendly territory."

It didn't matter. The dink, who shot at us, was gone by the time we received the answer. Not long afterward, we were pulled out by choppers and never finished our assignment.

Only The Strong Survive —
Larry's gun in Viet Nam

The next morning, I was on a large Air Force transport heading north to Camp Eagle, base camp for the 101. After a jittery first night, half of which was spent alone in a bunker listening to the bombs detonating, I awoke to find a large hole in the ground where the mess hall had been. That afternoon, I boarded a Huey Helicopter, the workhorse transport with skids and designed for quick entry and exit troop transport, that took me to the middle of the jungle to my new camp, LZ (landing zone) Vagel. I met the men of my section and saw my howitzer named, Only The Strong Survive.

It seems odd now, but at the time the boys seemed glad to have me there. Their former sergeant had rotated back to the states about a week before. They wanted a leader. Unfortunately for me, half of the ten men assigned to me also left in the following few days, which left me, SGT. Shake and Bake, with a bunch of teenaged green recruits to train . . . fast. At twenty-two years of age, I was the old man of the group.

I selected an eighteen-year-old man named Wayne Kuper from South Dakota as my gunner. He was smart, worked hard and followed orders well. I needed someone I could trust for this critical job. Wayne no sooner completed his on the job training when our section and gun were moved on to other locations, such as LZ Nancy and Camp Evans, to support and help fight battles. Most of the seven or eight LZs were established or at least close to completed.

LZ Nancy's bunkers were more progressive than most. Pallets from shipped bombs were placed on the dirt floor so that cots could be erected. They even had mosquito nets. I looked forward to not sleeping on the ground in the dark. The first night, I heard rats scurry between the wood slats of the pallets. I heard the whack sound of them being caught in the traps that had been set. I tucked my mosquito netting tight around my body. The thought of waking up to eye-to-eye contact with a rat caused me a lot of anxiety. A night's rest only lasted about four-five hours, but actual sleep was much less. The next day, we pulled the snared rats out of the bunker and put them in a pile. They were the size of footballs. My new luxurious hooch lost its appeal.

LZ Airborne, our next stop, was new. Our superior officers wanted the LZ to be established in quick order so that we could provide fire support for the infantry on Hill 937 more commonly known as Hamburger Hill.

The high mountaintop was picked as a fire support base used by Airborne because it would take the gooks a few days to hike up to the top. We never stayed long enough to get acquainted with them. The Air Force would bomb the top so that it was more level. Then the choppers brought in engineers with small bulldozers to dig holes approximately four feet deep, eight feet wide and ten feet long. As soon as the holes were dug, we were brought in with our howitzer to immediately begin shooting. While we fought, portable landing strip, timbers and tons of sand bags were brought in to make our underground living quarters. In our spare time, we created homes out of the pits. There was one entrance that also served as an exit. The air was cool in the north, but inside it was dark and damp. We lived like rats in a hole for a few short hours a day to sleep.

The purpose of being airmobile was to get to hard to reach places in short order. We immediately went into action bombing the VC in a surprise attack and left the mountaintop before the enemy could learn of our location. In the case of LZ Airborne, we broke our own standard and stayed too long.

I had assured Louise in my letters not to fear for my safety, as I was a far distance from the enemy. But on May 13, 1969, the Viet Cong overran our position. The attack started about three o'clock in the morning. The Vietcong, also known as Victor Charlie, VC, Charlie, gooks, zipper heads or dinks to the GIs, overran the perimeter, killing the infantry as they came. I thought the VC Special Forces (sappers), much like the kamikazes in World War II, must have been high on drugs as they crawled under the concertina wire, which ripped the skin on their bodies without slowing their forward motion. With no time to think through a strategy, I jumped into action. Our troops eventually won that battle, but not without a terrible loss of men. At the end of the siege, I was exhausted. As I collapsed on the ground, alive and relatively uninjured, I wept for the loss of so many men . . . boys, actually.

God what a mess!
I must be dreaming.

As I commiserated with myself, I spotted a *Playboy* magazine on the ground. Its pages flipped in the wind from the whirring blades of the hovering helicopters that had arrived to remove the injured and dead. When the helicopters landed, the breeze died down and exposed a page with a Gahan Wilson cartoon on it. The soldier covered in soot and blood caught my attention. The caption said, "I think I won." I tore it out and in addition to the statistics of the day, as I knew them, I wrote the following:

"13 May 69, LZ-Airborne, A Shau Valley. God what a mess! I must be dreaming."

I folded it up and carried the cartoon in my wallet for the rest of my tour of duty.

Larry was awarded the Bronze Star medal with "V" device—for valor that day. His Colonel described the reason for the award.

"For heroism in ground combat against a hostile force in the Republic of Viet Nam on 13 May 1969. Sergeant Laughlin distinguished himself in Battery C, 2d Battalion (Airmobile), 11th Artillery, during a ground and mortar attack on Fire Support Base Airborne, Republic of Viet Nam. Sergeant Laughlin immediately went to his howitzer, organized his section and began directing artillery fire on suspected enemy mortar and rocket propelled grenade positions. The outstanding example that he set for his men inspired them to remain in their position despite the constant incoming mortar rounds and sapper charges. Sergeant Laughlin's personal bravery and devotion to duty were in keeping with the highest traditions of the military service and reflect great credit upon himself, his unit and the United States Army."

The Bronze Star and write up didn't arrive until he was already home from Viet Nam. It was a wonderful surprise for us both. Larry was then, and still is, my hero.

While his heroism was recognized that particular day, the battle raged on as they tried to protect the soldiers on Hamburger Hill. While Larry was in Viet Nam, I worked a midnight shift at a Motorola plant near our house. I missed him most at night. This shift helped me keep my mind off my loneliness. I lived with my paternal grandmother, who catered to me. When I arrived home each morning, exhausted as I always felt sleep deprived, she'd have breakfast on the table for me. I'd eat and go to bed. Each day, when the mail came, she would wake me so I could read a letter. However, in May, two weeks went by with no word from Larry. I was worried. Finally I received a half page letter.

> *"Sorry I haven't written in so long. The last two weeks have been the worst of my tour of duty here. For more than ten days, we've fought for our lives non-stop. I haven't had a shower, a hot meal or a letter during all this time. I wanted to send you a quick note to let you know I'm still alive."*

Those weeks weren't the only time his remote unit was involved in combat. During one of those skirmishes, Larry was injured and sent to a field hospital. I didn't hear about this from the Army. I heard it from Larry in one of his letters.

> *I've been air-evacuated to a field hospital. I'm okay, just a broken foot from removing a hot round from the howitzer. We received orders to cease-fire and had to get the hot shell out of the gun so that it wouldn't explode. Kuper and I removed the gun powder and then positioned ourselves by the breech of the gun. My other men took a ramrod and punched the shell to dislodge it from its position. The men on the two guns on either side of mine scattered and ran to safety. This gun is of no use in hand-to-hand combat.*

The hot shell Kuper and I were trying to catch fell on my foot and broke it.

The first thing I did when I got here was to get some envelopes so I could send you this letter. This place is located on the South China Sea. It's really a beautiful view when looking across Cam Ranh Bay. You might know I don't have my camera or tape recorder. Fact is all I do have is a pair of hospital issued PJ's. They made me leave everything behind.

No one has said anything to me about going to Japan from here. I'd sure like that. Airborne did get hit the night I left, but no one was hurt. Last night they got it again, but I haven't heard a casualty report. When I lay down to go to sleep at night I thank God for you and all my family. I pray for the safety of the men up there. I hope they move off that hill before I go back. I think a lot of these soldiers in this hospital were injured in the A Shau Valley.

I'm going to close for now. I love you very much. I'll write tomorrow. Keep writing to the old address. They'll bring my mail.

Postscript: Caring is the distinction you give me; the gift that comes before a final carelessness. Only your gentle letters tattered, worn and memorized for the tenth time; your words tucked into my helmet for another reading takes me back to better days.

Your picture in my wallet; soiled with thumbprints reminds me of the happy times with you. Louise, you're the only thing that gives me the courage to drive on from the hideous nights to the break of dawn.

I love you,

Larry

I could hardly believe Larry wrote those words. It wasn't that he lacked emotion, but for a guy who buys a card without reading the words inside, it seemed too romantic. I loved it nonetheless. Years later, Larry confessed that he had copied the postscript from a book.

He said it was how he felt so he borrowed the words to send to me. I accepted the explanation and still appreciated the effort.

I tried my best not to worry Louise with the real horror I lived in Viet Nam. Seeing the devastation of the war and all of the injured soldiers brought into the small field hospital was the worst part. A few days later, I was flown to Japan.

I had few possessions with me when I was transported to the hospital in Japan. Things I had on my person were the cartoon I tore out of the *Playboy* magazine, half of a dollar bill that my friend, Bill Schammel, gave me before I left for Viet Nam, a letter my wife's Aunt Sue wrote to me a month after I arrived in the Nam and a marble. I was so touched by the letter and the symbolism the marble brought I couldn't throw either away.

May 1, 1969

Dear Larry,

Aunt Sue Moyer

Sam died last night. We gave him a quiet, dignified funeral. Only the immediate family was in attendance. We wrapped him in Northern Tissue and Father hummed Taps as I flushed him down the toilet. Elaine and Vince tossed apple blossoms after Sam as he cascaded out of sight. It was a sad affair.

Elaine is worried about Sam's little widow grieving. I can see that Cynthia is misty eyed all the time, but I think she is feeling a sort of sad relief. Sam had been looking poorly for some time; a slight green around the gills you might say. Lately he had been very cross with Cynthia, constantly nipping at her and he had become a terrible glutton, hogging all of their food. This may have been what killed him. Or it could have been his liver. He drank like a fish—but I mustn't speak ill of the dead.

We will never know what fatal malady caused Sam's demise. Vince offered to do an autopsy, but Elaine, as Cynthia's official interpreter, vehemently refused consent.

Sam didn't leave much of an estate. No insurance at all, I regret to report. However, their home was free and clear so Cynthia has no worries on that score.

I'm enclosing a marble for you to remember Sam by. It was one of his favorites.

Keep this marble, Larry, to remind you that a better life is waiting for you; a life where the worst casualty of the day will be the death of a goldfish. We pray God will keep you safe, and time will pass swiftly until you can come home to normalcy. We are anxious to see all of those beautiful children you and Louise are going to have.

Much love, Sue Moyer

I knew the love and prayers of the folks back home would carry me through this horrific way of life. While I was in recovery, a military representative was passing out Purple Hearts. He stopped to give one to me.

"I don't want it. Look at the men lying in beds on either side of me. That man has no arms. The other one has no legs. Some of these fine men have neither; some are blind. My surface wounds and broken bones in my foot don't rank high enough to earn the medal. Get the fuck out of here."

I had thought my country was in this war to win it. I could not believe the annihilation of these young men and then the government was handing out trinkets. It was like we were kids with a scratch and a piece of candy would make it all better. They could kiss my ass.

While I convalescing in the hospital in Japan, Louise received a telephone call from Sandy Clarstrom. Ron had been severely injured and shipped to the same hospital as me. The doctors were threatening to remove one leg from the knee down. Ron was very depressed. Louise wrote to me right away to tell me the bad news. As soon as I had read her letter, I looked for Ron. I found the bay where he was. The nurse told me, Ron was all the way at the end.

While Ron and I were in the NCO Academy, we had a gruff talking master sergeant who had a saying he repeated regularly. In a booming voice, I cried out as I marched down the sickbay toward my friend.

"I care less."

Ron responded in a weak but cheerful voice.

"Lock."

I visited with Ron every day until he was sent to the states. Once there, he was examined by more experienced doctors, who were able to save his leg. Thank you, God.

I also recovered. On the same August day that I received orders to return to the combat zone, President Nixon declared that soldiers who had been injured did not have to return. My orders were changed. Instead of returning to Viet Nam, I was assigned to go to the demilitarized zone in Korea. The DMZ wasn't exactly a pleasure trip, however. In fact, it was as dangerous as Viet Nam.

A day after I arrived in Seoul, Korea, I met a Colonel from Ohio, who recognized my name from my football days in high school. The Colonel asked me if I would like to join Special Services and play football for the Army. His team needed a line backer. The servicemen in this outpost territory needed the respite from the grind of their usual routine and the special services unit was important. It didn't take much persuasion; I was ready to sign on the dotted line. I think it was Devine intervention.

There were about six teams in the region, and each one played all the others at least twice during each season. One of the teams boasted a former professional player who was exceptional. The Colonel made it quite clear that they had lost to the other powerful team before.

"Larry, as captain of this team, it is your duty to make certain we don't lose another time. Now, I want you to rally the team and win the game. Am I clear?"

Even though this was not a wartime command, I respected the Colonel's rank and followed orders in kind.

"Yes sir. Consider it done."

The Colonel looked to either side of him to see if any of the other guys were listening. Then he leaned in close and spoke in a low voice.

"If you're successful, there will be a case of beer waiting for you and the team."

The reward would be worth the effort. "No problem sir. We'll win."

When I saw the size of the guy I was confronting, I knew I was in trouble. I intentionally jumped offside, and hit the professional player so hard that it knocked him out of the game for a quarter. My teammates were astonished.

"Larry really rang that fella's bell."

It was all for naught, though; our team lost the game anyway. But, there was still a case of cold beer waiting for us. The Colonel howled with laughter.

"I don't think I've ever seen anyone do anything that dumb."

He was right. While I suffered during the entire second half as the other player cleaned my clock every chance he got, it had earned me celebrity status. I was voted MVP of the team for the season. Further, the Colonel was so impressed with my ballsy approach to winning; he kept me in Special Forces for the remainder of my tour of duty. My assignment was to inspect Army base movie theaters and command a group of Korean KATUSAS (Korean Augmentation Troops to the United States Army), who served the Army in administrative jobs.

Chapter Five

Larry returned home to Arizona from overseas in March 1970. It had been a long year for both of us. Our first stop after I picked him up at the airport was church. In his dress greens, Larry walked up to the altar, knelt down and prayed.

I was thrilled to have him home. We took a week's vacation at my parents' cabin in Camp Verde, AZ. We returned to live at my grandmother's house. She had planned to go to Michigan for the summer, which gave us six months to find our own place to live. I went back to work at Motorola and Larry found a construction job.

The month after Larry returned from Viet Nam, I discovered I was expecting our first child. We were so excited. On Mother's Day, five weeks into the pregnancy, we had a family picnic with my parents and siblings in our back yard. We were playing volleyball when all of a sudden I felt a warm sensation as if I had wet my pants.

I hurried into the bathroom and discovered I was bleeding. I hollered out the bathroom window.

"Mom, come in here and help me, please."

My mother ran into the house, stood outside the bathroom door.

"What's the matter? May I come in?"

I was crying so hard I could hardly speak. I whispered a barely audible reply.

"Yes."

My mother entered the bathroom. She looked at me with her soft brown eyes; a gaze of love that was always there when I needed her. I knew she felt my anguish.

"Are you cramping?"

"No."

She put her arms around me and patted me on the back.

"Sometimes, this happens, but it's not always reason for concern. Come into the living room and let's chat while you rest awhile. Perhaps the game was too strenuous for you."

I cleaned up and did as she suggested. As usual my mother was able to lift my spirits by simply being there to empathize with my situation.

"Do you think I'm going to lose the baby?"

"I don't know, but what you should keep in mind that sometimes a miscarriage is nature's way of aborting an imperfect fetus. Time will tell."

I had chronic problems for another two and a half months. Finally, on July 30, 1970, I was at work and began experiencing excruciating cramping. My supervisor helped me to the nurse's office. The pains continued to get worse. The nurse suggested I have my husband pick me up and take me to the emergency room. We only had one car and I had driven it myself. I convinced her I was okay to drive and went home. Larry had been sleeping as he was working a graveyard shift at his new job at the Sheriff's Office. As soon as I arrived and told him what had happened, he jumped out of bed, dressed and took me to the doctor's office, who confirmed I was losing the baby. The doctor gave me a heavy sedative to alleviate the pain and help me to sleep.

"Take her home and let nature take its course."

There was nothing else to do, but wait until I miscarried. Aborting a live fetus was not legal; neither were there sophisticated ultra sounds that could be performed.

We went back home. Once there, the labor pains I experienced caused me to double over. Larry called my mother, who came over immediately. They watched me writhe in agonizing pain. My mother called the doctor again.

"The pain Louise is experiencing is way more than it should be. I've been through this myself and I don't remember having this much difficulty."

The doctor agreed.

"Tell Larry to bring her to Scottsdale Memorial Hospital right away. I'll meet them there."

He performed a D&C while I was under a general anesthetic. Once I recovered, I would be physically fine. My emotions, however, were another matter. My doctor was there when I awoke.

"We don't know what caused the problem, but I can assure you there was no growth beyond the first six weeks. I do not believe this will prevent you from having a healthy baby in the future. You'll just need to wait a few months and try again."

As disappointed as we were, we were resigned to the fact that it was God's way of protecting us and the baby from a lifetime of potential challenges.

❦ ❦ ❦

We spent the summer getting reacquainted with each other and our mutual friends. In the fall, we found a house to buy that fit both our price range and lifestyle. It was only two bedrooms, but had a family room that was eighteen by thirty feet; the same square footage of the rest of the tiny, eighteen thousand dollar house. We bought all of our furniture at auction and with of the help of my real estate agent, mother, from model home sales.

Larry had been hired at the Maricopa County Sheriff's office as a deputy a few months before we moved in. When he graduated, we had the party for the entire class. With the lights dim and the black lights glowing, we danced to "In-A-Gadda-Da-Vida" by the Iron

Butterfly. The music was so loud during the instrumental interlude that our commissary issue speakers vibrated off our concrete blocks and board shelves.

We had warned our neighbors that there would be noise, but it wouldn't have mattered if they had called the police. Our house was filled with them.

Larry bought a big Honda that he rode back and forth to work at his Deputy Sheriff's job. The motorcycle was a cheaper alternative to buying a car. Or, at least that's how Larry justified it to me. Since he worked odd hours, we couldn't car pool so I agreed.

Even though his bike was not built for the dirt, early one Saturday morning, Larry set out for a ride to Payson through the Bloody Basin desert. He took two friends with him; namely, David and Steve. They were family friends from my hometown in Michigan and had recently moved to Arizona. It was mid-July right after a heavy rainfall in Northern Arizona. Larry gave no consideration to how this weather may have impacted the environmental conditions. He was ready to ride.

"Okay, boys, I'm going to show you the beautiful desert of Arizona. Follow me."

We found the terrain rough going as the usual hard desert floor was soft, which made maneuvering difficult. This, of course, did not deter us. We were on a weekend adventure. I strapped the supplies on Steve's motorcycle. He was the youngest member of our party but his bike was the largest.

He was a bit hesitant as he was the least experienced rider of the three of us, but he knew the blanket, two quarts of water and a pint of Jack Daniels would be invaluable provisions on our journey.

"I don't mind carrying this stuff, but don't go too fast so I can keep up."

He appreciated being permitted to tag along. As the topography got tougher, he had a progressively harder time keeping up. One at a time, each of the bottles and the blanket came loose and fell to the ground. Rather than stopping to retrieve the lost gear, he kept on riding. He was concerned with losing his way unaware of the danger the desert can hold for those who travel unprepared. When we stopped for a break, I noticed the bottles were gone.

"Steve, why didn't you tell me you lost the water?"

"I tried to yell, but you couldn't hear me over the engine noise. I was worried I'd get too far behind so I didn't stop."

All I could think was that he was a moron. I knew he was a novice in this environment, but water is a required staple on whatever type of journey.

"I guess when we get to Payson; we can replace what we need."

We headed down a very steep embankment south of Childs, AZ, but could not cross the normally calm Verde River because it had swollen beyond its banks due to the heavy rains in the north. Our spirit of adventure was greater than our common sense. We had traveled sixty miles, but could go no farther due to the condition of the desert floor. I knew we were on the brink of trouble.

"Look guys, we can't go back. The mountain is too steep to ride up because these bikes are too big and heavy. I know our location, but it's going to be a bitch getting out of here. Our only recourse is to leave the motorcycles and try to return home on foot."

They didn't argue with me, as they were clueless on how to proceed. I was their leader and responsible for their well being. We pushed the motorcycles back up the mountain as far as we could, but with very little progress. The steepness and the one hundred ten degree heat hindered us. I knew the Verde River was now our only mode of transportation. To allay my companions fear, I acted as if I'd done this many times before. Frankly, it was all I could do to not let them know my own apprehensions and frustration with the situation.

"I know neither of you is a big outdoorsman, but I've been camping and hiking my whole life. I'll get us out of here if you'll listen to what I tell you."

The river rampaged, overflowing its banks and carrying trees on the current. The terrain along what little bank was left was very rocky and treacherous making it impossible to walk.

"There is only one way we can follow the river. We have to get in it. If we do, we can find a log and try to float to Bartlett Lake at Horseshoe Dam. It shouldn't be any more than ten miles the way the crow flies. Can you both swim?"

They both nodded their heads in slow motion, but their wide eyes had looks of terror in them as they gazed at the river. Like robots, they followed my every command without question.

"I'm going to watch for a log that will support all three of us. When I jump in, follow me and swim to the log as fast as you can. This won't be easy. Try to get your body out of the water and over the log as much as you can and hang on."

By river, the trip was more like twenty-five miles. The force of the rushing water propelled us through the narrowing canyons. It was more dangerous than I was willing to admit. It called for bravado.

"Hey, this is better than a wild carnival ride. Yee Haw. Hang on cowboys."

On at least two occasions, David and Steve, who rode on the front of the log over the rapids, were completely submerged before I went under. There was no turning back. The three of us accepted the challenge of the river for about six hours, but we made little forward progress toward any civilized destination. I screamed at them over the roar of the river to move toward the shoreline. When we were within an arm's reach, we let go of the log and crawled up the embankment. Exhausted from fighting to hold on to the log, we lay sprawled out on the ground for several minutes. Steve was the first to complain about thirst.

"This water is not really safe to drink without purification equipment, but we have no alternative. Hell, the pioneers did it. We can too."

David was not fooled by my optimistic remarks.

"Larry, do you know why so many pioneers died at an early age? They drank the dirty river water."

Humor, no matter how bad, was welcomed to lighten our spirits.

"Very funny, David. We'll rest a little while, then we'll hike to Highway 87. It can't be far to the east of our location. We can hitchhike to Payson."

I was mistaken about the distance and with no way of carrying water; we only made it four or five miles. Even though our feet were getting blistered from our wet, knee high boots, we were glad to have them on. We encountered several snakes and the leather protected us from their strikes. It was probably the best luck we'd had all day. I told the guys we needed to take turns blazing our trail. Again, Steve was first to object.

"Yeah, right, Larry. The fucking snakes can bite me for awhile."

"Stop whining. We're doing the best we can. We still haven't seen the Beeline Highway in the distance. I think we're getting too far from the river."

Nightfall was imminent. We had hiked for three or four hours with nothing to drink.

"We need to find some shelter. I haven't seen anything on our trek that would provide cover, but start looking for a bare spot where there aren't cacti or snakes."

We came upon a small hill that was large enough for all three of us. It was covered with crushed granite that would provide minimal comfort and there was no cactus to roll over into during the night. It was only about fifteen feet across and was one of the few places with no snakes in sight. As dehydrated as we were, there was no chance of making it back to the river in the dark.

"This will home for the night. In case you don't know snakes are cold blooded and have been known to cozy up to a warm body during the cold, desert nights."

David cringed as he thought about the snakes.

"Oh shit. This is fun. Got any ideas to keep them away from us?"

"Well, don't move much in your sleep."

Steve did not appreciate my attempt at humor.

"I hate snakes and I don't think this is a bit funny."

I reverted to my sergeant in charge demeanor.

"Here's how we're going to handle this situation. Don't get up at all at night and whoever wakes up first should throw a couple handfuls of gravel around. If the gravel hits a snake within striking distance, it would rattle and warn us of its proximity."

"Sure, that'll work if it's a rattle snake."

"Listen, David, I don't have all the answers."

We lay down in the dirt fairly close to one another so we could garner the warmth from each other's bodies. We were dog-tired from the hard ride and the long hike; sleep came easily. In the early morning dawn, I awoke to the sensation of a long cold object lying next to my body. I feared the worst had happened. All I could think of was snake.

I remained still for an hour or so until David, who was sleeping, facing me opened his eyes. Without speaking out loud, I mouthed snake to him. His eyes grew big as saucers as he very slowly backed away from me. I whispered a plan.

"Find a big rock and hurry. Keep quiet and try not to move much. At the count of three, I'll roll toward you. Throw the rock as hard as you can at the snake. Hopefully, it'll scare it away or kill it."

So David counted . . . 1 . . . 2 . . . 3. I rolled; he slung the rock and the snake moved. Only, it wasn't a snake, it was Steve's arm. Fortunately, David was a lousy aim and missed.

This, of course, startled Steve, the target. David and I were howling with laughter.

"What? What's so funny?"

We told him I thought his arm was a snake and David the great white snake hunter was going to kill it.

"You could have broken my arm if you hit it."

"Well, quite bitching. He didn't hit your arm and you're fine."

Steve was not the least bit amused.

"No I'm not. I'm hungry and thirsty."

"You know, Steve, if you hadn't lost our damned water bottles, you wouldn't be thirsty. Shut the hell up."

Enough said. We got up and headed back toward the river.

"I know if we follow the Verde, we'll eventually get home."

Steve was still whining.

"You said that before."

With clenched teeth, I glared at Steve. He knew by my look that he needed to get moving.

On the way, I found some water trapped among some rocks. We got down on our knees and scooped up what we could into our hands to drink. It wasn't much, but enough to hold us for a little while. Finding it restored my credibility with the guys and we pushed on.

The river was still raging and violent, but we found another log and jumped in. Sounds like sport, but the water was frigid from the recent rainfall and the exposure to the blistering July sun was a dread. We stopped talking and accepted our fate.

After spending what seem like unending hours and only going another few miles, I yelled to David and Steve.

"We need to get out of the water and rest. I'm worried one or all of us will get hypothermia."

It was a struggle, but we managed to get out of the river. David was first to speak once we dragged ourselves onto the shore.

"Damn, I was afraid we were going to drown. This is getting scary."

Steve stood in one spot and shivered.

"What's hypothermia?"

Not believing he was that naïve, I explained what could happen.

"Hypothermia can cause your body temperature to drop resulting in an inability to perform tasks. It also causes confusion and serious malfunctions in the body. We need all of our faculties functioning at normal levels to have a chance of surviving this predicament."

David tired of his cousin's unending stupidity.

"Yeah, Steve, we'd hate to leave you behind. The snakes might get you before we could come back and find you."

I was worried they would engage in a fistfight so I interjected another plan.

"Let's go guys while we have plenty of daylight. I don't know how far we'll have to walk this time."

We had walked about a mile and were still in the middle of nowhere, or so I thought when I spotted a cable system high across the river. We learned later it was a sheep's crossing and used by ranchers to move their animals across the river to the valley for the winter. We scrambled up a small hill toward the mirage and discovered a road at the top of our climb. There was a speck in the distance coming closer and getting larger. It was a Jeep. We all screamed in unison.

"Stop, stop. Help. Save us."

The driver saw us running toward his vehicle, screaming and crying. The man and his wife stopped to find three, wet, cold, tired men with swollen lips from an insufficient drinking water source and cactus quills sticking out of their clothes. He rolled down his window.

"What the heck are the three of you doing way out here?"

We could barely speak to explain what we had been through, but we had smiles on our faces. I finally managed out a short comment.

"Thank you so much for stopping and saving us. We were running out of options."

"Well, I'm glad we came along when we did. You guys look terrible. Hop in. We were going to camp out, but changed our minds when we saw the river. It looked too dangerous to set up a tent nearby. We're headed back to Scottsdale. We'll be glad to give you a ride."

The man's wife spoke up.

"When was the last time you boys ate?"

"We haven't had food or water since yesterday morning."

She smiled a warm smile and opened her car door. She walked to the back of the Jeep and opened the rear access.

"We have plenty packed that we don't need. Help yourself."

I think we ate all of their food that didn't need to be cooked and drank all of their liquid beverages. Then we slept for the rest of the time it took to get there. Without a ride, we probably would have had to spend another night out in the desert. I didn't know if I could have kept David and Steve motivated. The fact was I was becoming less brave myself.

All the while Larry and our friends were on their adventure; I was at home and worried. I had a sick feeling in my stomach that something had gone terribly wrong. I had no idea where Larry was. I couldn't imagine any good reason that would cause them to be so late. I called the Sheriff's office and asked if they'd begin a search and rescue mission. They told me to wait until Tuesday and call again if I hadn't heard from Larry. There was a forty-eight hour waiting period before they could start the search. At this point, it was only a couple of hours passed the time I had expected him.

"You don't understand. I know something has gone wrong. My husband is very responsible and should have been home two hours ago."

"Sorry, lady. He probably stopped to have a beer with the boys. Call us Tuesday if he doesn't get home."

I couldn't explain the little black cloud that followed Larry around in one phone call. Larry was one of their own deputies but that wasn't cause enough to change the rules. After several hours of worry, Larry finally called me late Sunday evening.

"Hi. We're in Scottsdale. We got stuck. I'll tell you the whole story later, but will you come and pick us up? This really nice guy and his wife gave us a ride this far, but I can't ask them to take us any farther than they were already going."

I exhaled a sigh of relief as I collapsed in the chair next to the phone.

"Are you okay?"

"Sure, besides tired, bruised and scratched up a bit, we're fine."

I was so happy they were safe; I didn't ask any more questions.

"I'm on my way."

The next day, Larry took a crew with plenty of muscle, a couple of trucks and a winch to haul the motorcycles from their resting place. Once again, Larry had amazed his friends with one of his death defying adventures, where he survived with only some bruises and scratches. I made an appointment for him with his doctor to get a gamma globulin shot. I knew drinking that dirty water could cause him problems later on.

He hadn't learned any lifetime lessons from this trip. Instead, it was added to his list of stories he told to entertain his friends. Not long afterward, he had another misfortune of a different sort on that big Honda. As he was approaching a busy intersection, a car turned left in front of him. Larry had to lay the bike down to avoid hitting the vehicle. He skidded across the intersection with fierce momentum and came to a stop under the front end of a semi headed directly toward him. Fortunately, the semi driver saw what was happening, slammed on his brakes and came to a screeching halt before hitting Larry. The driver who had caused the accident stopped momentarily after his left turn and then took off not knowing if Larry had collided with the semi. Larry paved the road with his skin. After the wounds healed, he sold the Honda and we car-pooled.

Chapter Six

Once given the go ahead, we practiced every day to make a baby without much luck. A year later, we went to Carol and Dan May's house for a Tupperware party. Carol May, who used to be Carol Masterton, was the one who had originally convinced me to date Larry. While the men watched TV and drank beer in one room, the ladies played stupid games in another. Carol served a spiked punch much to the dismay of the Tupperware lady. We didn't care what she thought. We figured as long as we bought stuff, it should make her happy. Because Larry and I had imbibed too much, we stayed the night in the guest room. Our lovemaking that night had good results. The booze made me relax more and not think about getting pregnant. Of course Larry likes to joke that I could never go to a Tupperware party again.

At first, my pregnancy was at risk, but with the proper care and plenty of prayers, we surpassed the danger zone. Six weeks before my due date, however, I had to lay down the law with Larry. No more motorcycle riding until after our baby was born.

Larry still loved the thrill of riding so he had purchased a dirt bike called an AJS. He and our friend, Dan Dunn, would go riding on Saturday or Sunday afternoons and come back covered in dirt, but happy. One day, Larry returned with a broken collarbone. Seems they'd been trying to recreate Evil Knivel jumps. I told Larry, in no uncertain terms; that I'd prefer he'd quit riding long enough to ensure our child had a birth father present. He acquiesced. I guess it was an easy decision since his arm was in a sling.

Larry and I attended baby classes together. It was the beginning of a generation of fathers who were allowed in the delivery room. He was determined not to miss out on the action. There were two couples in our class who boasted they were going to have natural childbirth after hearing our instructor nurse tell us about medication options. The nurse stopped her lecture.

"All childbirth is natural. Some is with pain and some is without."

I liked her philosophy.

On a bright sunny April morning, I had an overwhelming need to scrub the kitchen floor. I began having contractions in the middle of my job. I called the doctor's office and they advised me to go directly to the hospital. I finished my job first. I guess I was making certain our nest was clean.

While I took a shower, Larry made certain my bag was packed with last minute items I might need. We went to the hospital. I think Larry was more excited than I. While we were in the labor room, I could hear a lady screaming in the next room. It frightened me. I talked to the nurse about it.

"Should I be worried? My pains aren't as severe as hers. Is there something wrong with me?"

She patted my arm and leaned in close so no one would hear.

"Honey, you are fine. Sometimes childbirth is more difficult for some women. I promise that her contractions are no worse than yours."

The only pain reliever I had was one shot in my hand where the nurse found the best access to my veins. I dreaded it, but was thankful for the relief it brought.

Once in the labor room, Larry had plenty of rude comments to make as he saw the birth canal reflected in a huge mirror on the ceiling. When the doctor came in, he greeted us both and then took out a huge long needle to medicate me. What Larry hadn't noticed was that the doctor had inserted a sleeve that matched the length of the syringe needle into the birth canal. When the doctor slid the needle into sleeve to inject the medicine, Larry grabbed his face with both hands.

"What are you going to do . . . deaden her tonsils?"

The party began. Larry cheered me on as if he was at a football game.

"Go, go, go."

I laughed, the nurses laughed and the doctor laughed. Larry just shrugged his shoulders and kept it up. When the doctor delivered Jason, Larry jumped up and down. The nurses showed him to us and then took Jason to other side of the room to clean him up. Larry rushed over to see our son again. He tried to uncover him, but the nurse yelled at Larry.

"What are you doing to that baby? Keep the blanket on or he'll get cold."

Somewhat embarrassed, Larry followed her instructions.

"Sorry, I was counting fingers and toes to make certain they were all there."

Then Larry ran back over to where I was. He saw the doctor was standing at the end of the gurney with a needle and thread.

"Now what are you doing?"

The doctor explained he was sewing up the episiotomy. Larry chuckled.

"Take an extra stitch for me, doc."

I swear nothing is sacred with Larry. He gave me a kiss.

"I love you. Jason is perfect and I couldn't be more proud. Now, I have to go tell everybody it's a boy."

In his excitement to share the news of Jason's arrival to our waiting family, Larry took a wrong turn from the delivery room and entered another delivery room. He didn't do this once; he did it twice and witnessed two more births with the same enthusiasm as our son's. Needless to say, April 17, 1972 was a very special day for us.

By the time Jason was only a year old, Larry rode a Yamaha 360 motorcycle for his desert excursions. Chalk it up to young and dumb or that I was convinced Larry was invincible, I agreed to allow Jason to ride on Larry's motorcycle. My baby sat on a pillow, which Larry placed on the gas tank. Larry drove up and down a new home construction area across the street from our house going God knows how fast waving to me as I watched. Jason had on my helmet, which was so big for him that it would not have helped one iota in the case of an accident. When they returned home, they were both exhilarated. Jason has inherited Larry's need for speed, which he has demonstrated on many occasions as the years have passed.

Early one Saturday morning in 1974, Larry and I were lying in bed talking. The house seemed unusually quiet, but it was because our two-year-old son, Jason, was still sleeping. Larry began getting frisky, which was nothing new. Lovemaking was an everyday occurrence in our marriage. While in the midst of ecstasy, we heard squeals of laughter.

Larry stuck his head out from under the covers and looked back over his shoulder. Jason was standing next to our bed, sleepy eyed, but giggling. I tried to wriggle out from underneath Larry, but he held on to me.

"Don't move . . . he doesn't know what we doing."

I held the covers down by my side so that Jason couldn't get under them should he decide to join us. Instead he, who was like a monkey, climbed onto our bed with little effort.

"Horsey ride, Daddy?"

"Sure, buddy, hop on Daddy's back and hang on."

Jason didn't hesitate. He crawled up over Larry's rear end and onto his back . . . on top of the covers. Now, Larry was laughing.

"Isn't this fun, Mommy?"

"Not any more."

I couldn't get up because I was not dressed. I was concerned it would prompt more questions from Jason. The interruption was enough to quell the moment. Larry pushed his arms up and down a couple of times to entertain Jason, but then stopped.

"Let's go have some breakfast and then I'll give you another ride later."

At first, Jason objected and didn't move. I was getting hot from Larry, the blankets and Jason on top of me. I wanted to get up.

"Jason, sweetie, this is fun, but now it's time to get up."

"Okay."

He jumped off the bed and ran out of our bedroom toward the kitchen. Larry and I scrambled out of bed and dressed. We hugged each other and stifled the urge to lock the door. As we walked out of the room, I tapped Larry on the shoulder.

"If you don't mind, I believe I'll sit out the next horsey ride."

🐛 🐛 🐛

To help make our little family well rounded, we decided to get a dog. To say that Larry is not a big pet lover is an understatement. Throughout his childhood, his family had a few dogs, which lived in their own little houses outside. He told me he felt sorry for the dogs when the snow was deep, but to him they were mostly a chore. He and his brother, Kenny, were responsible for feeding them. That was the extent of his interaction with the family pets. My childhood experience with our family's dog was the opposite. Our dogs were allowed wherever we were, usually had people names and were an integral part of the family. Consequently, Larry and I differed on how our pets were to be treated. Specifically, Larry's opinion was that a dog lived outside, but I thought that a pet should live inside.

In 1974, we bought a registered Golden Retriever, who was named Popeye by our son, Jason. He was trying to say puppy, but it didn't come out quite right and the name stuck. Popeye was smart, fun and instantly fit into our family. Jason was two years old when

Popeye joined us. They were the best of friends. Popeye followed Jason everywhere. When they were in the back yard, Popeye would take Jason's arm in his mouth (Golden Retrievers are bred to have a "soft mouth") and take him to the sandbox to play. He'd stand guard the entire time Jason was there.

Life was mostly good. Larry, anxious to increase his earning potential and employment options, had returned to ASU and used his GI benefits to finish the degree that Viet Nam interrupted.

One day, Larry arrived home from school and work early. The weather outside was great so Larry picked up Jason and Popeye and took them to the park. All the kids in the park gathered around Popeye because he was so playful and friendly. As usual, he followed Jason everywhere including going up the slide steps and sliding down with Jason. Popeye was a hit.

On the drive home, Larry noticed the Humane Society sign and decided to stop in to get advice on getting Popeye dipped to prevent ticks. He was still a puppy and although Larry was worried about pests, he didn't want to harm him. Larry gathered Jason in his arms, hooked Popeye to his leash and went inside.

The entry room was full of people with their respective pets; mostly cats. Popeye was instantly aware of the other dogs and cats and was anxious to play; hence, pulled furiously on the leash. Jason, also fond of animals, squirmed in Larry's arms to get down, but Larry held on tight. Larry walked up to the reception counter.

"Excuse me. I'd like to get some information on getting my dog dipped for ticks if he's old enough."

The clerk was young and had a perky smile and attitude. She inquired as to Popeye's age. Larry told her Popeye was four months.

"You've come to the right place and your cute dog is old enough. We have a tank for that purpose where you can dip your dog yourself for only three dollars."

Larry was glad he had stopped by.

"That's reasonable. I'll do it. I don't have any cash. Will you take a check?"

The clerk was agreeable. Larry had to move Popeye's leash to the same hand that held Jason, which was a feat. He reached in his pocket for his checkbook with his other hand. Balancing child and dog, Larry wrote out a check and handed it to the clerk.

"May I see your driver's license please?"

Larry managed to get it out of his wallet of his back pocket without dropping Jason or letting go of Popeye.

"Why are there so many people here? You are really busy."

"Oh, the vet is in. Everyone is here to get checkups and shots for their pets."

"Is he old enough to get a rabies shot?"

"He sure is."

Larry looked around at the crowd to decide if he wanted to take the time and determined it was a good idea.

"How much does it cost?"

"It's only seven dollars for the shot and the visit."

He pondered a moment because he knew he didn't have cash for that either.

"I'll need to write another check for the seven dollars."

He went through the same check writing routine. Sounds simple enough, but not when your dog is trying to find a girlfriend, anxious to catch a cat and your son has had enough of being held. Larry finally finished and handed the new check to the clerk.

"May I see your driver's license?"

Larry's fuse was burning fast.

"Can't you see I'm having trouble here? Can't you look at the check I just gave you and copy the information from there?"

The girl stepped back a couple of paces at Larry's angry reply.

"Well, I guess I could. I didn't think of that."

Larry waited impatiently as she took his first check out of the cash drawer and copied the information onto the new check.

"Sir, obviously, you're going to have a long wait for your turn to see the vet so you might as well dip your dog first."

"Fine, where do I go?"

She pointed toward a hallway.

"Go down there, turn right at the first intersection and continue until that hallway ends. Then, go out the door. The tub will be on your left."

Larry grabbed onto Jason, who was nearly out of his arms and yanked hard on Popeye's leash.

"Come on, let's go."

As he started off, the clerk called after him.

"Sir, oh sir."

Larry stopped and turned toward her.

"What?"

"You forgot the Vaseline."

Larry snapped back in a loud voice.

"I don't want to fuck him, I want to dip him."

There was a hush in the room after a few gasps. The poor little clerk, whose hands now covered her blushing cheeks, straightened her shoulders as she mustered the courage for a response.

"It's for the dog's eyes."

Chapter Seven

gave birth to our second son, Jacob Lee on April 9, 1976, three weeks before Larry graduated from Arizona State. In spite of his hard work in school, the new affirmative action laws were having an opposite effect on Larry's ability to find career employment. Our former neighbors, who had moved to Point Barrow, Alaska; the northern most point in the United States told Larry of a job opening for a business manager at the Naval Arctic Research Lab. They had written us of how well they were adjusting to their life there. Larry wanted to apply and worked to convince me.

"You know how much I like camping and adventure. You'd have friends there and our children would have kids their age too."

I was tired of struggling financially, which made the prospect of the benefits of a five-year commitment desirable. In addition, our friends told us there was a bookkeeper position available for which I would qualify. With Larry's new business administration degree, he was a great fit.

"All right, let's go for it. I'll make arrangements to get you an airline pass to fly up there. I'll bet not too many of the candidates will go to the trouble of showing up in person."

The more we discussed it, the more excited we became. We called our friends, who were anxious to have Larry stay with them. We both applied and as I suspected, Larry was the only candidate out of fifty-two applicants who volunteered to interview in person.

Larry flew to Fairbanks without difficulty, but on arrival, he discovered that Wien Airlines' employees had gone on strike. For the first time in the years of flying on airline passes, Larry didn't depend on me to figure how another route when something went wrong. There was only one small commuter airline flying to Barrow. Larry approached their gate agent and presented his pass for Wien.

"I was supposed to fly up to Barrow today for an interview. This job opportunity is really important to my family and me. Would you please accept this pass?"

They understood his dilemma and even though they'd receive little compensation, they did have an empty seat.

"We have room for you and are happy to take you along, but I'm not certain how you'll get back. This flight operates round trip once per week and you happened to be here on the right day."

Without hesitation, Larry accepted their offer.

"I'll worry about that on the way home or I'll wait a week up there if I have to."

He loved the ride to Barrow and watched as the pilot followed the Alaska pipeline for much of the six hundred mile flight. When Larry arrived, our friends were there to greet him equipped with a heavy parka for Larry to wear.

His interviewer the next day was impressed with Larry's innovation in getting to Point Barrow on his own. Larry thought the job would be great and hoped he had been successful.

That night was Larry's first experience in the land of the midnight sun. He and our friends stayed up late with a premature celebratory fanfare. In what should have been the middle of the night, there was a loud knock at the door. Larry volunteered to answer it. The visitors were children.

"Can the boys come out and play baseball?"

"Well, they're in bed sleeping. Why aren't you?"

The kids didn't bother to answer him. They just scampered away. Larry watched them go and realized it was so light outside that it could have been daytime. He went back into the kitchen.

"This is incredible. How do kids know when to sleep and when to play? Obviously, those kids didn't."

Our friends explained school was out, but they put their children to bed at the same time every night so that they could keep their own schedule. That night was an exception for them. As soon as they said that, a loud horn began to wail. It startled all of them, but especially Larry.

"What's that?"

"Polar bear warning signal. There must be one wandering close to town."

Larry gave that some thoughtful moments, but decided it would all be part of the adventure. The next morning, Larry faced the challenge to find a way home. Our friends had heard of a bush pilot, who was heading back to Fairbanks in an old DC 3 cargo plane loaded with a dog sled and its crew. Larry went to the landing strip to introduce himself to the pilot.

"Say, do you have room for one more person?"

"Sure, happy to have you along, but I have to tell you that you'll have to ride in the back with the cargo . . . only have two seats and both are taken."

Larry felt fortunate to have a ride so told him he didn't mind. He went back to our friends' home and packed his clothes to be ready for an early flight the following day. As it turned out, he rode the entire flight sitting on the dog sled with an Alaskan Husky drooling on his shoulder. In Larry's words, he rode a dog sled from Point Barrow to Fairbanks, Alaska. True, after a fashion.

He returned encouraged and ready to move us. Our friends were as excited as Larry. The candidates had been narrowed down to two people with Larry being one of them. Unfortunately, a man who had a degree and more experience was awarded the job. About two months later, our phone rang and it was the successful candidate.

"I've reviewed your resume and want to offer you the bookkeeper position."

I was mystified. I thought I had written in my cover letter that I was interested in the job only in the event my husband received the position for which he had applied.

"Gee, I'd love to, but you have the job my husband wanted. I am afraid it was a package deal."

The man thanked me and apologized that he had gotten the job and not Larry.

With college completed, we had no income besides my part time income at the airline and Larry's weekend warrior monthly pay. No job prospects were imminent so Larry requested full time summer duty from the National Guard, which he had joined after returning from Viet Nam. This was a good decision that proved invaluable in helping to keep our family solvent. The colonel at the guard offered him employment at their facility in Flagstaff, Arizona where he helped manage the process of other guard units as they came and went for their two-week summer duty.

We hoped this would provide some experience in management for him in addition to having an extra income. While this was tough on me being home with two small children and working part time myself, we needed the money to make ends meet until he found real, long term employment.

At the end of his tour of duty, our friend, Allen Wacker, hired Larry to roof houses, which helped to supplement our income. I had picked up extra hours at work so now we both worked full time. It required a full time babysitter, however, so we selected a pre-school that took babies and toddlers. Jason was four and Jake was seven months old. It didn't matter if Larry or I delivered the boys, the same thing would happen each morning. Jason would run through the day care building to the playground out back so he could see us drive around the building to exit. The fence was wood with big slats that crossed one another and caused gaps. He'd stick his little hand through the slat to wave goodbye, while he stood on his tiptoes to look through another. Larry remarked to me how it broke his heart to watch Jason's morning routine.

"Do you think they're mean to him? Why does he do that?"

"I hope not. He never has marks or anything on him. It makes me cry every time too."

I took the kids to pre-school one day on my way to work and when I arrived at the school, the director advised me that one of the children had contracted infectious hepatitis.

"We have advised the county medical examiner, who will bring in a team to test all of the children. There will be no cost to you."

I was shocked that the cost seemed to be her biggest concern.

"I certainly hope not. But what happens if we find out our children have hepatitis?"

She shrugged her shoulders and had no answer to that.

Two weeks earlier, Jake had been very ill with what our vacationing pediatrician's substitute diagnosed as double ear infections. Larry had stayed home to care for Jake as Allen was more sympathetic than the attendance requirements were at my job. On one particular day during his illness, I arrived home from work to find Larry sitting in a chair with Jake lying in his arms. My baby was so pale; his skin had a transparent look about it. I feared he was deathly ill. I rushed over to cradle him in my arms. He didn't have a fever, but he was limp. Larry also looked worn out.

"What's happened today? You both look terrible."

Larry nodded his agreement.

"He's been throwing up all day and he's had diarrhea, but don't worry, I saved all the nasty diapers for you. They're in the toilet."

We couldn't afford the new invention, disposable diapers. Like my mother, I rinsed the soiled diapers in the toilet to remove the excess, wrung them out by hand and put them in a pail to haul to the washing machine. Larry didn't participate in that chore, though I did appreciate his willingness to change Jake's diapers.

When I heard about the hepatitis, I told the medical team about the incident even though Jake had recovered by the time the blood tests were administered. Jake's test proved positive, but not active. They suggested Jake had contracted hepatitis in addition to his ear infections, which would explain the violent vomiting and diarrhea.

The nurse on site gave Jason and me gamma globulin shots and insisted I take Jake back to his doctor. His pediatrician told me that the county had to be wrong, as Jake looked fine. I told him about the one day when Jake had been so sick. He proceeded to take two vials of blood from my baby's groin while the nurse and I held him down. Jake was wailing, and I was crying and wishing I had kept my mouth shut. The results were inconclusive, although, months later we learned the doctor had tested him for the wrong type of hepatitis. Since we had received such conflicting information, Larry chose not to have the gamma globulin shots as he thought it was a waste of time. At the end of the next week, he and Allen went hunting for a long weekend.

By the end of their hunting trip, Larry's urine had turned coffee colored, a primary symptom of hepatitis. I took him to the emergency room as soon as he came home and they admitted him for two weeks. He had caught the infectious hepatitis from Jake, but had a much worse case.

Larry's illness was a chronic, aggressive type of hepatitis that was damaging his liver. The doctors were baffled. Nothing they tried stopped the aggression. They took a biopsy of his liver and sent it to a specialist in another state. The only cure that could be offered was steroids and long-term bed rest. He was home for six weeks and seemed to be fairing well.

My sister, Laura's, wedding was planned in January. Jason was the ring bearer and I was the matron of honor. At the reception, Larry's pallor turned yellow.

"Are you feeling okay?"

He shook his head no.

"I feel exhausted."

I collected Jason, who was busy running around with the other children. We had left Jake home with a babysitter. The next morning, I took Larry to the hospital. He was there another week. That began a six months recovery period. He was so weak; he couldn't even hold Jake, who was ten months old. He couldn't work either. Our babysitters, who were sisters, lived next door and took turns caring for the boys while I worked. I don't know what I would have done without them. They washed our clothes and folded them, cleaned the house and were sweet to our children. Larry felt helpless as he watched them do the simple chores he was unable to accomplish.

I had another idea, which was to pray. I think the latter was supportive of the doctor's efforts. By June, Larry had finally rallied with only two percent of his liver intact. It was another example of his Murphy's Law persona; what can go wrong does for Larry.

❦ ❦ ❦

I met Allen Wacker when I served in the National Guard after Viet Nam. Allen, a couple of years junior to me, had been married and divorced and was still single when I met him. His marriage produced one son with whom Allen maintained a close relationship. However, his sights on romance were dimmed by his busy life style. He owned his own roofing business, served in the National Guard and divided his spare time between hunting and fishing.

Allen adopted our family as his own and thoroughly appreciated occasional home cooked meals with us. His agility as he maneuvered around a rooftop didn't match his massive stature. His height and size masked his gentle nature and humorous personality. We were wowed by the first of many Christmas Eves we shared together when he brought us a platter of home baked cookies he had prepared in a traditional baking season with his mother.

Since Louise didn't have a spark of interest in tracking Bambi, Allen and I became deer and elk hunting buddies. I have always had an immense respect for safety, expertise with guns and fairness in sport. I have been a hunter in the pioneer spirit, more than a trophy hunter. Safety conscious, I insisted each of our boys attend gun-handling classes before they were twelve years old. My family has all learned to eat the game I catch, provided I stick to elk and deer.

During one hunting adventure, Allen and I went to St. George, Utah where in addition to the dry climate; there was also cold wind and snow. Unlike Allen, who was always prepared, I didn't think of small details. The trouble began on the very first day Allen and I arrived in camp. I realized right away I'd forgotten to bring my lip balm. I hated to ask Allen because I knew I'd hear a ration of shit about what I should pack. But, I was desperate.

"Hey Wacker, did you bring Chap Stick?"

He bellowed his response as if in anticipation of a request.

"Why?"

"I forgot mine. Let me borrow yours. My lips are getting dry and chapped already."

Allen reached in his pocket and pulled out the small tube and threw it at me.

"Bring your own next time."

This went on for the whole long weekend. Allen lost patience with me quickly. Each time he had to dig the lip balm out of his pocket to throw to me, more words were exchanged and the pleasantries were fewer.

"You are really a pain in the ass, Larry. I can't believe you didn't bring anything for chapped lips. If you weren't my good buddy, I wouldn't share mine with you."

"Sorry, Allen, unlike you, I didn't make a list."

He muttered expletives under his breath.

"Well, next time make a list."

On the way home to Arizona, Allen and I stopped alongside Interstate 15 for a pee and beer break. Allen opened the passenger door and stepped out. I exited the driver's door and walked around the back of the truck to get a beer. I pitched a beer to Allen, who had stayed near his door to take care of his business. I turned my back to the road and unzipped my pants to pee.

"Hey Allen, throw me your Chap Stick."

He set his beer on the bed of the truck and reached in his pocket to retrieve the lip balm, but couldn't throw it without letting me know how he felt about it.

"You sorry SOB, Larry."

I knew I was getting on Allen's last nerve. I'd probably used his chap stick more than he had. As soon as he threw it to me, I dropped my pants to the ground, bent over and proceeded to apply it to my butt. Allen started screaming.

"What the hell are you doing?"

I stared at him, shrugged my shoulders and then put my hands in the air.

"Where do you think I've been putting this all weekend?"

Allen grabbed his beer and started chasing me. He seized a couple more bottles as he ran past the open cooler box at the end of the truck. He threw all of them at me and bent down to pick up rocks or whatever he could snatch. I ran down the highway with my pants around my ankles in hysterics. If Allen hadn't been laughing so hard at the sight of me struggling to run practically naked, his anger might not have subsided. The reckoning that it was all a joke would not have sunk in.

When I arrived home from the hunting trip, the first thing I told Louise was how I had tricked Allen on the way home from our hunting trip. Allen has never leant me his lip balm again.

For that matter, after I've told the story to our friends, no one, including my own wife will loan me a chap stick.

Months later, Larry and I were vacationing in Hawaii with Jason and Jake, and I vindicated Allen. I worked for an airline, which provided travel perks and compensated me for the low salary. The summer of 1980, Larry and I took Jason, age eight and Jake, age four, to Honolulu for a long weekend. We flew to Los Angeles, but had to stand by for a flight on another airline to get to Hawaii. We had to sit in the terminal for ten hours before we were able to secure four empty seats. The flight was cheap, but our boarding priority was low. The first three hours the boys played with their cars, as they were accustomed to this drill. The next hour, however, they chased each other in the waiting area as I tried to be discreet and get them to sit down. They were supposed to act like gentlemen, but even I couldn't corral them for such a long period of time.

I must say, that when they were running around, they were quiet about it. I'd hear an occasional giggle, but otherwise they kept close to us and away from other passengers. For this I was grateful. When we weren't granted boarding on the second flight, we walked down the hall for some tasteless, but expensive airport food. Larry had become increasingly more impatient.

"If we don't get on the next flight, I'm going home."

I had spent so much time planning this little getaway that I refused to allow him to make me feel bad.

"Suit yourself, but the boys and I are going if we have to wait all night."

We finished our meal and went back to the crowded gate area. Larry had a look of doom on his face with his mouth turned down in a frown.

"There are more people here this time than the last flight. We aren't going to get on."

"It's probably a bigger aircraft. Quit your bitching."

Fortunately, we did get on the plane. When we arrived in Honolulu, we took a taxi to our high-rise hotel, located on Waikiki Beach. Since we had stayed there before, we received a fruit basket in our room as a thank you. Jason spotted it as soon as he walked into the room.

"Hey Mom, can I have an apple?"

It seemed he was always hungry. He didn't eat big meals; rather, he liked to graze all day.

"Of course you may. Help yourself, but don't forget to wash it first."

Jake joined his brother as they rummaged through the basket to see what else was there that they liked. Larry and I unpacked.

Each morning, we had breakfast at the hotel patio snack shop and hit the beach running. We prepared our nest for the day and placed our straw mats and spread out our towels on the warm sand. We had plenty of room in spite of the beach being crowded. I slathered the boys with sun tan lotion (there was no sunscreen then) and put zinc oxide on their noses. Both of them were good swimmers so they took off to play in the surf with their boogie boards. Larry and I sat on the beach and watched. I loved the warmth of the sun against my skin. It wasn't as hot as Arizona; especially, with the soft breeze cooled off by the ocean.

"Ah, this is paradise. I could sit it here for hours."

And, we did. Larry tapped on my arm to get my attention.

"Remember our first trip here when we were worried we'd be too fat to sit on the beach?"

I gave him a dirty look as I recalled the rotten trick he'd played on me.

"How could I forget?"

We had traveled there for a seminar because I was an officer on the board of directors for our credit union. While I attended classes every day, Larry lounged on the beach. The first afternoon I had free, I joined him. As a very wide-hipped lady in a white bathing suit passed us, Larry leaned into me to whisper.

"I've been coming here every day for three days and watching the people. I've seen lots of men bigger than me, but I haven't seen anyone bigger than you."

What a creep. He had always loved to tease me at every opportunity and that was no exception. This trip, I was experienced and didn't worry about my size, which was pleasant, not fat.

"You're lucky I let you come back here with me."

He laughed, as he knew I was kidding. He took my hand and held it as we settled back on our mats. We had brought chips and fruit to the beach so munched on them throughout the day. Late in the afternoon, we persuaded the boys to get out of the water. We bought sandwiches and more chips from the hotel patio snack shop and headed to our room.

We showered off the sand and took the table and chairs from our room out onto the veranda so that we could dine as we watched the sunset. Afterward, we went back inside and all watched television for a little while, but the boys were worn out and went to sleep early. Since Larry and I couldn't leave the boys alone, we went back outside on the porch and listened to music that was carried up on the breeze from the outdoor bar below us. As romantic as the setting was, our budget didn't include champagne so we clinked our beer cans instead.

The next day, we were going to take them snorkeling at Waimea Bay. Larry headed downstairs with the boys while I gathered the necessities for our excursion. When I reached the area where the banks of elevators were, all three of them were sitting on a bench with the same pose; legs crossed and arms folded. I had to stop and take their picture they were so cute. We walked the two blocks to town and bought some frozen peas to take with us to feed the fish. We hopped on the bus and rode the few miles to the beach. We rented our gear when we arrived there. Jason loved wearing his snorkel gear and fins.

Jason, age eight — ready to snorkel   *Jake, age five — learning to tie his shoe*

"Take my picture, Mom. I look like a monster from outer space."

That was his favorite pose from the entire trip. Larry doled out a handful of peas to each of us along with instructions.

"Now, don't drop the peas all at once. Let go of one or two at a time. The fish will come closer and you'll get a good look at them. You won't believe how many different kinds and colors there are."

Jake was only four and was a bit apprehensive when he'd drop a few peas in the water. The fish swarmed him, which at first made him want to swim away. But, when he realized they weren't after him, he was braver. The coral reef looked like a garden of colorful flowers, which made us eager to go closer toward the outer edge. The four of us kicked our way around the reef for an hour before Jake and I retired to the beach. Larry and Jason swam around until they felt they had seen everything in the cove.

We played on the beach and took turns getting buried in the sand. At sunset, we went back to the hotel and waited for an elevator in the lobby. In spite of there being about ten of them, it seemed to take a long time. As we waited, a few more people gathered. We walked onto the elevator and turned to face the doors. As they closed, Larry and I saw Jason through the crack on the other side. Larry slapped at the panel and tried to hit the open button, but it was too late and he couldn't stop it. The two teenage girls, who had boarded before us were worried. One of them apologized for getting on ahead of our family.

"What are you going to do?"

I tried to remain calm so as not to alarm them.

"We're going to our floor, which is fifteen, and hope that Jason remembers our floor number."

Even though he was eight years old, Jason was a seasoned traveler. He had been taking trips with us since he was a year old. We thought it best to wait for him there because if we tried to go back down, we might miss him. The girls stayed with us. I began to think terrible thoughts. He doesn't know our floor. Someone might snatch him. It seemed we had waited for hours, but in reality it had only been a few minutes. Larry paced back and forth amid the elevators. The girls offered to take another elevator down and look for him. I punched the down button and prayed for a quick response.

When we heard the ding of an arriving elevator, we all turned our attention to the door. It opened and there stood Jason. The girls and Jake cheered. I had tears of joy in my eyes and Larry rushed toward the elevator. Jason bowed to the Asian gentleman, who held the door open for him. The man returned the gesture and smiled. Larry and I hugged Jason, but Larry was the first to speak.

"I was so worried. I'm proud you remembered our floor number."

I held Jason's hand and felt the clammy coldness. While he beamed with pride, I knew he had also been frightened. His voice quivered a bit when he spoke.

"I knew which floor, but I couldn't reach the number fifteen. I had to wait for a grown-up to help me. That man was nice, but he didn't speak English. I had to shape numbers with my fingers and point until he pushed the right button for me."

I hugged him, again, for his cleverness and quick thinking. The girls gathered around us for a group hug.

"For a little kid, you sure are smart."

They left us chattering to each other. They were amazed at how well it turned out. I, also grateful, looked up toward Heaven and said my thanks. We went to our room, showered and changed clothes and headed to McDonald's for dinner. Afterward we went to the beach and watched the sunset. The sky was ablaze in pink, orange and purple. It was lovely to see the hot sun sink into the sea. I almost expected to hear it sizzle as it went down.

We took the boys to visit the sights such as Pearl Harbor and toured the USS Arizona memorial. They had lots of questions about what had happened. The somber crowd around us spoke more of the reverence than we could explain. We decided a catamaran cruise would be more to their liking, but after forty-five minutes on the boat, Jason came to sit by me and put his head in my lap. He looked as green as I felt.

"Are you going to be sick?"

"I think so."

The captain heard our conversation and brought us a bucket. This was evidently not the first victim of the rough sea on his boat. As Jason hung his head over the bucket, I rubbed his back.

"We'll be back on shore in fifteen minutes. Try to hang in there. Besides, if you throw up, I will too. This bucket isn't big enough for both of us to use at the same time."

The thought that he wasn't alone in his misery made him cheer up.

"Okay."

And then he puked. I gagged and then I prayed we'd make it to shore before I threw up. It reminded me that Larry and I had made a deal when Jason was born. Larry had barf duty and I had poop duty. For whatever reason, the latter was easier for me to handle. We had stuck to our bargain until this time. As I tried to look away from Jason's regurgitation, I noticed Larry sitting on the other side of the boat chuckling. I glared at him as my lunch was creeping up my throat. I patted Jason on the back.

"This ride is fun, isn't it?"

Jason looked at up me. His greenish face showed no joy.

"Well, before you threw up, anyway."

I turned my head away from Jason and could see the shore. I began taking deep breaths through my nostrils.

"Yea, we made it."

Jason and I jumped off the boat first as soon as we anchored by the shore. We were both happy to be on solid ground.

We spent our last day on Waikiki at the beach. After a couple of hours, Jake was a tired little boy and needed a nap. He lay down on one of the straw mats and I covered him with towels so he wouldn't get sunburned. While he slept, the tide came in and swamped him. The waves went clear over his small body and dragged him out toward the ocean. I ran after him and pulled him and the mat up to safe ground. He never stirred.

Because of the constant wetness of our bottoms on the sand, I had developed a small, uncomfortable rash. I had rummaged through my girlie stuff and found a sample container of Aloe Vera. It was just what I needed to handle my discomfort, but I hadn't told Larry what I did to fix the problem.

We took one last swim before we packed up and headed to the airport. Larry and I carried our belongings to the hotel locker room. We took turns, one of us watched the boys in the water while the other took trips to the hotel. I was walking back to the beach when I saw Larry search in my purse for lip balm, which he never remembered to carry himself. He found the Aloe Vera container I had used and flipped it over to look at the ingredients. I was about ten yards away and stopped to see what he'd do.

He opened the lid of the container, stuck a finger in and as he began to apply the contents to his lips, he raised his head and we made eye contact. He stopped, looked at me and shook his head no. I nodded my head yes and we knew that Allen would be satisfied. I couldn't wait to tell him.

Chapter Eight

Larry had returned to work for Allen roofing houses after convalescing from hepatitis. This was difficult for him in his weakened condition, but in a gesture of friendship, Allen was considerate in giving Larry time to get back into shape. The blistering Arizona heat, however, was a tortuous challenge and on a rooftop it couldn't be avoided.

In the fall of 1977, the tide changed for us. My mother had spoken to a close friend she worked with in real estate sales about Larry. Mom knew her friend's husband was the Regional Manager of a State Farm Insurance Claims office. Never one to mince words, Mom was always in a sales pitch mode.

"My son-in-law is in desperate need of a desk job. He's smart, talented, handsome and athletic. He graduated from ASU and was a football player there."

Her friend didn't hesitate to offer help.

"I'll speak with my husband tonight to see if he will get Larry an interview."

The timing was perfect as State Farm was in a hiring mode. Larry was granted an interview, scored well and was hired. We were both ecstatic. It was a career position with benefits, a company car and decent pay.

Larry's mentor on the job was Francene Adcock, whose father was Larry's manager and whose husband, Jim, also worked at State Farm.

A couple of weeks into the job, his coworkers enticed him to join them for the weekly Friday night happy hour at the nearby Fiesta Inn. Larry offered to drive. As it turned out, most of his passengers were women.

When they returned to the company parking lot a couple of hours later, after countless war stories Larry had told, Francene asked Larry where he had been injured when in Viet Nam. Larry jumped out of the car, shot them a moon, and pointed to his behind.

"Right here."

The girls howled with laughter and went to their respective cars. The next Monday at work, Francene, talked to Larry about what happened Friday night.

"You know we love you and thought your moon shot was hysterical, but I found out that it was captured on the security video camera in the parking lot. You are being summoned to the front office."

While this happened before the days of reporting sexual harassment, Larry was panic stricken that he was about to lose the job he loved.

"I don't know what I'm going to tell Louise."

He took a deep breath, fought back the tears that threatened to fill his eyes and slowly headed for the front office. When he arrived, he introduced himself to the boss' Executive Assistant.

"I'm Larry Laughlin and I have an appointment with Clem."

She shook her head as if disgusted.

"Tsk, tsk. Have a seat."

She pushed the button of the intercom.

"Larry is here to see you."

Larry stared at the vice president's door. It seemed larger than life. He sat with closed body language, legs crossed and arms folded and this seemed to make his body shrink in comparison. He watched as the door finally opened, but ever so slowly.

Inside the office were all the people he had gone to happy hour with the Friday before. Shrieks of laughter filled the room as they were all in on the joke, including the vice president and his assistant. Larry didn't get fired for mooning the girls; rather, this initiation gave him the new nickname of Moon. They also clued him in to the fact that the camera was not even turned on. It began the long-term friendships forged during his twenty years at State Farm. I dare say; had it happened in this decade, the ending would have been quite different.

During these memorable years when Larry worked at State Farm in Arizona, I worked for Hughes Airwest, Republic Airlines and Northwest Airlines without ever changing jobs other than an occasional promotion. The benefits provided opportunities for endless travel. We took advantage of this privilege every chance we had. We started out small with weekend trips to California, flying to Utah for a day of snow skiing or going to Ohio to see Larry's family. We branched out and went to Hawaii a couple of times and then we went international.

Larry and I were envied in our family for our long weekend trips such as the time we went to London. When we arrived at Heathrow after the long flight, we didn't want to waste time on sleeping. We ventured out together to see the sights with some other airline employees we had met on the flight. After perusing the flea market near Piccadilly, we decided to head to Windsor Castle. We had to stand in queue at a bus stop for what seemed like forever. When the right bus to get to the train station finally arrived, the neat line became a mass of people pushing and shoving to get on. Whoever said the English are proper hasn't been to London.

The whole time we waited, Larry kept commenting on the pallor of the English girls.

"These women could use a long day in the sun."

I shushed him fearful someone would hear. I didn't want anyone to think he was rude. When we finally secured seats on the bus, Larry turned to the girl next to him and in a loud voice announced his opinion.

"You're the first good looking English girl I've seen since I've been here."

At first, her chin dropped giving Larry an incredulous glare. Her reply relayed her displeasure at his comment.

"I'm an American, you turkey."

This caused laughter from the men on board, but the women turned away from Larry, the ugly American. I stifled a giggle and pretended I didn't know him.

We stayed at the only Irish hotel in London, which had been advertised in an employee airline discount guidebook. It was fate, as we had no idea of where to stay. The weekend we were there was Memorial Day weekend for us and a Bank Holiday for London. It was also the weekend of the annual soccer match between England and Scotland. Larry was in heaven as along with the Scots, there were plenty of Irish. He knew he must be related to many of the men in

Larry, Louise and new Scottish friends

the hotel. That evening we saw an American woman seated alone in the crowded bar. Larry tapped her on the shoulder.

"Do you mind if we join you and share your table?"

She smiled pleasantly at us.

"Please, sit down. I don't like being here alone. I'm waiting for my husband, who is a bit late returning from work."

Larry, who does most of the talking with strangers, drilled her with questions.

"Where does your husband work? How long have you been here? Are you going to stay here long?"

She was happy to accommodate his inquiries and we learned her husband was in the military and assigned to the American Embassy. She had been there a couple of weeks and had seen the sights we had come to see. Further, she was lonesome and bored in the daytime when her husband was at work. Larry invited her to go with us the next day.

"Instead of staying at the hotel by yourself, why don't you meet us in the morning and be our tour guide?"

She looked at me as if to see if I objected. I didn't and told her so.

"Yes, please join us if you can stand a gabby Irish-American."

She nodded.

"I'd love to."

We set a time and place to meet in the hotel lobby. Larry turned around and began making friends with the many Scotsmen there for the soccer game. The next morning, we set out for our tour. We went to lunch at the Grenadier Pub, which was over eight hundred years old. It had been in the movie, *Around the World in 80 Days*. The age of the buildings amazed us. I don't think either of us had seen a building older than one hundred years before. One wouldn't know the history that each building could offer by looking at it. At first glance or in the case of the pub, our second or third glance wouldn't reveal its age. It was well preserved. This trip was a turning point for my interest in history. Because I have always been a visual person, I was intrigued and imagined the stories that could be told if the walls could talk. The places we wanted to see, such as Hyde Park and Buckingham Palace, seemed to be another block ahead so we walked instead of taking the bus. We had a grand time. It's such a wonderful place to sightsee.

The last day of our weekend, we went to the Tower of London with our airline friends. The Crown Jewels were spectacular. We acted silly when we saw the many suits of armor in one hall and teased Larry.

"You could never have been a soldier in that era because you wouldn't have fit in any of these get ups."

We couldn't imagine the poor horses that also wore some armor and carried a passenger as well. Duly impressed and hungry when we finished the tour, we headed for a pub. Unfortunately most were closed for the holiday. We found one open that served ale but no food. The six of us went inside for warm, bitter ale. I hated the taste, but mostly I didn't like that it wasn't cold. I ordered a vodka and tonic and received a nasty warm drink. They don't use ice.

While there, Larry made friends with everyone in the pub, which is nothing unusual, but one kind fellow who said he owned the closed pub down the street had heard us grousing about being hungry and unable to find a source of food.

"Be my guest and come to my pub. I'll open it up for you and give you a hot meal."

Larry immediately accepted on everyone's behalf.

"Give me twenty minutes to get the lights turned on, open the kitchen and turn on the music."

We all trooped down the street and the man greeted us at the door.

"I must apologize as I've checked the larder and I have no food I can cook to serve you. But, I have plenty of ale and some snacks."

We offered to pay, but he said he was happy to treat. He turned on the microphone and turned up the music. We sang, danced, ate peanuts and crackers and drank our fill.

In the course of conversation, we discovered that the kind gentleman was not the proprietor; rather, he was the janitor. We insisted he take money at that point because we didn't want him to get fired.

Larry and I had been invited by our new American friend from the hotel to go to the American Embassy for dinner that night so said our goodbyes, left some pounds for the gentleman and took our leave. The others stayed a while. When we met up with our friend at the hotel, we all realized that it was Memorial Day and the Embassy was closed for the holiday.

Other than craving a balanced meal, we weren't too disappointed as we were exhausted by now. We had a few more drinks in the bar with our American friends and Scottish buddies and went to our room to sleep for the few hours left of the night.

We had an early morning flight and hoped the seat next to us remained empty so we could have more room to finish our rest. A young, American girl who had been visiting her brother sat in the empty seat next to us. As politely as he could, Larry encouraged her to move to a row where there were a few empty seats. I joined him in a persuasive manner.

"You know, it's okay to move after we take off."

I pointed to a row with three seats in the middle unoccupied.

"If you go over there, you could stretch out for a more comfortable sleep."

She wasn't convinced.

"Are you sure it isn't against the rules?"

"Oh no, it's fine. I work for an airline and I know."

She wouldn't budge. We probably should have moved, but by this time, we had our things positioned where we wanted them and I didn't feel like picking up and moving either even though I was in the middle seat. Larry ordered a bloody Mary and settled in.

"I'm going to drink this drink and go to sleep."

It had the opposite effect as he was too wired from our weekend to rest. After several Bloody Marys, evidenced by the pile of stirrers that looked like a pick-up sticks game in front of him, he started telling stories.

He engaged in a conversation with the young girl, who had finally woken up.

"Why were you in England?"

"I met my brother there and we traveled for six weeks around Europe. He stayed on to attend school."

The flight attendant came by with food and offered some to the girl first, but she declined. I remembered my first flight and Larry's first experience and guessed she didn't know it was a package deal.

"You know you don't have to pay for the food, don't you?"

Her face lit up and she rang her call button. When the flight attendant returned, the girl spoke up.

"I've changed my mind, if that all right."

She received a kind, knowing response and was immediately presented with a tray. Larry kept up his inquisition.

"Are you going to college after the summer?"

"Actually, I've been accepted to Julliard on a music scholarship."

Larry raised his eyebrows and pursed his lips as if he were impressed.

"What instrument do you play?"

She explained she played the piano and violin. Larry was too quick to tell her he was also musically inclined. Now, I was worried. It was a lie. I couldn't imagine where he was going with this conversation. The girl repositioned herself in her seat so that she could look past me and give Larry her full attention. She took the bait; hook, line and sinker.

"What instrument do you play?"

A grin crept across Larry's mouth.

"A swinette."

"What is that?"

And here came the punch line.

"It's a string stretched across a pig's ass and you pluck it with your teeth."

She excused herself and left. I moved to her window seat and we had more room for the remainder of the flight.

We continued our travel as often as we could even though most of our trips were limited to long weekends. September 1981 was no exception. My long time friend, Carol May, Larry and I traveled to Ireland together for a four-day weekend. Dan, Carol's husband, was supposed to go, but was forced to cancel at the last minute due to a work commitment. Carol and I both worked for the same airline and managed to take advantage of a great cheap deal on the trip.

We flew to Shannon in a DC-8 with an interior configuration of three seats on each side of the aisle. The fuselage was long and narrow, which made us feel like we were sitting in a bowling lane. Carol is about 5'11" and had such a small space for her long legs that the passenger, who sat in front of her couldn't put his seat back without crushing her kneecaps. In spite of the cramped space and eight-hour journey, Carol, Larry and I managed to entertain ourselves the entire time. We laughed, drank, told stories and slept.

As soon as we arrived in Shannon, Ireland, we hit the road to soak in as much countryside as we could. We stopped by a bed and breakfast first that a friend I worked with had recommended, to ensure we had a place to spend the night.

"I have two goals while I'm here . . . have fun and find another Laughlin."

Carol exchanged glances with me, but responded to Larry.

"Good luck with that."

The first was easy, but the second proved to be a challenge. We drove to the Cliffs of Moher on the west coast. We watched as the waves of the wild Atlantic slapped against the walls of the cliffs. Each day of travel with Larry and Carol was like having a circus troop with us. Carol loved to dance around with her arms extended and kicking her long legs in the air, but most fun to watch, for me, was the smile displayed on Larry's face at every new sight. He was truly in his element. He and Carol tried to talk with an Irish brogue the entire time. Carol loved the Burren.

"Ah, would ya look at the lovely landscape. The Burren goes for miles."

I took a more realistic point of view.

"Where the heck did they get all those rocks?"

Carol twirled around.

"From the ground, lassie."

I took nearly a whole role of film on the 35MM camera I had borrowed from my sister. I also had my trusty Instamatic camera, but these views deserved better. The air was close to frigid because of the winds that swept off the cold ocean. I practically had to drag Larry away as he was mesmerized by the countryside.

"Let's head back to Shannon. We have reservations at Bunratty Castle."

We reached the car and climbed into the small compact. Larry was our chauffer for the trip. The passenger seat was reserved for the navigator and the responsibility of back seat rider was to yell at the driver.

"Keep left, keep left."

I often rode in the back for two reasons; one, the front seat provided more room for Carol's legs and two; I rather enjoyed having a legitimate reason for being a back seat driver.

Bunratty Castle is nestled along the Shannon River and serves a traditional fifteenth century dinner each night. On arrival, we were escorted to the parlor for mead, a fermented, honey drink, and conversation. The castle, with its turrets and grey walls looked as I expected. The inside had tapestries hanging on the walls, which helped to reduce the bone-chilling air from the expanse of the brick and mortar in the room. In spite of the dull color, I was transformed into a Cinderella fairy tale. The ladies in waiting played their harps and violins for the noisy guests, who chatted amongst themselves and toasted one another with their drab green, glazed pottery glasses. Larry had already made friends with another Irish-American from San Francisco named Mr. O'Casey.

"Allow me to introduce you to my wife, and our friend Carol."

The gentleman was quick to laughter and joviality like Larry. There was a kindred spirit between them. The master of ceremonies called out to the crowd that must have numbered about one hundred.

"My lords and my ladies may I have your attention please."

The voices of the guests lowered like a ripple effect across the room until there was silence. Everyone was focused the speaker.

"Our first order of business is to follow the castle tradition of electing a Lord and Lady of the manor to preside over the evening's events. Please shout out your recommendations to me now."

There was a buzz among the crowd, but in short order, a gentleman cried out as he pointed to his nomination.

"How about the tall gent and his wife? They seem like a perfect, stalwart couple."

I had to crane my neck to see whom he meant, whereas Larry and Carol were nodding their heads in agreement. Sometimes I felt as if I was in the land of giants. I'm not particularly short; rather, everyone around me seemed tall. However, when I saw the couple, who had been recommended, I agreed, they looked regal enough for the job. Their posture was so erect; they looked like Barbie and Ken dolls. The crowd burst out in a round of applause indicating their agreement. They were beckoned to the front of the room where capes of velvet were placed on their shoulders and their heads were adorned with crowns. Cheers erupted.

"Long live the Lord and Lady of the Manor."

After the tourists participated in the election, beautiful women who played soothing music, sang and entertained us. About an hour later, we were led down a flight of stairs to the dining hall for our dinner. The walls of this room had been painted white perhaps to add an air of cleanliness to where the food was served. We were seated at long tables that filled the room. We had lost Mr. and Mrs. O'Casey in the resettlement, but as if on cue, Larry and his friend stood at opposite ends of room, their glasses raised and hollered their salute to one another.

Carol sat across from me so that we could engage in conversation more easily. Larry was seated next to and across from some older American ladies who were traveling together and whom we would bump into on more than one occasion on our self-tour.

The cuisine we were served was chicken with gravy, red wine and other finger foods, primarily, because we had no forks. We

Louise and Larry at Bunratty Castle feast

were provided a dagger with which to eat should our fingers not be sufficient. We wore cloth bibs to protect our clothing. Larry became the instant entertainment for the guests at our table. He picked up his chicken with his hands and bit into it like a dog would have done.

"Grrrrrr."

He tore off a bite and slapped the remainder on his plate. Carol and I were taken aback as he grabbed the bib of the lady sitting next to him and wiped his hands. We burst out laughing and the lady squealed with delight.

"Oh, young man, you are so much fun."

Encouraged by her response, he stepped up his play-acting. He motioned to our server, who was one of the ladies who had played the music beforehand.

"May I help you sir?"

"Ay, you may but please first tell me your name."

She blinked her eyes and curtseyed.

"It's Funella, my lord."

"Is there any chance I could have more mead instead of this red wine? I don't like it."

"Certainly sir. Tis an easy request you've made. I'll come right back to serve ye."

When she returned, she brought the mead in a crockery pitcher that matched the one that held the gravy. He smelled the contents and without hesitation, picked up the pitcher and drank from it. The lady across from him gasped.

"Why are you drinking the gravy?"

He thrust the pitcher toward her.

"Try it, you'll like it."

She faltered as she brought it closer to her face, but the strong aroma was unmistakable. Not fond of the wine, herself, she drank greedily from the pitcher. Her companions shrieked with delight.

"That young man has put a spell on you."

The lady did not let on as to what the contents were; rather, she winked at Larry and handed the container back. While this scenario transpired, the master of ceremonies approached me and whispered in my ear.

"Are you with the gentleman next to you or is the lady across from you his wife?"

In a low voice, I replied to him. "I'm the lucky one."

He grinned and shared his intentions.

"We like to pick out a person from the crowd and put them in the dungeon as part of the entertainment. His food will probably get cold, but we'll bring him another plateful. Do you think your husband will go along with the scheme?"

"Are you kidding? He'll love it. The center of attention is his favorite spot."

He left me and walked up to a podium, which was set a foot higher than the guests, to make an announcement to the crowd.

"There is a scalawag among us who is trifling with the ladies."

He walked over to Larry and asked him to stand.

"This is the offender. Shall we let him go free or throw him in the dungeon?"

Practically in unison, the crowd roared back their decision.

"Throw him in the dungeon."

The MC led Larry to a cave like area with bars at the front end of the room. He opened it up and with little effort, pushed Larry inside.

"In you go, rascal. There'll be no dining for you."

We all continued with our meal. The master of ceremonies addressed Larry periodically in a voice loud enough for all to hear.

"Knave, what say you now?"

Larry played the part well by raising his fisted hand out through the bars and shouting his retort.

"Mead for my friends and death to my enemies."

Everyone cheered and kept eating. After about twenty minutes, Larry complained. He leaned his face against the bars and cried out.

"Hello? Anyone remember I'm still in the dungeon?"

The master of ceremonies finally dragged him out of the cell and had him kneel before the Lord and Lady.

"Knave, what say you now?"

Larry with hands clasped as if he were praying, replied with sarcasm.

"Praise the Lord."

The crowd roared at Larry's reply while the Lord and Lady counseled with each other. They granted forgiveness to him and sent him back to his seat. The guests applauded Larry as he went back to his seat. He bowed his thanks and sat down.

"I was about to starve to death. I didn't think they were going to let me out of there."

Carol shook her finger at him.

"That's what you get for being a scoundrel."

Funella appeared with another meal in hand, which Larry ate with gusto.

We left the castle and went next door to Dirty Nellie's, a tourist pub that was packed with patrons and the local rugby team. We could barely maneuver our way from one room to the next. Larry, not hampered by the crowd continued his bad boy behavior.

"It's elbow to asshole in here."

As he passed by one of the little old ladies we had shared a meal with, he pinched her on the rear. Carol and I shook our heads. I was glad Carol was with me, as perhaps people would think Larry was her husband; not mine.

On our way to Kilarney the next day, I took out my sister's camera to change the role of film. I had forgotten her instructions and exposed the entire roll of film I had taken our first day. I was not a happy camper. I put the camera away and took out my trusty Instamatic.

"I'd better stick to what I know."

Carol commiserated with me and reminded me that we had used the cheap camera for some of the pictures of the dinner the night before. I was relieved to know all was not lost.

Some friends where I worked advised me to stop in Kilarney and attend a songfest in the back of the Laurel's Pub. When we arrived, the ladies were there too. They recognized Larry and called to him.

"Young man, we're over here. Come sit with us."

I grabbed Larry's arm and dragged him in another direction.

"Enough is enough."

We sat on the opposite side of the big room. The folksy entertainment was fun and interactive. We sang loud and long in the songfest and thoroughly enjoyed ourselves.

The third day, we arrived in a seaside resort named Kinsale on our way to County Cork. It was a quaint little village that looked like it could be a movie set. Typically, we stopped at a pub around two in the afternoon to have sandwiches and ale. We discovered the Irish drink their beer colder than the English, which I greatly appreciated. We chatted with the locals while we ate and moved on to the next stop on our journey. This particular afternoon, we met Emer and Michael Ramsden at the Pub. She was Irish and he was English. They owned an antique shop in Dublin and were in Kinsale to close up their summer home.

It was raining and cold outside, but the small fire burning in the fireplace brought warmth to the pub. Even though I had not become accustomed to the unusual odor of the peat moss and found its pungent scent somewhat offensive; the heat compensated for the odor. Regulars of small pubs such as this one brought their dogs with them. As the master sat on a bar stool, his faithful companion would settle on the floor beside him or stretch out in front of the warm fire. The animals were gentle and used to strangers petting them or scratching them behind the ears. Dog lover that I am, I took advantage of the opportunity as we relaxed in the chairs by the fireplace. Emer, who had an effervescent quality about her, engaged us in conversation and told us about the area.

"You really must stay in Kinsale tonight. Tomorrow is supposed to be sunny. This is a delightful little town worth seeing. There's no use in going from one dreary little town to the next or so it would seem with today's weather."

We agreed to stay. Because our trip was short, we knew we wouldn't be able to see everything on our list of destinations. Our concern was finding a place to stay, as September was the end of the tourist season. I was certain we could rely on Emer to give us advice.

"Could you recommend a bread and breakfast near here that is still open?"

Emer was eager for us to see the beauty of the area.

"There's a bed and breakfast a block or so from our cottage. I'm certain I saw their sign out for business. Why don't you go there and then come to our place for cocktails?"

We accepted her offer. After chatting for another hour, we left to check into the B&B. Fortunately, they had two rooms available. We put our suitcases in our respective rooms and headed out to the Ramsden's home. We had a couple of bottles of liquor in our car, which Larry gathered up to take inside.

"You know, Larry. We're not in America where it is customary to bring your own booze. They invited us. You might insult them if you carry in those bottles."

He grumbled a bit, but left them behind. When we got inside, Michael apologized to Larry.

"I'm sorry, mate. I've checked the liquor cabinet and it's empty. However, we have a wine cellar. Please join me to select a bottle of wine?"

Since Larry did not like wine, he was not a connoisseur. He looked at me in an attempt to protest, but I motioned him on. When they returned, they had three bottles between them. Michael opened the bottles and set them next to the fireplace to breathe. The peat moss that was burning smelled like incense, which made me feel a little swimmy headed. Larry held back his disappointment at the beverage choice, especially, warm wine.

I noticed his jaw looked tight as if he was clinching his teeth. Carol and I just went with the flow. Soon, other guests, a doctor and his wife, arrived. Like Michael and Emer, it was a mixed marriage only the doctor was Irish and his wife was very proper English. Because she was pregnant, she drank Sarsaparilla in extreme robotic mannerisms. Larry loosened up with each glass he drank.

"I'm not much of a wine drinker. In college, we drank Ripple, Red Mountain, Strawberry Hill or whatever."

Carol and I cracked up, but Michael looked quizzically at him as he'd never heard of any of those brands. Emer, who was the salt of the earth, told a bawdy joke that broke the ice. She and Larry were two of a kind. The evening was filled with laughter, mostly Larry, Carol, Emer, the doctor and I as we shared anecdotes. Mrs. Doctor complained she was getting hungry. We apologized that we had stayed so long and interfered with their dinner plans. Emer jumped up and addressed us.

"We've loved visiting with you. Why don't you join us for dinner?"

I was thankful, as I was hungry too. It was now nine in the evening; seven hours since we'd had lunch. Michael, who had acted arrogant toward us, rather enjoyed his host in charge routine.

"Because of the late hour, most restaurants will be closed, but I know the owner of a lovely restaurant in town. I'm certain he'll accommodate us."

When we arrived, the maitre d' peeked out the door to announce the restaurant was not open for business but then he recognized Michael who spoke with him.

"We have out of town and out of country guests. We're sorry to impose on the late hour, but could you please oblige us?"

The man nodded his consent.

"The only thing we can offer is the soup of the day and cheese."

Michael moved forward toward the door to hold it open for us.

"That would be perfect."

We trooped in single file and were led to our table. We had a wonderful cream of tomato soup, Larry's least favorite, and Brie. Michael handed Larry the wine list and addressed him with a hint of sarcasm.

"You did such a good job earlier in the evening selecting the wine, why not do it again."

Larry found the same wine we had been drinking and marveled that it was sixty dollars a bottle; a hefty price for 1981. We had drunk all three at the cottage. We ordered two more.

On a tight budget for this trip, the three of us had intentionally eaten late in the afternoon to avoid expensive dinners. When the bill came, all of the men feigned reaching for their wallets. The doctor spoke up first.

"Allow me."

Not to be undone, Larry chimed in.

"No, I'll pay."

Michael stood and removed his wallet.

"You're my guests tonight."

Everyone acquiesced. We said our goodbyes and parted ways promising Emer we'd write. We did exchange Christmas cards for about three years and then unfortunately lost touch. I sent her a subscription to Arizona Highways as she loved Arizona and we wanted to thank her for a lovely evening.

The next day we strolled through the town. It was picturesque, but we were anxious to see Blarney Castle so we left. There is a legend that holds the king of the castle stuttered. He was advised by one of his subjects that if he kissed the stone in a certain manner, he would have the gift of gab. Since, in his case, his speech impediment was psychological, he was able to speak eloquently to his kingdom after he followed the advice. Larry was especially anxious to participate; for what reason I don't know as he already talked a lot. We arrived early in the afternoon. Carol and I carried umbrellas to shield us from the slight drizzle. We skipped along the path to the castle, held our umbrellas high and warbled.

"Singing in the rain, we're signing in the rain."

That gave me an idea. I handed Larry my umbrella and ran ahead about ten feet. On my command, Carol and Larry clicked up their heels in opposite directions. I captured the photo at the perfect time to catch them in the air. We entered the castle and climbed up to the second floor where we found the place for the special kiss. To do this, one has to bend over backward over a crevasse and kiss the wall behind it. When Larry was finished, he jumped up with a big smile on his face.

"I French kissed it."

I expelled a heavy sigh. "Here we go; now he'll never be quiet."

Afterward, we went into a small garden area called Sherwood Forest. Carol and I continued our silly act. We bantered back and forth.

"Robin, Maid Marion, where are you?"

We headed back toward Shannon as our return flight was the next morning. During our weekend travels through Ireland, we had visited several churches along the way and discovered a wedding in progress each time. Carol was amazed this happened so often.

"Ireland's September must be like America's June."

Quick on the comeback, Larry educated her.

"Winter's coming. Those good Irish Catholics have to get married to keep warm."

Carol didn't believe his explanation.

"Yeah, right."

We arrived in Tipperary where we stopped to use a pay phone to call the B&B where we had stayed the first night to reserve our rooms for that evening. When we stopped to park, we found ourselves right in front of a downtown church. Sure enough, a groomsman walked outside. Carol was flabbergasted.

"We can't believe how many weddings we've seen in the past three days.

He smiled at her.

"Winter's coming."

Carol and I stared at each other and then looked for Larry and wondered if he had paid the guy for saying that. Larry was in the phone booth and innocent. We had a quiet dinner that evening at Dirty Nellie's where we had celebrated our first night. Our fun trip was over, but we were happy for the memories we had gathered in our whirlwind four-day excursion.

At breakfast the next morning, we were joined by an Irish couple from Donegal Bay and two girls, who looked as if they were in their twenties. A bed and breakfast is so much more fun than a hotel. We sat at the table of strangers as if we were family. Larry, as usual, broke the initial silence.

"I've been in Ireland four days and I still haven't met another Laughlin. I'm so disappointed."

One of the young girl's eyes lit up with a twinkle and she spoke right up.

"My last name is Laughlin."

Larry could hardly contain his excitement.

"Where are you from?"

"Los Angeles."

Larry, who felt immediate disappointment, put his head down with his chin resting on his chest. The rest of us laughed out loud. I put my arm around his shoulders to console him.

"Honey, you looked in the wrong country."

An Irish gentleman explained that our name meant fresh water fisherman and offered the solution.

"You need to travel to Donegal Bay, where we're from. There are so many Laughlins there; I have to step over them as I exit the pubs."

Now, we howled with laughter. In spite of his joke, Larry was encouraged.

"The next time I come here to visit, I'll do that."

We found out through extended conversation that the girl, Lori, spelled her name Loughlin. Larry had researched genealogy, but could never quite get back to the home country. I thought he should expand his search.

"You may be related to Lori. For all you know, you could be an O'Loughlin, O'Laughlin, McLaughlin or MacLaughlin and so forth. Laughlin may be the Americanized version of your name."

Larry's take on the conversation was that by the time he found out his true origin, he might not even be Irish; he might be Scottish. I'm an incurable optimist and told him not to be sad.

"Even if the Laughlins are not Irish, your grandmother O'Donnell's husband was, which still makes you one with this country. Larry smiled and the others cheered. He had, indeed, come home after all.

Chapter Nine

I don't think anyone was ready for the hilarity, a diet challenge offered at my office. Several of my friends and I, at work, decided we would compete to lose weight. The latest rage in 1983 was the liquid Cambridge Diet, which consisted of a powered formula that one mixed with water. One particularly dreary rainy morning, my coworkers and I went to the cafeteria for our morning break. I decided to make hot chocolate, which I had never tried before, out of my powdered drink. I was tired of the cold drab taste and wanted a change. I put the mixture in a Tupperware glass, added hot water and snapped the lid shut.

Several executives, who had come to visit the office that morning, were also in the cafeteria for coffee. The Vice President of Sales, for the entire western region stood ahead of me in the line. The last thing I remembered seeing before I shook the hot mixture was the crisp blue pin stripped suit that the VP wore.

After only two good shakes, the hot chocolate blew the lid to the plastic container off and exploded. Chocolate erupted like lava flowing from a volcano. It dripped from the light fixtures, the cafeteria equipment, the ice cream machine, the Vice President's head and everyone else within a ten foot radius. No one was spared. The cafeteria workers, secretaries, big shots, coworkers all had splatters of some volume on their clothes or faces. People shouted. The VP, who was known for his stern and grumpy demeanor began screaming.

"What the hell was that? Who did this?"

I could see the back of the man's neck turn red in between the streaks of liquid. Chocolate covered the back and shoulders of his suit. I grabbed napkins and tried to dry the drink off people's clothes.

"I'm so sorry. I'm so sorry."

I realized my efforts were fruitless. If I could have crawled under the ice cream machine, I would have. I was so embarrassed. I backed away from the group far enough to turn, scurry out of the cafeteria and return to my desk. I threw the Tupperware container into the trash on my way out to get rid of the evidence.

One of my coworkers stopped by my desk.

"I ran into Vern. He wants to know who the SOB was that caused the accident in the cafeteria. I told him I thought you worked in administrative services. He didn't respond with kindness. He told me that if you didn't, you would be."

Louise and I made several close friendships with my coworkers at State Farm. One couple, Don and Debbie Hancock, had children the same ages as ours. We frequently went on weekend camping outings at Sycamore Creek near Sunflower, Arizona. We slept on the ground in tents, cooked on a camp stove, played volleyball with our kids and sang songs around the campfire at night. One morning, I was washing my face in the creek. I heard Don laughing. I turned to look at him and saw why. He was upstream relieving himself in the rushing creek headed right toward me. I guess it was all part of the outdoor fun.

One memorable Saturday, Louise and I invited Don, Debbie and their kids to join us for a swim and barbeque at our house. We lived in a tract home in a nice friendly neighborhood. Our pool nearly consumed our backyard, but we had a big enough covered patio to house four lounge chairs. There was an olive tree next to the porch that provided additional cooling shade.

Don and I sat in our chairs, sipped our beer and watched our children scream with delight playing games of tag and Marco Polo. Louise and Debbie were inside preparing food. We had to drag the kids out of the pool to eat, but once at the small picnic table, they ate hot dogs and hamburgers, potato salad and chips with gusto.

At dusk, our wives took the kids indoors to watch a movie on television, then joined us back outside to enjoy the unmatched Arizona sunset. The sky turned variations of orange and pink. My conversation with Don led to discussions about explosives and firepower in Viet Nam. That's when I got this great idea.

"Hey, I have some gun powder from the National Guard Armory in the garage. Let's show the kids how it works."

We rushed indoors all excited about the lesson we were going to teach our children. We knew our boys would love to watch gunpowder burn. We weren't too sure about Don's little daughter, Jennifer. For that matter, we weren't too certain how Louise or Debbie would feel, but we didn't care. We thought it'd be cool.

"Come on, boys, we're going to show you a trick. Jenny, you might like this too."

Everybody came outside with us to our front driveway, including our wives. Don and I were feeling quite proud we were so knowledgeable about this stuff. We poured a trail of gunpowder down the length of our two-car driveway in the depression between the slabs. Louise was apprehensive about our impending trick.

"Larry, is this a good idea? Really, it's getting dark. Can you see what you're doing?"

I waved her away. "We know what we're doing. We're both experienced handling this stuff."

We made a really small pile at the end of the snaking powder. We tried to light it with a match, but for some reason, it didn't catch. Ten minutes into our demonstration, the kids started complaining. My son, Jason, the oldest of the group was the spokesperson.

"Dad, we'd rather watch a movie. This is boring."

We were convinced they would like this once we got the powder to burn. "Hang on, guys once we get this going, it'll be great."

I noticed Louise and Debbie stood back by the garage door. Both of them had their arms folded over their bodies. This needed to go well because I could tell they were getting aggravated at our nonsense. When it still didn't light, both of us dummies got down on our hands and knees with our faces only two inches from the pile. We gently blew on the gunpowder as we lit it.

All of a sudden, it flashed. Boom! It jumped five feet into the air with such a bright glow that it looked like daytime. The kids squealed with delight, but Don and I had burned our faces. We had no eyebrows or lashes. Louise took off running across the street.

"Don't touch your face. I'll go get some Aloe Vera stems from the neighbor's plant."

When she returned, Debbie and Louise doused our faces with the goop from the inside of the stems. Once we were properly attended to, Louise went into the house and returned with a big wooden paddle.

"Bend over boys. Now we're going to teach the kids a lesson on what the consequences are for playing with fire."

The kids clapped and jumped in line when Louise handed Jason the paddle to go first. They were each allowed to give us a swat for doing such a dumb and dangerous trick.

It was another story to spread through the office.

Larry and I planned a long weekend trip to Puerto Vallarta, Mexico with a coworker of mine and her husband, who seemed to be a jack of all sports. He suggested we go scuba diving. Larry was all for it. He had tried it once on a trip to Acapulco before he was inducted into the service and thought it was great fun.

My friend's husband had his own scuba gear and offered to teach his wife, and us, how to dive. He was certified, but the rest of us wouldn't have to be in Mexico. The two of them came to our house for dinner and a lesson. It seemed simple enough in our backyard pool, but when the real excursion transpired, it was a much different story.

The day after we arrived in Puerto Vallarta, we headed to the wharf where we could rent scuba gear and hire a craft to take us out on the ocean. The actual diving boats were way out of our financial range so we settled on a thirty-foot fishing boat, whose captain assured us that he knew a great place to take us and could accommodate our needs for a much lesser price.

We motored twenty-five miles out to sea to some islands. One of the things I hadn't taken into consideration was my woeful experience with seasickness. By the time we reached our destination, my stomach churned and I had a headache. Like my comrades, though, I was anxious to try my hand at scuba diving. I thought being in the water would calm my innards down. I thought wrong.

We swam about forty feet away from the boat, where our friend stopped to give us last minute instructions as we treaded water. I put the mouthpiece that provided my oxygen in my mouth and took a deep breath. I gagged right away so I took it out, moved my mask off my nose and tried to inhale fresh air and compose myself. Then I tried again. We all had issues with too much buoyancy as we had not rented the proper weights along with the other gear. My heart began to race as the anxiety grew in me. I felt claustrophobic with the mask on and my mouth filled with rubber. As soon as I swam underwater, my mask filled with water and covered my nose because I didn't have a proper seal against my face. I swam up the couple of feet to the surface, took the hose out of my mouth and raised my mask to empty it. I knew this was a mistake for me. Larry was under the water right beside me. I tapped him on the arm, made an up signal and then I pointed to the boat. There was no way I could do this. I'm a good swimmer and didn't worry at all about the swim back to the boat; especially, with the fins on. I felt like a dolphin I moved so fast.

The captain must have been watching us as he was at the top of the rope ladder when I arrived. I took off my mask and handed it up to him and did the same with my fins. The boat bobbed on the waves, which made the climb difficult. It was at that very moment that I realized the advantage of hiring a diving vessel, which would have had a platform to swim onto to get back into the boat. Nevertheless, I managed. The captain helped me on board when I was within his reach.

"Problemo, señora?"

He helped me take off the heavy tank on my back. I slipped and flopped onto the deck like a dead fish.

"Sí, I'm sick."

He didn't understand and my limited Spanish vocabulary failed me so I pantomimed throwing up. He nodded his head.

"Sí, Sí, yo comprendo."

Good, he understood. He pointed at a bench at the back of the boat, put his hand on my elbow and guided me there. Then, in Spanish, he told me to sit down. At least, I could understand him. I sat down, but the motion of the boat caused me further uneasiness, which was exacerbated by the smell of the diesel fuel and smoke from the engine that quickly encircled me. I tried to get up to escape the odor, but the captain pushed me back down. He held up one finger.

"Un momento, por favor."

Okay, fine, I would stay there for a minute or two, but I knew I needed to find cleaner air to breathe. He left me and I put my head down between my knees. I figured it worked to avoid a fainting spell, perhaps, it would stave off vomit. I didn't hear the gentleman return because of the noise of the engine. Instead, I felt the cold water as he dumped half a bucket of seawater on me. As I lifted up my head to protest, he emptied the rest in my face. I choked and spit the salty taste out. He started to leave and I knew he was going for another bucket full. I yelled out to him to get his attention and when he turned around, I held up my hand to stop him. I rose from my perch and headed toward the center of the boat to lie down on the warm deck. I had been seasick often enough that I knew where the least motion was.

I put on a tee shirt, rolled up a towel to put under the back of my neck to support my head and lay down. With my eyes shut and my hand covering my nose to try to avoid inhaling the diesel fuel that drifted my way, I tried to rest. I was only there five minutes when I heard Larry holler from the bottom of the ladder.

"Hey, someone take my gear so I can come up the ladder."

I could hardly move from my spot, but it didn't matter as the captain was already on his way. He followed the same routine that he had with me. Larry came over to me to see how I was.

"You doing okay?"

"Not really, I am nauseous, but trying not to throw up. Why did you come back so soon?"

"I have to poop."

I rolled over away from him and curled up into a fetal position. I didn't want to think about his issue. Larry asked the captain where the toilet was. The captain didn't understand him so I turned my head and yelled over my shoulder.

"Donde està el baño?"

The captain showed Larry to the bathroom. He was in there for a good twenty minutes and when he exited and came directly toward me.

"I have a problem."

"Now what?"

"It won't flush. It was like a funnel only the bottom has a closed flap. I tried to pump the handle and it didn't work. I filled the whole thing up with icky, gooey, peanut butter like crap."

I started to gag and couldn't respond verbally. The captain rushed over to us as he probably thought I was about to lose my breakfast and didn't want me cluttering his deck.

"Es problemo?"

Larry's face turned red, which is unusual for him as there isn't much that embarrasses him.

"Sí, señor. "

Larry pinched his nostrils and then spread his arms wide.

"PU grande. No flush.*"*

The captain understood immediately and tried his best to respond in English.

"I take care of."

Larry shook his head no.

"You don't understand. This is *muy PU grande.*"

The man nodded his head.

"Sí, I do."

Larry shrugged his shoulders and tipped his head at the same time. There was a smirk on his face.

"Okay, I'm going back into the water."

The captain helped him put his gear back on and Larry jumped into the ocean. For the next twenty minutes, the captain lowered his bucket on a rope into the sea and hauled the water up. He carried the full container into the head to flush down the offending plug. Each time he exited the bathroom, he'd shake his head as if he was trying to get the stink off him. He also muttered expletives in his native language, which I understood as those were the only Spanish words my husband could remember and had taught to me. I watched, but didn't let on that I knew what he was saying. I also noticed that each time he dumped a bucket of water into the toilet, he'd walk over to the port side of the boat and peer down into the ocean water. I suspected he was watching to make certain the *PU grande* was clearing the trap door in the funnel commode.

By his third trip, I had moved to the opposite side of the boat from the ladder and hung my head over the edge to barf.

I could hear Larry and the others swimming back to the boat as they spoke in loud voices to each other. The captain heard them too and put his bucket down to help them onto the deck. When they saw me, they all started laughing and made fun of me vomiting.

"Yow, I've never seen you look so green."

"Hey, are you feeding the fish?"

Larry was the last to comment.

"Geez, I'm sure glad we didn't have to swim through that to get to the ladder."

I couldn't help myself as I knew I would get the last laugh. "Yeah, well you just swam through the *PU grande*. How do you feel now?"

We had to explain that one to our pals on the trip home. I managed to drink a soda, which helped to settle my stomach. The captain let Larry and the other guy fish on the way back, while my coworker and I basked in the warm sun. We saw a number of beautiful sailfish fly out of the water, but the boys didn't catch anything worth keeping. When we were within thirty feet of the dock, the engine on the boat quit running. I wanted to be onshore so badly that this additional delay was intolerable. We were within the low wake zone and there were several boats coming into and going out of the marina. The captain kept trying to restart the engine and I had had enough.

"Larry, please go ask him to have someone tow us in. I can't take too much more of this."

I think Larry and our buddy offered to dive in with a rope and pull the boat to the pier, but the captain wouldn't let them as it was too dangerous. He finally conceded the engine wouldn't crank and called out to a fellow fisherman, who got us to shore. All in all, that day was the worst fun I have ever had.

Chapter Ten

I n October 1984, my vice president advised me the Phoenix reservations office that I managed was being closed. The employees would have three choices; move to Los Angeles, move to Minneapolis or leave. My only offer was to move to Los Angeles, which at the time did not seem to be a viable option. Neither Larry nor I were interested in living there. We had purchased a new home the year before and had pushed our financial resources to the max using both of our salaries. I thought quitting my job would be a worse decision. On an impulse, I decided to take some drastic action. I called Larry to discuss my idea.

"Are you sitting down? I just heard we're closing our office, but I was also told the Atlanta reservation manager has resigned. What would you think if I asked for that job?"

At first, Larry was stunned at the closure statement, but the transfer held some intrigue for him.

"Would we be able to go there first to see if we like it?"

"Probably not, I don't even know if it will be a possibility, but I need to take immediate proactive action to find out. My senior vice president arrives today to make the announcement to the office."

Larry was silent a few moments before he spoke.

"Okay, go ahead and find out about it and then we'll decide. I'd have to get a transfer and I don't know if that is feasible."

I hung up the phone, got up from my desk and walked over and closed the door. I went back, sat down and took some deep breaths while I pondered what I would say. I knew my guest would be arriving at any time. When I had mustered enough courage, I opened the door and went back to my desk to make a list of pros and cons. It wasn't even ten minutes before I heard a knock on the door and saw my senior VP standing in the threshold. I had met him only one other time and found his demeanor to be aggressive and stern. He talked fast and it had been difficult to get a word into our conversation. I decided I needed to speak first, to spit out what I wanted to say. I rose from my desk and walked briskly toward him and extended my hand to shake his. I was thankful at that very moment that a management professor had our class practice handshakes until we had possessed a firm, confident one.

"Arnold, welcome. Please come over here and have a seat." I grabbed another chair and placed it so that I faced him. "I have a proposition to make."

His eyebrows rose as if surprised and his mouth opened to speak, but I beat him to the punch.

"I heard the manager in Atlanta is leaving and I want her job." I didn't say anymore; rather, gave him direct eye contact and waited for a response.

He sat up, clapped his hands together and rubbed them back and forth as if he was in deep thought.

"I like your attitude. It takes some backbone to say what you want. Let me think it over and get back to you."

He rose from his seat. I took his cue and stood up. I smiled at my own bravado and was glad I didn't have to shake his hand again right away as mine was clammy and shook some. He put his hand on my shoulder to steer me toward the door.

"Let's go tell your management team our news."

My team waited for us in a conference room away from the reservations office. This was not good news for them as neither of them would consider the options desirable. Before we returned to the reservations office, the vice-president stopped me in the hall.

"I need to make a couple of calls. Is there a place where I could talk privately?"

"Certainly, you may use my office."

I escorted him to the door and left. I went to the ladies lounge to gather my thoughts. I wasn't ready to face anyone else yet. When I exited, I saw the VP down the hall and he waved to me. I walked toward him. He met me halfway.

"The job is yours, if you really want it. You need to give me an answer tomorrow before we make the closure announcement to your office."

Then he left. I scurried back to my office, shut the door and called Larry.

"The job is mine. Should I take it?"

Larry was startled, but there was excitement in his voice.

"How much time do you have?"

"Twenty-four hours."

Now he was stunned and stuttered.

"Whoa . . . I, I need to see if I can transfer."

I felt dizzy, but we didn't have time to catch a deep breath. "Could you ask now?"

"I guess so. I'll call you back."

I paced back and forth in my office for what seemed like an hour when the phone rang.

"My boss called a man he knows in Georgia and there's an opening. He gave me a great recommendation and I have a job."

"Wow, this is incredible. I wonder what our kids will think. We'll talk to them tonight."

We hung up and I went back to business as usual, the best I could. I took some time to talk to the assistant managers to get their thoughts about their prospects. The next morning after I had been in my office fifteen minutes, one of the reservations agents came to see me.

"Hear you're moving to Atlanta. How come?"

I was so surprised. I don't know that I was drooling, but my mouth was definitely agape. "Who told you that?"

"Easy . . . news travels fast at State Farm. My husband works there too, remember?"

I pointed to a chair. "Have a seat."

We chatted for a few minutes and I pleaded with her to keep the information confidential. I would share the news myself at the appropriate time. I worried the news would be too interesting to keep quiet, but she kept her word.

After my VP arrived, I accepted the position, shook on it and we called the union steward to come to my office. As a courtesy, I liked to advise her of important information before the general population. We all went into the reservations office. Following typical procedure for any announcement, I stood on the window side of the room mid-way through the area.

"May I have your attention, please? Put your calls on hold as I need to speak to you for a moment."

I waited until I heard the sales calls turn into a low buzz of gossip.

"For years, rumors have circulated that our small office would close. I'm sorry to tell you, it's finally true."

Now that buzz became progressively loud chatter contained with objections, declarations and questions. I held up my hand to silence them.

"I understand how difficult this is for all of us. We will schedule small group discussions on your options, but for now, your choices are to move to the reservations offices in LA or Minneapolis. Of course, some of you, with enough seniority, will be able to bump another person at the Phoenix airport. As for me, I'm not going with any of you. I've been offered the manager's position in Atlanta and I have accepted."

At first, there was an eerie silence, but slowly they applauded my promotion. The remainder of the day was fraught with an occasional interruption of someone in tears or sidebar conversations. It was one day I didn't concern myself with statistics in call handling. I thought I'd be there to transition the group to their ultimate job destinations, but my boss called me the next day and told me to pack my bags and go to Atlanta. He wanted me to spend a week there shadowing the current manager before she left. He also suggested I take some time to look for a home. As he had requested, I left a day later.

My mother, who was a top-notch real estate broker, joined me at the end of the week to help me preview houses in Peachtree City. It was a location recommended to me by my predecessor because it was convenient to the airport and was a beautiful little town. I was grateful to have Mom with me as I needed her advice. One evening after work and an afternoon of house hunting, we were trying to relax in the hotel room. Emotion overcame me and I burst into tears.

"What have I done? I don't know if I'm able to manage this office. It's four times bigger than my other one. I also heard that the former manager did not endear herself to these people. There have

been whispers about another Yankee bitch has come to town. They don't even know me."

She cradled me in her arms; something moms do best and rocked me gently.

"Louise, you can do anything you set your mind to doing. Be yourself and they'll find out fast that you're kind and smart."

Flora N. Walters — Mom

I took her counsel and when I went to work the next day, I told the operations supervisors to move some calls to our overflow office in Detroit. I wanted to have group meetings with every employee. They offered to make up the schedule and asked me how late in the day the last one could be arranged.

"I want to speak to every shift. I know we can't do this in one day, but I'd like to be finished by the end of next week. You set the time and I'll be there."

I spent the rest of my week talking to every employee who reported to me. I told them all about me, my family, my sense of humor and my participative style of management and let them ask me questions. I concluded my meetings with a comparison of them to me, which helped me break the ice and gain their confidence.

"I want you to know I'm not a full blooded Yankee. My mother was born south of the Mason-Dixon Line."

This caused an eruption of laughter and chatter. I silently thanked my mother for her support.

When Larry flew to Georgia on Friday of the second week, I drove him by his new office, which was near the airport and within a mile of mine. It seemed too good to be true. On Saturday, I took him to see the final three choices on my list. Larry was impressed with Peachtree City.

"This reminds me of my roots in Ohio. I'm looking forward to experiencing four seasons again."

I was relieved that he liked the houses I had selected and the location. This had been such a rushed decision without any advanced knowledge of our new environment that I hadn't realized how nervous I was about his approval.

"Wait until you see the cart paths that wind throughout the city. We can take long walks and maybe even buy a golf cart to drive to the store."

❧❧ ❧❧ ❧❧

I had worked at State Farm for five and a half years and was reluctant to leave my friends and my sense of security, but I knew the transfer Louise was offered to Atlanta, Georgia would be a good opportunity for her. When I had seen the area where we would live and work, I became more enthused. When I left,

State Farm in Arizona, Don and Debbie wrote a poem and had it framed:

Moon

Once in a while a fellow comes your way
And when putting him to words, it's hard to say.
Now this ol' boy came from the big Midwest
Back where they claim football is at its best.
He came out West to play at ASU
Where he found Frank Kush and the Devils damn tuff too.
He's an All American boy, and that ain't no joke,
He served his country in Nam as Chief of Smoke.
After the war, he strived for peace
It seems his love for man does never cease.
As Deputy Sheriff he put in his time
A trying to keep peace while fighting crime.
After a while he figured it can't do no harm
I'll quit this job and work for State Farm.
Well I need not tell you how he did with them
As an adjuster and negotiator, he's a gem.
His unique wit and humor, they are unsurpassed
And our memories of him will forever last.
We remember all the good times and fun we had
Bushnell Tank, Sycamore Creek and the water that's bad.
The Moon shot on camera, cannon powder burns slow.
Another match, a puff, up in our face it did blow.
He's a Sun Devil fan—that's written in the logs
But before long he'll be shouting "How 'bout them Dawgs."
With Jake and Jason and Louise, his wife
They are off to Atlanta to start a new life.
Well, Moon this is not goodbye, we want you to know,
For again you'll return and the laughter will flow.
Let's just say adios, we'll see you soon
And know that Atlanta will have a new Moon.

It was bittersweet to leave our friends for a new opportunity.

🌿🌿 🌿🌿 🌿🌿

We selected a new home that had to be constructed from the ground up. This meant we had to live in a rental house for four months. Larry and Jason began their driving trek to Georgia on November first. Jake was only in the third grade so Larry decided he could get farther, faster with one passenger. I flew the opposite direction to Arizona to pick up Jake and then flew back to Georgia. We had it timed so that we'd all get to my hotel about the same time. When we joined forces, we set out to see our family's new surroundings.

The first stop was at the building site of our new home. We drove through the neighborhood and passed by the school that Jake would attend. Then we went past Jason's school, which was closer to where our new temporary home was located. It was the only affordable place I could find to live for such a short duration. Larry walked through the front door, took a look around and came back to the living room where I was.

"It looks like a barn. Everything is brown."

Moving to a state we had never seen was traumatic enough, but we also had to leave what we had considered to be our dream house in Arizona.

"I'm sorry. Nothing will look good to you after what we left behind."

We rented three beds, three small dressers and a table with four chairs. We didn't even have a refrigerator; rather, we used a cooler that we kept outside. There was a sitting area next to our dining room that had a built-in bench with two inch brown cushions on it. This became our living room. Our television sat on the floor. Even though my company was paying for our accommodations for three months, I didn't spend any more money than I had to. This was my naiveté. I was a tad resentful that no one had bothered to explain the extent of my relocation budget and upset with myself for not asking. Had I the chance to do it over again, it would have been considerably different. At the very least, I would have rented a refrigerator.

For Christmas, we had a small tree with homemade ornaments. The boys were interested and happy to participate in cutting strips of construction paper and stapling them in rings to form chains. Larry, who had been the least satisfied with this move as his job wasn't quite what he had anticipated, made a great suggestion.

"Why don't we string some popcorn like we did when I was a kid?"

The boys punched each other in the arm and giggled.

"Right, Dad. How do you string popcorn?"

I went to the kitchen and reached for a pan, oil and popcorn seeds. "As soon as we get some popped, we'll show you."

We had made fun out of a forlorn situation. That night when we were in bed, Larry made another good suggestion.

"Let's go shop for remote control cars tomorrow. It might be fun to have races outside."

I agreed before I knew how expensive this venture was, but we extended ourselves to make up for the lack of family, friends and the sparkle that Christmas usually brought. Everything we purchased required batteries so we also purchased rechargeable batteries and a charger. The next morning the boys were anxious to open their gifts. We had a rule that they had to wake us up first. Larry was the most excited he'd been since he had started his new job. It seemed as if I had apologized often for our dismal life even though we both knew it was temporary. We hated the house we were in. It was drab, cold and uncomfortable. I hopped out of bed to join the boys. It was freezing so I stopped to put on a robe and slippers and my best smile.

The boys tore into the packages.

"Wow, look at this? And . . . did you see what I got?"

They both spoke so fast, I couldn't keep up with who said what to whom. Larry helped them load the batteries and had the boys stand up, remote in hand, for the first race. They each pressed the power button. Nothing moved. We weren't savvy enough to charge the batteries first, therefore, nothing worked. Jason, who like his father had a short fuse, pitched his remote onto the built-in couch.

"What a bummer."

He plopped down onto the couch and traced the buttons on the remote.

"Jason, I know you're disappointed, but please keep in mind the reason we give one another gifts is to celebrate the birth of Jesus. In other words, there are more important things to consider today than your presents that don't work."

"I know, Mom, sorry."

My intent was not to make him feel guilty or worse than he did; rather, to bring the focus back to more important things. I knew he understood and that his mood would be temporary, but I also knew that my entire family was homesick and felt sorry for themselves that we had nothing else to do. Ever the Pollyanna in the family and feeling responsible for moving everyone away from our familiar surroundings, it was my job to lift their spirits.

"Who wants to play cards?"

Jake, my best ally in these emotional situations jumped up off the floor where he was sitting.

"Can we play Crazy Eights?"

"Sure."

I waved Larry over and gave him a help me look. He got up and headed to the table.

"Great idea. Come on, Jason; see if you can beat me."

We played for an hour, but by then everyone was bored with the game. We had another twelve hours to pass in the day before the batteries would be charged. By that time, we'd all be in bed. I grasped at every idea for activity.

"Why don't we all go for a walk? The fresh air will feel good."

We bundled up in sweatshirts and light jackets. We didn't have winter coats, yet, as they weren't needed in Phoenix. We walked outside and the cold air slapped us in the face. We looked up to the sky expecting the sun and only saw grey clouds. Larry took my hand.

"This is fun."

We only walked around the block because we were too cold to go farther. By that time, Larry's feeble attempt at being cheerful was over.

"I hate this place. We live in a barn, we have no furniture, our refrigerator is a cooler and my job sucks."

I leaned into his shoulder and rested my head. I felt guilty for his misery. "It'll get better in February when we get into our new house and spring comes."

When we went back inside the house, the boys ran to the charger to see if the batteries were good enough to run their cars. They weren't. Jason was quick to point out the obvious.

"This is boring. We don't have anything to do. We don't know where the kids we met at school live so we can't play with them. I hate it here."

I already felt terrible and his disappointment stabbed at my heart. The boys played in the empty living room with our Springer Spaniel mixed breed dog, Bandit, and tried to watch the one station on television that we had reception for all day. We didn't even have

cable hookup. I decided right then that I didn't care what the cost, I would make certain we had it on the next business day. The bright side to our day was our meal of turkey, dressing and all the trimmings. It was the only tradition we engaged in that day that felt right. I even made Christmas cookies; the kinds where you buy a roll of chocolate

Bandit, our Springer Spaniel Mutt

chip or sugar cookie dough, slice it, bake it and put frosting on it. The boys enjoyed doing that, at least.

It wasn't until the following day they could play with their new toys. After an early car racing event between the boys, I went to our neighbor's house to meet them. They were very nice people, who had two little girls. That didn't make the boys too happy, but it helped. When school was back in session, they made new friends, who they discovered lived close to us, which alleviated after school boredom.

🌿🌿 🌿🌿 🌿🌿

I was assigned a claims territory in Griffin when we arrived in Georgia. My actual desk was in Riverdale, thirty miles away, but my office while on the road was the trunk of my car. State Farm had closed their Griffin office a couple of years earlier, but after six months, I convinced them to reopen it due to the overwhelming workload in the rural town. Another claim representative, secretary, claims processor and two estimators were added. I was relieved.

I was anxious to fit into the new Southern culture where I lived and worked. The first time I called to get a statement from a customer who had been in an accident, I was met with resistance because the local folks there didn't trust a Yankee.

"Who are you?"

"Ma'am, I'm your claims adjuster from State Farm and I need to get the necessary information to settle your claim."

She hung up on me and promptly called her agent, who told her it was okay to give me information. Mr. Ogletree called me to let me know he had cleared the way for me to finish my job.

In order to communicate well with the claimants, I learned to speak Southern. I enunciated my words with a twang and ended my sentences with an elevated word tone, which made them sound like questions. Further, I used words in a different manner. For example, I'd tell my customers to carry their car instead of take their car to the designated body shop. Other phraseology, I was quick to acquire included hey; not hi, crank the car; not turn on the car and click on the light bub (bulb to northern folks); not turn on the light. It was a slow process, but I was accepted. My wife tells me that my open, honest and humorous personality served me well in making new friends.

One of the estimators, Don Henderson, known as Gomer to his close friends took me under his wing. He called me his little fat Yankee buddy. The whole staff teased me because some of their food traditions were foreign to me. Because of this, they all delighted in watching me try new cuisines.

Gomer, the other men from the office, and I had a weekly routine of eating breakfast at Miss Lucy's cafeteria. The first morning we went, I followed close behind Gomer and tried to order what he did. I became distracted and lagged behind a bit. When I caught up, I wasn't quite certain what Gomer had ordered, but thought I had heard him say something about grits and tried to play it cool. I perused the selection and gave my order to the server.

"Give me one of them grits."

The server furrowed her eyebrows when she looked at me.

"Where you from, boy? Them ain't grits. That's my sausage gravy."

I blushed from embarrassment. "I knew that. I was just joshin' ya. I'll take a biscuit with gravy."

Gomer and the boys never let me live that one down.

⚔ ⚔ ⚔

One day our work crew went to a nearby barbeque restaurant. Of course I had eaten BBQ before, but not like this. When I bit into the cornbread, there were some hard pieces in it. I thought they were weevils or something similar. I tried to be subtle and spit them into my napkin, but it didn't deter me from eating the good parts. Gomer noticed.

"Why do you keep spittin' in your napkin?"

"There's something hard in my cornbread."

Gomer guffawed with a big belly laugh.

"Aw, that's the cracklin' you can eat it."

"What's cracklin'?"

"It's fried pig skin. It won't hurt you."

Another memorable time, Gomer and I were invited along with the rest of the business unit to go to our boss' house for dinner. Generally, this would have been held at a restaurant, but my supervisor's children were both physically and mentally challenged. Getting out for an evening was difficult. Instead, he and his wife hosted a steak dinner at their house.

Gomer cleaned his plate and fancy dessert much faster than I. When I was served my French pastry, I took my time and enjoyed the pleasurable flavor. Gomer glanced over at my dish that was empty except for the doily and scratched his head.

"Aren't you going to eat that?"

"What this? It's paper."

"Dadgum, I done et mine. I thought it was a bit chewy."

The two of us became such good friends that I stood up as Gomer's best man for his short-lived second marriage.

We made trips everyday to our building site to see what construction changes had been made. One thing that Larry and I both enjoyed was watching the progress on building a new home. It was our third experience and I knew this house would be as welcoming as the last one. We had taken great care in selecting exactly what features we wanted.

We moved into our new house the last week in February 1985. We felt immediate relief in the comfort of our own furniture, which had been delivered. To celebrate, Larry and I arranged for sitters for our children and planned a snow skiing trip with some of his former co-workers at State Farm, three weeks after our move.

I worked the day we were scheduled to leave for Tahoe, so I called my boss before Larry picked me up to go to the airport terminal.

"Hey, I wanted to remind you I'll be gone for a long weekend."

He was glad I had called as it had slipped his mind. He also had some information he needed to share with me.

"I know you and your husband just moved into your new house so this might be a tough pill to swallow. We've been negotiating a deal for a new office in Detroit, Michigan for that past few months. We've decided to close your office and consolidate it with a new one. I'll be in your office next Wednesday to make the announcement."

At first, I was speechless and insulted that he didn't trust me with inside information. I could feel my face turning red. Tears formed in my eyes.

"Why didn't you tell me before we moved into our new house?"

He sounded apologetic, but he wasn't convincing.

"Well, I knew you had put five thousand dollars in escrow funds and I didn't want you to lose it."

I rose from my desk and closed my office door while I silently counted to five before I responded. He didn't deserve my holding back for a full ten second count.

"That's not a good enough answer. Now, I have seventy thousand dollars in a house I'm not going to live in. This is outrageous. How am I going to tell my family I've ruined their lives again? When is this going to happen?"

I didn't care, at that point, if he fired me, I deserved better treatment and I knew it. He shied away from any specifics other than it could take about three months or so.

"Perhaps this skiing weekend will help you sort though any communication dilemma you have with your husband and children."

I couldn't believe the cold, indifferent attitude he demonstrated. Before I slammed the phone down, I muttered a farewell of sorts. I couldn't imagine how to begin to tell Larry about the closure and interruption in our lives; especially, after the past four months of quasi-happiness we had endured. I left my office and went outside to wait for him.

I carried on joyful conversations as we drove to the airport and throughout boarding the plane. I'm surprised Larry didn't suspect anything was amiss. I must have put on a good act. We settled into our first class seats. Larry remarked how lucky we were to sit up front in more comfort. He did enjoy my flight privileges.

"I'm really looking forward to this trip. I love first class with free drinks. Our house is great and my job has improved. This is all going to work out fine just like you said."

I didn't respond as I didn't know what to say. I nodded my head in agreement. I dreaded this conversation. All I could think of was how my family would feel, the huge amount of financial investment we had made in this new house, how disrupted our lives had been for the past four months, how our Christmas had been dismal being away from family. We loved our new house and I couldn't bear to see the look on my family's faces when I told them. Further, I didn't want to move to Michigan. It was my birth state and when I lived there as a child, I had loved it. But, I had grown apart from my connections there and loathed the thought of six months of intense winter weather.

When the flight attendant brought us drinks, she recognized me as the manager of the reservations office.

"Say, have you heard the rumors about Republic closing the Atlanta flight attendant base?"

She thought I'd have some inside scoop because of my job. I had to choose my words carefully. I didn't know about her position, but I knew about mine and I felt devastated.

"Sorry, I don't have any information about the in-flight base."

Larry leaned over and whispered to me.

"I'm sure glad we don't have to move again."

This was the intro I needed to broach the subject. As gently as I could muster, I put my hand on his and looked directly into his eyes.

"Not for at least three months."

I knew I had made too light of the topic, but the retort spilled out of my mouth. I think if Larry could have jumped out the window, he would have. Worse, he might have considered pushing me out first.

"What do you mean?"

I explained the discussion I had with my boss before I left the office that day.

"That's how I found out my office; the second largest in the system was being closed. Everyone who wanted to go would be transferred to Detroit."

I took a deep breath before proceeding. I tried my best not to cry about it for fear the flight attendant would notice and press me for more information.

"I don't know exactly when it will happen, but it will be approximately three months."

Larry went limp. We both had more drinks than the law would allow. When we reached Tahoe and the safety of our friends' companionship and empathy, we agreed to forget about our news and have a good time.

When we left Atlanta, David and Penny Boyd had moved to San Francisco for David's job. We told them what happened and they were particularly sympathetic about our plight. They were still living in a studio apartment. The others also felt badly, but we did not have the same kindred relationship with them as we did with David and Penny.

We stuck to our agreement and didn't give work another thought or discuss it further after the initial announcement to our friends. The Boyds had driven to Lake Tahoe to meet up with us. Penny had made dozens of homemade chocolate chip cookies for our trip and a wonderful pan of lasagna. We appreciated coming home from a day of skiing and not having to cook. We made a salad, warmed up some garlic bread, uncorked the wine and sat down at the table. I noticed one of the women only ate salad and bread.

"Hey, why aren't you eating the food Penny cooked. It's delicious."

She tipped her head back and forth toward her shoulders.

"I don't eat any Italian food."

The rest of us exchanged glances.

"Why didn't you say something this morning when we discussed what was for supper? We could have stopped on the way home and picked up something for you."

She explained she didn't want to be any trouble, but her actions spoke louder than words the whole rest of the trip. Seems there wasn't much we could do to make her happy. I had bigger fish to fry with my job and chose to ignore her.

We wanted to be able to signal our group while we skied to keep up with one another. Not everyone was on the same level of expertise. Every time someone rode the ski lift, he or she would scream out our code word for the weekend. You could hear it echo on the mountain.

"Clambake."

We had borrowed it from an Elvis movie. Larry and David's voices were particularly noticeable. We would listen for the code word response and knew we weren't far behind or ahead of one another. The other skiers probably thought we were nuts and maybe we were a bit, but we were on vacation . . . so who cared?

Our best day, we had put on our skis and ridden the lift midway up the slope. We stopped there to peruse the map to determine who was going down which run and the degrees of difficulty. All of the women were huddled in a group talking. I don't know if it was Penny or me who moved wrong, but the results were that our skis became entangled. When we each tried to step to the side, it caused us to be tripped up and we fell. We were sitting on the backs of each other's skis. As we tried to get up, we started to slide and then spin.

We spun all the way down the slope on our rear ends. We looked like a pretzel flying down the hill out of control. We reached the bottom unscathed except for the tears from laughing frozen on our faces. We made life long memories on that trip.

When we returned to Atlanta, I went right to work on trying to keep my office afloat as people left in droves for other jobs. The announcement we'd move in three months was premature. We didn't close the office until six months later. Larry and I discussed our situation and determined living in Detroit was not going to work for us. Larry requested and was granted another transfer back to Tempe at his old office. We put our house up for sale and Larry drove back to Arizona with the boys before school started in September. They took their clothes, bikes and other essentials, but we left our household goods. We figured we'd move them when we sold the house. Larry settled in with my parents for a month until he could find an apartment suitable for him and the boys. This began his tour of duty as Mr. Mom, and he was a working mother to boot. We thought the house would sell in a short while and I would quit my job when it did. I began my two year Monday through Friday separation from my family while I traveled to Michigan to work.

It was a nice plan, but it didn't work out well. I flew to Phoenix from Detroit every weekend for a year. Our beautiful, new house still hadn't sold as it was among the first ten of ninety in the subdivision. The builder could offer a much better deal to perspective buyers.

My job was going well. I helped to manage the largest office, nearly nine hundred people, in our company. Six months after our grand opening, I was promoted to Director. As proud as I was of my accomplishments, they didn't hold a candle to my first job as mom and wife. I was tired of commuting. The winter months were difficult.

Often, I would only be home for twenty-four hours and return on Sunday in the middle of the night to a snowstorm. I remember one night; I walked to the long-term parking lot by myself at two o'clock in the morning. I was more concerned with the cold than I was my safety. When I reached the freeway in my car, there was one lane, in the middle of the road that had been plowed. The snow storm was close to a blizzard state. Having spent my driving years in Arizona, I was not an expert in this weather. Mine was the only car for the first thirty minutes until some moron came flying up behind me and tailgated me. I slowed down to force him to go around me instead of me moving to the unplowed lane. He honked his horn, instead. With the utmost care, I moved over to the right lane and he passed me. He intentionally moved farther left so that he created a rooster tail of snow that covered my car and windshield. I drove blind for a few minutes, which scared me. I made a silent vow to do whatever I could to fix my miserable situation.

Chapter Eleven

The year our son, Jake was in the fourth grade, I was home, in Arizona, for the Christmas holiday. We attended the children's mass at our church. Our priest invited all of the children in the congregation to join him on the altar. He told the wonderful story of the birth of Jesus, which explained why we exchanged gifts in honor of His birthday. Then he posed a question to the group.

"What present would you want Jesus to bring you if He could come here right now?"

Many little hands shot up to be chosen to respond to the question. The priest pointed to each child as he gave each an opportunity to answer.

"I want love in my heart."

"I want peace on earth."

And so on . . . Jake, eager to have his gift pronounced, waved his hand with vigor. The priest finally pointed to him.

"Yes, son, what do you want Jesus to bring you?"

"I want an Air-Jammer, Road-Rammer."

The priest quickly lost control of his young audience. The congregation clapped their hands at his brave attempt at sharing the Christmas story.

"I think I'm done here. You may go back to your seats."

Larry and I had slunk down in our pew even though we were laughing like the rest of the people around us. As funny as it was, I had concerns, as I had not been able to find the toy he wanted so much. I hoped his Christmas morning wouldn't be ruined when he opened presents. I was thankful for the lesson of the birth of Christ as I could focus Jake's attention on the true meaning as opposed to what Santa Claus contributes.

Fortunately, my concerns were allayed, as he was pleased with what he did receive. He didn't tell us of his disappointment that Christmas. However, as the years passed and we told this story about him, he always had the same response.

"I still never got an Air-Jammer Road-Rammer."

I had never considered our older son, Jason, the more sensitive of the two boys, but it turned out that he was. For Christmas, 2005, Jason gave his brother the prize Jake had lusted for since he was nine years old. Jason found a new, still in the package toy of Jake's dreams. I think Jason learned the valuable lesson that it's better to give than receive well for he was as excited to give his younger brother the gift as Jake was delighted to receive it.

By May 1986, I was as frustrated with our living conditions as were Larry and our children. I asked my mother to fly to Georgia and hire a different realtor for me to sell our beautiful but as yet unsold house. My mother was still an ace in real estate. When she arrived, the dogwoods and azaleas were in bloom. Spring was everywhere. The neighbors greeted her with open arms. She visited every yard sale in the neighborhood. Then she flew back to Arizona. We picked her up at the airport. I was anxious to hear which realtor she selected to sell our house.

"So, tell us. What do you think? Can we sell the house? Did you find someone to get the job done?"

Mom had a real thoughtful look on her face.

"Why don't you move back to Georgia? It's beautiful. Larry could transfer again and you should find a job there."

Larry and I looked at each other. We had no immediate answer to her question. We dropped her off and headed back to our place. John Denver's song, *Country Roads*, was playing on the radio. I initiated a serious discussion.

"Why were we so anxious to come home to Arizona?"

Of course, we both knew the answer was that our roots were there.

"She's right, you know. It's the second dream house we've built and didn't get to live in very long."

We talked about what had seemed simpler times such as the day Larry was out watering our new lawn in Georgia. It was the first time we had ever planted grass seed. In Arizona, we had always had sod we rolled or desert landscaping. Jake, who was in the third grade, stood there and watched his dad.

"Dad, did you notice how the grass grows right up out of the ground here?"

We recalled the burst of color of the azaleas in the spring from an otherwise unnoticeable bush and the fragile beauty of the dogwoods that true to their legend only bloomed at Easter and were hidden among the pine trees. Our discussion led right to autumn as we talked about the leaves turning colors and the smell of them burning. It had, frankly, taken us back to our individual childhoods. We had made some great new friends in Georgia, and realized that now we were in a constant state of flux.

The fact that Larry and the boys lived in a one-bedroom apartment with meager furnishings in Arizona, I lived in Detroit in a room I rented from a friend and suffered from permanent jet lag were all good reasons why we should be living in our big house in Georgia.

"Let's move back. I'll find a job there."

Larry transferred to Georgia again; God Bless State Farm.

I commuted between Detroit and Atlanta each week for another year. It was a much easier; shorter flight and in the same time zone.

However, I grew weary from travel and the boys were tired of beans and weenies. I knew Larry could cook better than that, but he protested.

"I'm too tired to fix dinner when I get home from work."

Hmm. That sounded familiar. Then the icing on the cake spewed right in my face. Jake, who was in the fifth grade, gave Larry a Mother's Day card that read, "Happy Mother's Day, Dad." He gave me one too, but it still broke my heart. Larry knew how sad I felt that I wasn't mothering my children on a daily basis. My attempts at job hunting in Atlanta had not been fruitful. We weren't gaining ground financially, we were still apart weekdays and I was tired a good bit of the time from the travel. My husband had been so patient, but he empathized with me.

"I've decided to transfer to Detroit to be with you."

I was overwhelmed by his devotion and understanding. He knew I had a good job. It was probable State Farm would transfer him. We flew to Detroit and we looked at houses . . . again. We put our house on the market and sold it three weeks later. On the day, we closed the deal, and were literally sitting at the lawyer's office signing papers; I received a call from Eastern Air Lines in Atlanta, who offered me a job.

I had made a connection with the Chief Financial Officer and a Senior Vice President when I took them on tour of my office in Detroit. We went out to dinner and our small talk led to discussions of my commute. The VP, who had been a former VP at Northwest Airlines, knew me.

"Why don't you go to work in Atlanta?"

"I would in a heartbeat if I could find a job."

That conversation led to an interview and the job offer.

We made a quick decision to stay in Georgia. The problem we faced was that we had sold our house and now had the task of finding another. A coworker told Larry about a house in Brooks, fifteen miles south of Peachtree City. It sat on ten acres, had a cedar barn with a wood burning stove and a tractor with a bush hog to mow the acreage. We couldn't want for more. We bought it and became good friends with the original owners. This purchase meant that we could live together as a family for the first time in two years with our two golden retrievers, Murphy and Maggie and our little dog, Bandit. Brooks was rural, which required we practice our Southern accents more. Peachtree City was considered an airline town because of its many residents in the business. It was more cosmopolitan.

We bought the boys an ATV for Christmas with strict rules that it could only be driven in the three acre fenced pasture until we knew they were experienced. They made a track and put five hundred miles on it during the first week. Four of the ten acres were landscaped with hundreds of trees. Each weekend during the fall, we'd spend a few hours raking leaves. It was a family activity even though it was work.

Larry taught Jason, who was fourteen, to drive the tractor. Part of Jason's job was to haul the trailer full of leaves to the wooded part of the property to dump the load. He usually had a couple of dogs

Jason, Jake, Murphy and Maggie

and Jake sprawled on top of the leaves in the trailer. On one such day, Jason stood next to Larry with rake in hand.

"Dad, why we can't we wait to rake until all the leaves are finished falling?"

"Because this is fun being outdoors and working together."

Jason looked quizzically at Larry and shrugged his shoulders.

"Okay, whatever you say."

🍂🍂 🍂🍂 🍂🍂

Our boys had always done some chores and we prided ourselves that they understood that television and games weren't their only pass times.

They were active in Boy Scouts. Larry attended every camping trip and enjoyed each minute. My involvement was more administrative; promotion council type duties. We were committed to ensuring our boys were well-rounded good citizens. They earned badges regularly and each achieved Eagle Scout rank. I have always maintained that the Boy Scouts first required merit badge should be sewing. Although proud of their achievements, I grew tired of changing patches so often on sleeves or adding the merit badges to their sashes. These days they use Velcro.

The boys also played soccer and football. Larry coached the latter. He was and still is an attentive Dad. Jason believed everything his dad told him. Larry loved to tease the boys just as his Uncle Chuck had done to him when he was young. Larry convinced Jason that buffalos were born with wings.

"They have to cut them off while they're babies. Otherwise, buffalos would be flying around and pooping in mid air. Yuck, what a mess that would be."

Jason loved to eat Buffalo wings.

"They taste like chicken to me."

Larry could be a bit disgusting at times. Jason and Jake also believed for a very short time that hot dogs came from dog's wieners.

Jason was independent and innovative. We were convinced that he was like MacGyver on the television show. We could send him out in the woods with a toothpick and he'd survive. When he was tapped out for the Order of the Arrow in Boy Scouts, we were very proud of him and knew he'd do well. Being tapped out is a Boy Scout ritual where everyone sits in a circle and the chosen boy is tapped on the shoulder by an anonymous scout. It is the process of being nominated for the Order of the Arrow award. The candidates spend a weekend in the woods at a Boy Scout campground with minimal supplies and have to use their good sense and training from merit badges to survive.

Not long afterward, Larry and Jake were tapped out on the same night. We were a bit concerned about Jake's survival skills. If his track record at home was any indication, we could send him out with a can of beans and a can opener and he'd starve. When he was issued his raw egg, one piece of bread, two matches and sleeping bag and pointed toward the woods, Larry had a twinge of doubt.

"Are you going to be okay out there by yourself, son?"

Jake's head nodded in a yes, but his quivering voice indicated otherwise.

"I think so, Dad."

Larry reminded him that if he was in any trouble to tell one of the observers. Fortunately, he survived just fine.

While Larry was at camp one weekend with Jake, I was out of town on business. Jason broke the rules at home and rode the ATV without supervision. Like his father, he had no fear. He climbed up an embankment and the three-wheeler rolled over backward on top of him. He broke his arm. He managed to get to his weekend caretaker's house. The neighbor had to drive him the sixty miles to camp to get Larry's permission to go to the emergency room.

Jake and Jason — broken arms, Scout uniforms

Larry volunteered to leave camp, but our neighbor understood the significance of the event and offered to take care of Jason. The following Sunday or, Sunday week as we'd say it in Georgia, Jason drove our tractor to the country store a couple of miles down the road. Jake and some buddies and the dogs rode on the flat bed trailer that Jason towed behind the tractor. Jake returned home with a broken arm. They claimed he had tripped in a pothole in the parking lot and landed on his arm.

The next day, Larry took both boys to the doctor. They both needed permanent casts. After they were finished, Larry and the boys had to walk back through the waiting room that overflowed with patients awaiting their turn. The doctor escorted them and then stuck his head through the door so that all of his patients who were within listening distance would hear.

"Don't be so hard on those boys now, hear?"

The mothers glared at Larry. The doctor chuckled, the boys snickered and Larry blushed. Years later the boys revealed the real story. Jake had fallen off the trailer; not tripped in the parking lot. I suspect Jason's driving might have contributed.

Right after we purchased the house in the country in Brooks, Georgia, Larry bought Jason a 1954 Chevy truck; at least he said it was for Jason. The truck was a classic with its oak bed, running boards and three on the column. The paint job was superb. Jason still had about eighteen months before he could get a driver's license. I thought it was an extravagance we could have lived without and questioned Larry's reasoning for buying it.

"Jason isn't even old enough to drive. Don't you think this is a bit premature not to mention that I think he should be able to help pick out his first vehicle?"

Larry was quick to defend his purchase.

"Well, for one thing, it'll probably take nearly two years to fix it up. If I'm paying for it, I'll pick it out. Besides, I want lots of metal around him."

Larry, not a bit mechanically inclined, had to pay a mechanic for every improvement made. While this truck was a big deal in Larry's eyes, I have to admit I thought it was fun to take a ride in it on occasion. Jason, however, had a look of dread in his eyes.

"Mom, the kids at school will make fun of me."

It didn't take much fear or sadness on behalf of my children for my heart to wrench a bit. I knew some parents spent way too much on vehicles where Jason attended high school, so understood his embarrassment. We were unable to financially keep up with the high rollers in town and we thought it was ridiculous for a high school student to drive a BMW.

"Jason, the truck will have to do. Please keep in mind that your dad doesn't even have to buy you a vehicle. This will be a lot of fun. You'll see."

One of the problems Larry could never seem to get handled with the truck was the battery staying charged. He named the truck, Old Blue as it has a certain Southern charm to it like the Southern humorist who used Old Blue as a name of a scoundrel of a dog in one of his stories. It had come to be a favorite story in our family. Now, if our Old Blue would only start on a regular basis, Larry would be happy, as it seemed he gleaned the most joy from the old truck.

❦❦ ❦❦ ❦❦

One August night in 1987 about nine in the evening, I was home alone with the boys. Louise was in Michigan working out her two-week's notice to leave her job and live full time in Georgia. The boys and I had just returned to the house from youth football practice. We were all sweaty as it was one of those stifling hot and humid Georgia nights. The boys turned on the floodlights on the back of the house so they could shoot a few hoops before coming in for the night. I went on inside to shower and cool off. I put on my underwear and walked back to the mudroom to check on the boys. I was watching them through the window when I remembered what the former owner, had told me when we bought the house.

"Your nearest neighbor is a mile away. You can wash your car in the nude and no one will see you."

It was true; our nearest neighbor did live a mile away. So I thought what the heck and paraded outside with just my underwear on. I sauntered over to Old Blue and tried to get it to crank. It didn't. Our house sat up on a small hill at the back of our land, just right for a push start.

"Boys, come over here and give the truck a shove down the hill. I want to get the battery charged up."

They jogged over to the truck.

"Where are you going, Daddy?"

"Aw, I'm just going down to the end of the driveway and back. I won't be long."

By the time I reached the end of the quarter mile driveway, Old Blue was purring like a kitten. I headed on down the dirt road a bit thinking I'd get it revved up good. One mile led to the next until I was about three miles from the house. I decided I'd better turn around and when I did, the truck spit and sputtered and stopped. I sat there in the truck on the side of the road talking out loud to myself.

"I can be so stupid. I'm forty-one, overweight, barefoot and dressed only in my under drawers."

There was no way in the world that I could get help. If I stood outside of the truck and waved down a vehicle, if one even came by, I knew what they would be thinking. Pervert came to mind. The same would happen if I stayed in the truck and waved my bare arm. I'd get the same response.

I wasn't ready for the Spaulding County Jail. So, my only alternative was to walk the three miles back down the gravel road on my bare feet and unclothed. I got out of the truck, pushed it to the side of the road and started walking. I looked up to the sky hoping the stars could provide some guidance or light. In spite of the many I saw, the moon was hidden behind a cloud. I could barely see my hand held out in front of me. I had to feel my way with my feet in the darkness.

I treaded lightly as I feared I would tramp on a snake crawling from the swampy side of the road or squish a big green toad between my toes. Only about a half mile after I had begun my trek, I saw the reflection of headlights coming up from behind me. Not wanting to be embarrassed or worse, arrested, I jumped to the side of the road and tumbled down the embankment. It was so dark; I didn't realize there was a ditch when I jumped. I rolled down about twenty feet into a swampy area. The ground moved around me. I had Kudzu wrapped around my head, neck and arms. Honeysuckle vines clung to the rest of my body as I fell. My imagination went into overdrive conjuring up a water moccasin wrapping itself around my neck at any moment.

I scrambled back up the hill as fast as I could; clawing at the damp ground as I went. When I reached the top, I saw that the vehicle had turned and not even come my way.

I sat down in the dirt to pick the thorns out of my feet and body. When I stood up, the backside of my under drawers were wet with mud, which caused a severe drooping effect. I regained my composure and continued on down the road. My feet were stone bruised and bleeding. It hurt so much that each step made me moan out loud. I thought I felt things crawling all over my body and kept rubbing and slapping myself to get them off.

I had reached an area of the road where the Live Oak trees hung over like an arch and had moss hanging from the limbs and dripping down low toward the ground. The air cooled down immediately on this stretch of the road. It was dark and spooky even at noon and it was worse at this time of night. I was startled when I heard loud crashing noise like tree limbs cracking and the sound of hooves connecting with brush on the ground. It frightened me so much; I crouched in the dirt fearing for my life. Whatever live creature was headed my way was moving fast. My heart raced at the impending danger. I covered my face with my hands and prayed. I hoped that I would never have to see what was about to eat me. It came out from the darkness of the woods next to the road and I heard a whoosh as it passed me.

All of a sudden, the night was silent except for the babbling of the creek and the sound of my heart still beating in my ears. I wondered if it was standing ahead of me waiting for me to move. Or perhaps, it was hidden behind one of the big oak trees. I decided not to wait and find out. I ran as fast as I could until I reached the other end of the archway of the trees.

There was a farmhouse a hundred yards off the road. A light from a utility pole shone down on the ground revealing the monster that had stopped in the nearby pasture. It was a deer. I exhaled a heavy sigh of relief. Thank God it wasn't Sasquatch after all. As I watched the deer standing in the pasture of a nearby house, I marveled at the sight of the creature. It stood there with its head up and ears erect listening to the sounds of the night and watching for the threat of potential danger.

I noticed a light on in the garage. I counted six beagles with their noses turned upright sniffing the air. They began to bark, howl and growl. They jumped up in unison as if they were soldiers on guard duty and ran down the driveway. I thought that deer better get out of Dodge. All of a sudden, they made a sharp left turn, picked up my scent and the chase began.

For the next half-mile or so, I ran as fast as my overweight old body would go. The dogs caught up with me and nipped at my calves and ankles. One actually jumped and reached my soggy, sagging underwear and ripped the ass end out of them. Thankfully, they tired of chasing me, turned around and went home. I had reached an intersection and lay down in the middle of it. The street lamps provided enough light on me that hopefully any approaching car would stop before running over me. My heart beat so fast I thought my head would pop. I stayed there until I caught my breath and then went on down the road toward home. I still had another mile and a half to go. As I passed our neighbor's house, I considered going there for help. But I changed my mind as I had only met him one time before and I looked a mess.

By the time I reached our paved driveway, which felt like carpet to me, I was nearly in tears. I could walk no farther. My feet were covered in blood blisters. I got down on my hands and knees and crawled up the driveway. I was so thankful that I had insisted Jake sweep the driveway every week as his chore. He did a good job. There were no stones. When I finally reached the house, I went inside to look for the boys. It was after midnight. They were in the family room watching a movie and eating popcorn. Jason looked up at me with a startled expression.

"Where have you been, Daddy?"

I was bewildered at his accusatory tone as if I were a teenager who had stayed out after curfew.

"Where have I been? I've been gone over three hours. Look at me."

I was covered with leaves, leeches and pond scum; scratched, bleeding, the back end of my under drawers was gone and I had dog bites on my legs. I finished telling them a bit of my terrible experience. Jake looked at me nonplussed.

"Daddy, you should shoot Old Blue."

Old Blue

I suspect it's difficult for people to believe that the Larry stories, as they've come to be known by our friends and family, are not a figment of my imagination. I sometimes wish they weren't true. However, they're all as factual as I can remember them. My move back to Georgia from Michigan to work at Eastern Air Lines only lasted four years as Eastern went out of business. This was highly appreciated time to be with my family everyday, especially, since the boys were in their teenage years.

These years were also chock full of Larry stories, especially, his hunting escapades. Larry joined a hunt club that was a few miles from our home in Brooks, GA. Larry learned that the hunting was much different in Georgia than in Arizona where you get enrolled in a lottery and can go for years without getting drawn. There were so many deer in our area of Georgia, at that time; a hunter could get five deer per tag. The other huge difference between Georgia and Arizona was the terrain. One can see for hundreds of yards with no obstruction in Arizona, whereas in Georgia, the hunting grounds were thick with trees. Because of that, one had to use a tree stand, which is basically a flat board with rails on two sides and an area on the back that opens to clamp around a tree trunk. They're large enough to hold one body and offer little comfort. They are open on the topside to give the hunter the ability to shoot in all directions. Larry's was painted green with a camouflage design. He had to inch the stand up the trunk of the tree until it was positioned high enough to view movement through the dense forest. I don't know if it was Larry's years of experience in hunting or his rifle training and qualification in the Army, but he was dead on accurate. He used to brag to the boys and me.

"I only need one bullet to shoot a deer."

That was a technically correct statement, but I had a simple retort to his comment. "Would that be the first bullet or the last one?"

It was a joke even the boys understood, but the fact remained that Larry's expertise usually required only the first bullet. Jason and Jake were always impressed when Larry came home with the game and claimed to have shot it with one try.

The night before opening day of deer season in 1987, the first year he belonged to the hunt club, Larry and I were out partying with friends until the wee hours of the morning. Larry slept in and ignored the early morning alarm. About eight o'clock, he rose and dressed in his hunting clothes.

"Where are you going? Weren't you supposed to be at the club before dawn?"

"Yep. Too late to go there so I thought I'd go out in the woods on our property this morning."

We lived on ten acres of land; half of which was wooded. "Yeah, right. I don't care if we are in the middle of nowhere. You're wasting your time."

I rolled over, closed my eyes, brought the warm covers up under my chin and snuggled in for more sleep. About fifteen minutes later, I heard a gunshot. I jumped out of bed and ran upstairs to look through the guest bedroom window. It was at the end of a long hall and had a view of the woods on the side of our house. I yelled at my kids, when I reached the top of the stairs. Their rooms were on either side of the stairway.

"Boys. Wake up. Come in here, quick."

The boys hurried out of their rooms, raced down the hall and joined me at the window. From our high vantage point, we saw a buck with huge antlers, about five points on each side, run out from the woods. He ran alongside the house below the window where we were huddled and into the woods behind our back driveway. Jason, our eldest son, spoke first.

"Wow, get a look at that. He's the biggest buck I've ever seen, but he doesn't look like he's been shot."

Jake, my sleepy eyed eleven year old, leaned into the cold pane of the window and tried to get a better look at the buck as he disappeared into the woods.

"Maybe Dad missed."

"Dad doesn't miss, Jake."

A couple of minutes later, Larry opened the front door and strutted into the house.

"Got my buck . . . right here from the front porch. Get up, get dressed and come out here."

We put our coats on over our pajamas. We were all excited to see what he was talking about. Even I was in awe of Larry's skill. "How did you do that so fast?"

"I stood on the front porch, got a buck in the sights of my gun and shot; job done."

"I heard the gun fire and woke up the boys. We saw a huge buck run past the house."

"Well, that wasn't the one I shot. Mine is down on the other side of the woods by our grape vines. Boys, I need some help."

Deadeye Laughlin was successful again.

A few days later, Jason, who was fifteen, thought he'd try. He went out in the woods, took an apple for a snack and waited. He sat in a pile of leaves with a blanket wrapped around him. He was so comfortable, he fell asleep before he had finished his apple and awoke to a small doe trying to eat it. He watched for a few moments and then shooed her away. He had a tag for a buck, not a doe.

"Go get your dad."

I don't think hunting was his thing.

The following weekend, Larry went to the hunt camp and came back with two more deer. Jake had a football game in two hours so Larry hung the deer high in the rafters of our open barn. His plan was to transport them to the butcher on his return. The hoofs were at least six to eight feet off the ground. Satisfied with his job, we left to go to the game. What he didn't take into consideration was our hay wagon that was parked near the deer. It was about three to four feet high. When we returned, our three, spunky dogs, Maggie and Murphy both Golden Retrievers and Bandit, our Springer Spaniel mutt, who were always there to greet us, lay in different parts of the yard and acted lethargic. Maggie, who chased our Jeep on a regular basis, lifted her head a few inches off the ground, looked at us, put her head back down and closed her eyes. Larry hurried down to the barn and discovered the dogs had jumped up onto the hay wagon where without too much effort they could reach the hindquarters of the deer. They had shredded off portions and eaten like pigs. There wasn't a scrap of meat on the ground.

Needless to say, they were in big trouble. Like kids, they wore their guilt all over their faces, not to mention, how miserable they were from their feast. Fortunately, it didn't make them sick . . . just uncomfortable.

"Damn dogs. You ruined two good deer. There was enough meat there to fill the freezer."

Other than cleaning up the mess, yelling and cursing, as he worked, I don't think Larry ever punished the dogs for their enterprising. Besides, I think he was a little bit impressed that they had figured out a means and could jump that high.

� ✧ ✧

The next year, on a very early foggy morning just before sunrise, Larry was sitting in his tree stand. After he had gotten his position stable, high in the tree, he doused himself with deer scent. Thirty minutes later, Larry heard some snorting in the distance. It came closer and got louder. He strained to see through the dark and fog, but heard the big buck before he saw him. The next thing he knew, the buck was rubbing his body against the tree stand. It was a big buck. It snorted louder and louder and rubbed harder and harder. The tree stand began shaking. Larry tried to get him in the sights of his gun, but the buck was so close beneath him, that all Larry could see were his own toes.

The buck was turned on by that doe scent. Larry was sweating despite the cold and tried to decide how to manage the situation. All he could think was that buck wanted to come up there and if it managed it would be none too happy to find Larry and not a lady love. Larry tried to adjust his position to avoid falling, but when he did the buck stopped moving and looked up. His eyes were opened wide and his nostrils flared. Large puffs of vapor escaped his nose. When the buck and Larry had eye contact, Larry screamed and the buck bugled at the same time. The buck ran away and Larry's honor was saved.

"I think I won!"

Larry, aka Santa

Louise, Biker Girl   *Larry, Bad Biker Dude*

Diane Sawyer and Larry. . .
Ho Ho Ho back at ya—2003

Larry and Charlie Gibson—2003

Lakes Cabin; Summer & Winter

Louise and Larry, 1997 at Jake & Nikki's wedding

Jake, Louise, Jason and Larry, 2003 at Jason and Jean's wedding

The same season and perhaps the winner of his hunting stories was the time that he and another fellow hunter were at the hunt camp. After a morning of hunting and no luck, they walked back to their respective cars . . .

The two of us chatted as we put our equipment away. I opened the tailgate of our Jeep and ejected a live shell from my gun. Without realizing it, I had incorrectly released the safety. The gun fired. The other hunter and I fell to our knees from the blast.

We exchanged startled looks. I was trembling.

"I'm okay. Are you okay?"

The man nodded his head up and down, but was too choked to speak. We slowly rose to a standing position and inspected the Jeep for damage. I had shot a hole right through the carpet on the backside. The bullet had penetrated the gas tank. I saw what I had done and began to sweat profusely from fear. I pointed to the damage.

"We should have been blasted to South Carolina. So much for safety! I am so sorry. I should have been more careful."

The other hunter ambled off to his car shaking his head in disbelief. I suspect he might have mumbled damned fool if he wasn't still speechless from the incident. I packed up and drove my Jeep with a hole in the gas tank and the fuel leaking back the few miles to Brooks to a body shop near our house. Since I was an auto claims adjuster, I knew the body shop owner, Mr. Green and his staff, Cooter and Booger. I was still wet with sweat and quaking when I pulled into Mr. Green's Body Shop.

"You boys aren't going to believe what I've just done."

By the time I was finished explaining, they were buckled over in laughter.

"Stop laughing. This is serious. We could have been killed. In fact, this stunt scared me so much that I may never hunt again."

Mr. Green regained his composure.

"Aw, Larry, we're just funnin' ya. Y'all can't help bein' a Yankee."

"Well, all y'all know how hard I've tried to overcome that title and get along with these folks down here so don't you go spreading this story around town. I'm embarrassed enough about being so careless and having to admit it to y'all. Besides, I really need your help. We have to take my son to Gatlinburg, Tennessee tomorrow to play in the junior football playoffs. I need this fixed right away."

Mr. Green gave me a ride to our house a few miles away to get our old pick up truck. When I returned, Cooter and Booger had already dropped the gas tank from the Jeep. They loaded it into the truck bed while Mr. Green gave me the directions.

"You take this on down to old man Pritchard's in Griffin. He'll repair the tank and then we'll install it on the Jeep. You're our little Yankee buddy and we'll take good care of you."

When I arrived at old man Pritchard's house, a gentleman dressed in overalls greeted me. He had a foot long white, scraggly beard with a permanent tobacco stain that ran the length of it. Mr. Pritchard took one look at me, ran his tongue over the gob of tobacco between his bottom lip and teeth and spat out the juice.

"Guess you couldn't get a deer so you shot your Jeep."

I knew the spreading of the story had begun. When I returned to the body shop to pick up the fixed Jeep, Mr. Green had also washed it.

"We can't have you drive into the fine state of Tennessee with a dirty Jeep. Those people will think you're a hick."

I thanked Mr. Green, Cooter and Booger for their promptness in getting my vehicle fixed, paid and left.

Months later, I was promoted to a supervisor job at another branch of State Farm sixty miles from our home. When I arrived the first morning to report for my new duties, the large, employee bulletin board had been cleared with the exception of two items; a picture of a deer and a picture of a Jeep. There was a caption underneath.

> **Larry, this is a deer and this is a Jeep.**

I was a legend at State Farm.

We sold our rustic country house in Brooks and moved back to Peachtree City in 1990, which reduced our long sixty-mile commute to work by fifteen miles of country road. We couldn't car pool as I worked on the west side of Atlanta and Larry worked on the east side. Both boys were going to school in Peachtree City. We often made two round trips in a day from our country home to town so the boys could attend sports or school functions. It was a relief to spend less time on the road and more at home.

Jason graduated from high school in 1992 and moved to Denver, Colorado to work, ski and snowboard at Keystone Resort. This was a great experience in his becoming a responsible, self-supporting adult. I missed him, but appreciated his independence and entrepreneurial attitude. The job opportunities were primarily for the winter sports, but Jason managed to land a job cleaning the executive offices for the resort in the summer. Within a month, he was managing the night crew and awarded Employee of the Month by his superiors. He also bought a small, cheap car and delivered pizzas as a second job. When he tired of that job, he sold the little car for what he had paid for it. His sales skills since a little boy had always been superior. We visited him for a week each winter and combined it with a ski vacation. To satisfy our longing to see him the rest of the year, we had to be content with weekly telephone calls.

Not long thereafter, Eastern went out of business. I was on the road again. I went back to work at Northwest Airlines. That was the good news. The bad news was I worked in Los Angeles, California. Fortunately, my good friend, Kathy Federoff, had an apartment there and was happy to share expenses. I flew home to Georgia every other weekend for three years, which was a benefit of working in the airline business. As long as there was a seat available, I went home. Larry and I were both discouraged about our arrangement. We were both lonely when we were apart. I had chronic jet lag from the cross-country travel. Larry once more held the title of Mr. Mom to Jake, but in spite of the extra expense of two households, we were better off financially. We accepted our arrangement philosophically, and waited until I could find employment in Georgia.

Worth mentioning here is the apartment Kathy and I shared. It was in Manhattan Beach, which is a classy beach city near Los Angeles. We lived in the shadows of several stories high homes only three blocks from the beach. All one needed to claim an ocean view was to be able to see a speck of it from some part of the dwelling. It seemed like a contest to build higher to get that view. Our apartment, however, was a renovated garage. Actually, it was only one stall of the garage. We had one room with an alcove for a kitchen, which housed a small bar refrigerator with a hot plate on top of it and a mini-microwave on half of the kitchen counter. The bathroom had a corner shower, small sink and toilet. One had to lean against the shower opening to close the bathroom door and use the toilet. It was definitely a one-person place for the bargain price of six hundred fifty dollars per month.

Our twin beds were aligned against two of the walls with the heads toward a common corner. We crammed a small three-drawer dresser in that same corner between the beds. There was another small dresser with a television across the room and a closet that jutted out into the walk space of the room. Though compact, it met our needs. Kathy's innate ability to decorate with very little served us well. We had a patio, which was the same size as our indoor living space, adjacent to our landlord's yard. Kathy's innovation made it inviting and useful. The front of our place was the alley where we were assigned one parking space. We took turns parking there. On the non-parking space week, the other person had to walk a few blocks. Since we worked together, we often carpooled. We lived like this for close to three years. In spite of our small claustrophobic-like space, we still remained great friends.

On occasion, Larry would fly to Los Angeles to visit me. One such time, he brought Jake with him. Kathy and I made a pallet on the floor for the boys. It was late when they arrived and Larry had had a few drinks on the long flight. We went directly to bed. Larry's place on the floor was directly below me. He thought his conversation to me was in a hushed whisper, but Kathy and Jake could hear him as clearly as I could.

"Weezie . . . could I come up there with you in your bed? I've missed you."

"Larry, hush and go to sleep. There's only room for one person in this bed."

He didn't accept that answer.

"I don't mind. I'll cuddle real close."

Kathy rolled over so that she faced the wall and covered her head with a pillow. Jake pulled the blankets over his head. They were both preparing themselves for a spectacle that I was determined wouldn't happen. Larry wouldn't let up his pleading so I relented.

"Okay, you can come up here, but no funny stuff."

Jake groaned.

Larry jumped up and crawled into the bed with me. He immediately started getting frisky, which was exactly what I thought he'd do.

"Stop it Larry. Do you realize we are all in the same room? It's so crowded in here, it's like we're all sharing the same bed."

"No one will know."

Jake couldn't take it anymore.

"Dad, please stop. It's too gross."

That made me embarrassed, but I laughed. "Don't worry, Jake. If he doesn't shush and stop moving around, he'll be back on the floor with you . . . or I will."

That made Larry give up his advances and he drifted off to sleep much to everyone's relief.

Under different circumstances; specifically, if I was twenty years younger and single, living by the beach might have been a pleasurable time. Kathy was sympathetic and understanding when I'd cry because I missed my husband and kids. We bonded like sisters and she is still an extended member of my family. My husband and children love her too.

Jake was a sophomore in high school during this time and called me at work in LA everyday when he got home. Back then; long distance telephone rates were based on the time of day. Since three-thirty in the afternoon was the high rate time, I told him to quit this habit unless he was bleeding and a band-aid wouldn't handle it. I phoned home every night when rates were lower and told him we could talk then. Within a couple of days of our conversation, he called me again in the afternoon. I don't know if he thought I lived so far away from home because it was fun or if he didn't understand high finance. Whatever the reason, it aggravated me.

"Jake, did you forget the telephone rules?"

"No, but my football coach just brought me home because he thinks I broke my neck."

I freaked out. "Why didn't you call your dad? What can I do from here?"

"I did try to call, but he's in a meeting."

"Okay, stay put. Don't move. I'll find someone to help you."

I called my friend, Dianne Maney, who drove to our house and took Jake to the doctor. Fortunately, it was a false alarm. That night, Larry, Jake and I set down some rules on how to handle emergency situations. Specifically, anything that required a parent's intervention or approval had to go to Larry since he was local. If he was unavailable, Jake needed to tell Larry's secretary to find him.

A week later, Jake called me at dinnertime and sounded like he was crying.

"What's the matter? Are you hurt?"

"No, Dad is making me eat pasta salad and it tastes terrible."

I could hear him crunch.

"This is the second night in a row that Dad made this salad. It doesn't taste at all like Kathy Kirby's pasta salad."

Kathy and her husband, Tom, were close friends of ours. This recipe was a favorite on our weekend camping trips at the lake.

"Put your father on the phone."

I had to wait a few minutes, as Jake must have hidden in a closet to call me and be out of Larry's earshot.

"Larry, why are you forcing Jake to eat the pasta salad if he doesn't like it and why is he crunching?"

"Because, I bought all those fresh vegetables, which were expensive. I soaked the pasta and veggies all night like the recipe said and the pasta never softened. I threw away the first batch, but we're eating this one; crunch and all."

I stifled a chuckle because I knew exactly what he had done. "Did you cook the pasta first before you marinated it?"

If I could have seen Larry's face, I knew it would look like someone had slapped him along side of the head and told him to get with it.

"The recipe did not say anything about cooking the pasta first."

In spite of his insistence to justify his actions, I asked him to take Jake out to dinner.

Halfway through Jake's junior year in high school, he moved to Ohio. We had gone there to visit Larry's family for Thanksgiving. Jake was amazed at the football program at Massillon's high school.

"Wow, I wish I could play here."

His team in Peachtree City had never had a winning season. Jake shared Larry's passion for football. Massillon's football history was incomparable to Jake's high school. Our nephew, Todd, whose family hosted the holiday weekend, planted the seed.

"Jake could live with us. We'd love to have him. I'll help him with weight training. It'll be great."

We talked about the prospect of Jake's potential move during the long drive home. Larry and I did our best to explain the magnitude of this decision to him. Our family already lived in three states and this would totally split us up.

"But, Mom, did you see that stadium and the weight room and the different uniforms? I can't believe it."

I noticed Larry wipe his eyes a couple of times and knew he was troubled by thoughts of providing an opportunity to his son versus living all alone. With me in California and Jason in Colorado, we would not spend much time together.

"Do you think we could fly to all of the games?"

"Well, you know how my flight privileges work. You'll have to fly stand by, but you can get there if you fly to Detroit first and then to Cleveland."

There were hours of long silences during the thirteen-hour car ride. Then we'd discuss the pros and cons over again. The one rule we set down in advance was that if Jake chose to make this move, he could not move back home until after graduation. By the end of the trip, Jake had made his decision to go. I whispered a silent prayer to myself that it was the right thing to do. I was more worried about Larry than Jake. Larry liked his family near him and didn't do well by himself.

Larry worked with an attorney in Griffin to draw up the paperwork to assign custody of Jake to our nephew and his wife until he was eighteen. It was the hardest thing Larry and I had ever done. The legal documents more or less said that our separate living conditions did not provide a healthy, home environment for Jake. We lived a rather bazaar lifestyle, not by choice, rather by necessity. Though we cried as we signed the documents, we knew it would be a great opportunity for Jake. This was the only way he would be allowed to play football in Massillon. It was an opportunity for him to be recognized and perhaps get a college scholarship.

❧❧ ❧❧ ❧❧

The first semester was tough on Jake. He made friends, but he missed us. He called me in California one night about six weeks after he moved.

"Mom, I changed my mind. I want to go back to Georgia."

My heart hurt to know he was so homesick. I knew how he felt as I too wished I could be at home. But I couldn't let him backslide on his decision, however hard the lesson.

"Jake. We had a deal. Things will get better, you'll see. We'll plan a visit home for you at spring break."

I was right. In time his friendships became more solid and his attitude improved. Even though he was competing with kids, who had played together throughout their youth and first two years of high school, Jake worked hard and made the team. Larry attended every weekly game. He flew to Ohio from Georgia every Friday afternoon and arrived in Massillon in time to see the game. I had to fly to Ohio from California and missed only two games. As exciting as it was to see Jake play in a big stadium with a big crowd, I think we were all miserable without each other. Larry was impacted the most by this separation as when alone, he had a tendency to sulk.

Howard and Gloria would invite him over for dinner or other activities, but he withdrew into his shell and felt sorry for himself. Occasionally, I talked him into flying to California to see me just to get him out of the house.

After Jake graduated a year and a half later, he moved home and attended West Georgia College. About the same time, Jason blew out his knee snowboarding. I went to Denver to be with him after surgery. Jason was also lonesome for family and moved home not too long thereafter. In 1993, I received a job offer in Atlanta. We were, finally back together again.

Larry purchased a Harley Davidson Soft Tail Custom motorcycle right before I left Los Angeles. I don't know if you'd call it mid-life crisis or keeping up with the Jones, but Larry's love for motorcycles never waned and he had to have one. His motorcycles became progressively more expensive; bigger toys for bigger boys. We had ridden for short rides, but one weekend he convinced me that we should ride up to our friends' cabin, which was about one hundred and ten miles away. My concern about the longer trip was how miserable my backside would feel by the time we arrived. The six inch wide seat was much narrower than my butt.

I packed whatever necessities would fit in a small flowered duffle bag that Larry would have to strap on the back of the sissy bar that doubled as my backrest. When I went outside, I found Larry polishing the chrome on his bike. It was already shiny. He turned around toward me when he heard me scuffing the paved driveway with my leather boots.

"You aren't putting that flowered bag on my Harley."

I looked at him and then at the bundle I carried. "Why not? It's the perfect size."

He stood up.

"It has flowers. I'll find one."

He managed to find an old Army duffle among the boxes in the garage. He held it up to show me.

"This is a duffle bag suitable for our ride."

I waved my hand at him in a pretend slap. "Whatever."

I transferred the items to his luggage of choice and he strapped it on the back of the bike. We put on our leather coats, helmets and leather gloves and climbed on.

We traveled on the winding back roads, parallel to the freeway. While the countryside was very scenic, it also added miles to the trip. We rode through a small retirement community when all of a sudden the Harley sputtered and backfired. The bang was loud enough to grab people's attention evidenced by the multiple houses whose curtains were drawn back ever so slightly. It sounded like a gunshot when it backfired again and came to a complete stop. The curious folks in the senior community peered through their doors. Since we were both dressed in black leather jackets and jeans and wore helmets that hid our faces, we looked like bad biker dudes. No one wanted to venture near.

Larry muttered expletives under his breath, got off the Harley and stared at the bike. This was his first encounter with a malfunction and he was stumped. As I slung my leg over the sissy bar to dismount, I offered some positive comments.

"I'm sure it's nothing serious. Try to start it again."

Larry's short fuse had begun to sizzle.

"It won't start."

I expected him to kick the tires at any moment. At least, that's what he does to a car when it breaks down. The motorcycle, however, would topple over from the force and he wouldn't want to dent the beautiful chrome. Instead, he took off his helmet and slammed it to the ground without any concern that he'd damage his safety device. He startled me. I knew from experience that I needed to take some action so he would quit fuming. He's so touchy about his things.

"I'll go borrow a phone and call Jason."

In 1994, a fortunate few owned cell phones. We were not one of them. I spotted a gentleman working in his yard on the next street. There was a green belt area much like a park between us. The short walk gave me time to remove my helmet, shake out my hair a bit to soften my appearance and begin smiling at him. It also gave him time to decide if he needed to flee or stay to satisfy his curiosity.

When I reached his house, I explained our motorcycle had broken down, which was the loud bang he'd heard and asked if I could borrow his telephone to call our son. Southern hospitality was commonplace in Georgia and he agreed right away. Besides, he'd be the envy of the neighborhood when he shared the inside scoop on the strange motorcycle people who had been stranded in their quiet village. The man and his wife were most helpful. She retrieved the yellow pages from the cupboard so that in addition to calling for a ride for us, I could call a tow truck. In between the phone calls, she asked me questions like how old my children were.

"Have you been driving that motorcycle long?"

Her husband harrumphed.

"Now, Mother, leave her to her business."

I smiled my most polite smile. "It's okay. I'd be curious too, if someone dressed up like me and knocked on my door." I gave her the answers that satisfied her.

Meanwhile, Larry pretended he knew something about the mechanics of a motorcycle and inspected his bike. A small, slumped shouldered older gentleman shuffled by Larry. He moved with intent on his destination, but at a snail's pace. Nodding a greeting to Larry, he pointed his shaky, bony finger toward the motorcycle.

"Having trouble with your motorcycle, sonny?"

Larry looked up to acknowledge the old man.

"Yes sir."

"Well, I'm going down yonder to the recreation center. You're welcome to come along and use their telephone."

Larry respectfully declined and explained that his wife had gone to borrow a phone to call our son. Without stopping his forward motion, the man continued his slow walk down the block and waved goodbye over his shoulder as he went.

I thanked my hosts and wandered back to where Larry was to give him an update.

"I couldn't get in touch with Jason, but I did reach Howard Brooks."

Our friend, who is about two years younger than we, delighted in Larry's antics. In fact, every time something like this happened to Larry, Howard would comment.

"Here's another faux pas for the book."

He was happy to rescue us in Christian City. When I talked to him, he chuckled and remarked that Larry would be the talk of the town for days. When Howard arrived about an hour later, the same little old man was hobbling back from the recreation center. He nodded his head in Howard's direction.

"Well, see your son got here okay."

He kept shuffling his way home. As soon as he was out of earshot, Howard belted out a big guffaw.

"So, Mom, what's for dinner?"

I giggled back at him. He's such a loveable guy. "Shut up, Howard."

We wound up going to Howard and Gloria's house and dined with him. Howard couldn't help himself and called me Mom all evening long.

We skipped the weekend trip. I told Larry that any travel farther than twenty miles wouldn't include me on the back of that motorcycle. I learned quickly a better name for his model of motorcycle should be a Hard Tail Custom unless the passenger had buns of steel. Larry agreed and upgraded to an Ultra Classic that had a wider rear seat, stereo and headphones so that we could talk to one another over the roar of the engine. Now, that was a nice ride.

Chapter Twelve

Our younger son, Jake, met his wife at the airline where they both worked. They had been dating for a year when they announced to us they were engaged and planned to marry the following summer. We knew Nikki well as she was a regular visitor at our home, but we had never met her family. I was happy for the kids as they seemed well suited and she had blended into our family life with ease.

I invited Nikki's mother and grandmother to our home to discuss wedding plans. While the bride's family usually paid for those arrangements, I had never given credence to that line of thinking. Larry's parents had split costs with my parents so I volunteered to help pay some expenses as well. We decided we would host the affair ourselves and rent a hall as opposed to paying a hotel or professional wedding planner. We had a pleasant conversation and each of us volunteered for activities and spent the remainder of the evening getting acquainted.

Another reason for initiating this discussion was that Jake and Nikki also told us they wanted to get married in the Catholic Church. None of Nikki's family was Catholic and while it wasn't a requirement by us, I wanted to help make it more palatable in case there was an issue.

Another of Nikki's grandmothers owned a wedding rental shop and volunteered to set up candelabra in the church, help decorate the food tables in the hall and make the cake of the bride's choice. Our church was being remodeled and under construction, therefore, our priest contacted the Catholic Church in a neighboring town for us. They were most accommodating and helped us set a date for August 9, 1997.

I accompanied Jake and Nikki to the new church to discuss the church's requirements with their voluntary wedding planner. It was quite an eye opener. I had never given any thought to seating protocol other than the bride and groom's parents sat in the first pew. As soon as the volunteer explained where the mother and father of the bride would sit in the first pew, Nikki blushed a bit.

"My parents are not married any longer. My dad is remarried and my mom is single."

The wedding planner looked at her seating chart and made some changes.

"No problem, we'll put your mother in the front row and your father and his wife in the second row. It wouldn't be appropriate for them to be seated next to each other."

Jake, Nikki and I looked at each other and shrugged our shoulders. I knew the lady helping us was a little uncomfortable with the discussion, but not surprised. Even though our church frowned on divorce, there were plenty of divorced Catholics. She continued on with her questions.

"Okay, that's settled. We can seat your maternal grandmother and her husband next to your mother."

Nikki's jaw tightened as if she wasn't certain how to proceed, but then she laughed a nervous chuckle.

"Well, my paw paw and granny are divorced too and both of them have remarried."

The lady's eyes opened wider.

"My, my, I'm not certain what we should do about this."

She adjusted her position in her seat as though she was trying to find a way to be more comfortable. I tried to ease her dilemma.

"You know, all of her family members are happy for her. In fact, she's going to ask her grandfather to participate in the ceremony . . . and her dad is escorting her down the aisle. I believe we can seat them all within the same proximity and they'll be fine."

The planner blotted her forehead.

"Well, that helps."

She asked a few more pertinent questions. Jake, Nikki and I all had the giggles over the situation, which probably didn't make the woman feel better, but it helped us. We set the date and time for the wedding and the rehearsal and left after we had perused the altar area. There were tall windows at the back with a rock waterfall on the outside. We were all pleased with the setting.

"This will be beautiful."

Nikki was especially pleased.

"I'm going to ask my grandmother, Paw Paw's wife, to set up candelabra so that the waterfall shows in the middle."

We all left in agreement. One task was crossed off our to do list.

Nikki's grandfather, a Protestant Christian, was the only person troubled about the wedding being conducted in a Catholic church. We determined the best way to overcome his objections was to include him in the ceremony. Our priest gave us a choice of five passages from the Bible. Nikki delivered the message to her grandfather.

"Paw Paw, would you like to read the first Bible scripture in our wedding?"

Nikki's grandfather cleared his throat as if preparing for an argument.

"Only if I can use my own Bible."

She had anticipated his response and was ready with the right answer.

"Of course you can. Which of these five verses would you like to read?"

When he reviewed the choices, a big smile crept across his face.

"Why, that one there is the one I would have chosen."

Another obstacle was overcome. Jake and Nikki met with the priest and followed his instruction. The rehearsal was two nights before the wedding because of overbooking at the church. We decided the best spot for the rehearsal dinner was a favorite barbeque restaurant in Fayetteville, Georgia, which was half way between where Nikki's family lived and where we lived. Our nephew, Jeff, my next older brother's son, was in town and led us in prayer. Jeff had struggled with substance abuse and was now sober. I was very proud of him. He looked good and was pleased to be included in our celebration.

The night before the wedding, we hosted a dinner for sixty family members of ours, who had flown in from Arizona, Kentucky and Ohio to attend the wedding. Our good friends, Howard and Gloria took care of the cooking and serving arrangements. Howard made his delectable low country boil with hot sausage, potatoes, small ears of corn and crawdads for the occasion. Larry and I rented tables and chairs and set up an out-door dining room in our back yard. It was a lovely setting with the mini-lake behind our house. I set up Tiki torches around the perimeter of the yard to ward off the mosquitoes. Poor Larry didn't get to eat with us as he made multiple trips to the airport to pick up evening arrivals. When he returned, there was only the broth, a cob of corn and shells off a crawdad, not exactly appetizing.

The next day was also my mother's birthday so we had a big cake and sang Happy Birthday to her. Howard and Gloria and two other couples who were mutual friends helped them clean up and they left. People like the Brooks don't come along very often. We feel blessed to have them as friends.

It started to sprinkle around nine o'clock. Some folks went back to the hotel to rest, but several of us moved a couple of tables into the garage, cranked up the music and drank beer. We partied until midnight, but then broke up the gathering. We had a big day ahead of us.

In the morning, several family members helped me blow up balloons with helium and decorate the reception hall. In hindsight, I would have selected another venue as there was much more work than I had expected. Further, I don't think any of us saved any money in the long run. But, no matter, we had fun.

One of our acquaintances, in fact, the gentleman we had purchased our house in the country from, was an Irish tenor. He had been the music director of the Methodist Church in Atlanta. As a gift to the bridge and groom, he agreed to sing at their wedding. His rendition of the Our Father brought goose bumps to members of the congregation. He also sang as the multitudes gathered for the ceremony.

The altar with the candelabra was beautiful. Everyone remembered his or her part without flaw and the Irish priest gave a wonderful sermon during the ceremony. He told the story of the people of Ireland, who climb St. Patrick's Mountain on a pilgrimage each year.

"You can not possibly do it alone. Someone must push you or pull you or walk along side of you to be successful. It's the same with marriage."

I had never understood why people cried at weddings since they were such happy occasions. I figured it out. Hearing the wise words of the priest and watching my baby leave our nest for good struck an emotional chord with me. It seemed bittersweet, but the newly married couple looked so happy, I cheered up right away. While we were taking pictures of the bridal party after the ceremony, Nikki's grandfather stopped me. He had tears in his eyes.

Jake and Nikki, wedding 8/9/97

"That was the loveliest ceremony I have ever witnessed. I forgot we were in a Catholic church."

"I'm glad you approved."

By the time we arrived at the reception hall, the party was already in full swing. People had food and the DJ had the music playing. He announced the bridal party as they entered the room. After a quick bite to eat, we removed tables from the dance floor and celebrated.

Nikki's grandmother had made the most beautiful cake I had ever seen. It was five layers and had hand-made sugar flowers cascading from the top down. I had to take several pictures to capture its beauty. It was truly a work of art.

Jake and Nikki said goodbye to their guests and headed to the hotel after midnight. We bid them farewell with thousands of bubbles we had blown into the air.

I had arranged a surprise of milk and cookies to be delivered to their room. I remembered how starved Larry and I were on our wedding night. There were too many things happening to enjoy the food that was served. It wasn't until they returned from their honeymoon in Savannah that I learned the hotel had messed up the order and delivered the treats a night early. Nikki and her bridesmaids, who had stayed in the room with her, enjoyed their treat instead.

☙ ☙ ☙

Our first grandchild, Madison, was born on December 30, 1997. We thought she was clever as soon as we saw her. She had been born via a cesarean section and had been taken to a small room with a plate glass window where she was placed on display so that her maternal grandparents, aunts, uncles and Larry and I could see the newest addition to our families. Her little body was purplish in color from the trauma of birth so her nurse had placed a large oxygen dome over her. It took only a few minutes to bring her skin tone to a pleasant pink. Jake was permitted in the room with Madison as the nurse took vital signs and checked her. He had to squeeze into the corner adjacent to the window and at the foot of the table where Madison lay.

Jake, who possesses an innate ability to entertain us with unique facial expressions, was fascinated with this new cherub. The nurse turned Madison over on her stomach and the baby immediately extended her arms with palms flat on the table and lifted her body up like she was doing a push up. She knocked the dome right off her head as she did it. Jake's eyes opened up wide and he contorted his face to show how impressed he was with the strength of his little daughter.

Our first opportunity to show off Madison to our friends was at a birthday party Howard and Gloria threw for Larry when Maddy was three weeks old. He loved this baby, but was unsettled at being called Grandpa.

"I'm too young to be called Grandpa. Now I know how my mother felt when she made her first two grandchildren call her by her first name, Helen."

The roomful of people laughed at Larry for being so vain. Howard, who loved to tease Larry, let him have it.

"What do you mean, you're too young? You're fifty-two years old, which is plenty old enough to be a grandparent."

One of the women in the room took her turn holding Madison, who had scrunched up into a fetal position on the lady's bosom.

She cooed at Maddy.

"I have news for you, Larry. This child can call you Shithook and you won't mind."

As crass as it seemed, she was right. Larry was a pushover for this baby. After much discussion, Larry settled on being called Papa and I was called Grandma, a much more difficult word to say when our granddaughter became a toddler.

Madison said small words by the time she was one; papa was one of them. I used to hold Maddy and pat my heart with my fingers;

the palm of my hand resting on my chest. I repeated the word over and over as I patted.

"Grandma. Say Grandma."

Maddy finally caught on and when asked to say Grandma, she patted her heart. When she was almost two, I made Larry buy me a video camera for an early Christmas present. I wanted to capture this endearing gesture. I readied my camera and zoomed in on Madison, who was busy coloring. Jake prompted her.

"Maddy, say Grandma."

She ignored him.

"Come on honey, say Grandma."

She put down her crayons, looked up at him for a brief moment. She had a slight scowl on her face for being interrupted, but she patted her heart. This thirty-second video was taken at the exactly the right moment as the next time we asked her she spoke the words instead. While I was a bit heart-broken, as I loved the gesture, I also appreciated her ability to get my attention verbally.

Papa, as Madison knew him, had a beard until she was almost four. That was the longest he had ever had one and he decided to shave it off one day. Simultaneously, he had been researching his genealogy and learned that his great grandfather was known as Pap to all his family and friends. Larry showed me the document.

"Look here. Elias Laughlin, aka Pap Laughlin. I think I'm going to have Madison call me Pap."

He saw her that very afternoon. She noticed his beard was gone right away and touched his face.

"Maddy, doesn't your papa look different?"

She nodded her head. Larry corrected me through the gentle instructions he gave to Maddy.

"Call me Pap."

Everything is literal with a child. For a few short months, when we showed Madison a picture of Larry with a beard and asked who it was, she responded the same.

"That's my papa."

I'd point to Larry and ask who he was. She'd grin.

"That's my pap."

Madison's two siblings, Chloe and Dylan, always knew Larry as Pap, but they also learned to say Grandma by patting their heart.

Chapter Thirteen

Larry discovered his alter ego in 1998 when he decided to play Santa Claus for Madison, who would be one year old. Her first birthday was on December 30th, six days after Christmas. She was a joy and he thought it would be a good way to stretch out the celebration.

When Larry had retired two years earlier, for health reasons, he declared he wasn't going to cut his hair again and he grew a beard. I pretty much ignored him because he had worn a beard on and off since we were married. With the exception of his Afro in the eighties, he had always had short hair. It was of no consequence to me, as no matter what he did, I knew he would be neat and clean, which was all I cared about. His mini rebellion was against all those years of wearing starched shirts and ties, having a conservative haircut and objections from some of his managers concerning his beard.

Two months after his last day at work, the State Farm office in Griffin, where he had first worked when we moved to Georgia, needed some help. His former manager asked if he'd consider working on a consulting basis.

"Sure, I can do that, but I'm not cutting my hair or my beard."

Desperate for coverage in the office, his old boss didn't object.

"As long as you look professional, I don't care."

Cleanliness had never been a problem for Larry. He pulled his hair back in a ponytail low on his neck. He looked a bit like Sean Connery to me. He worked an additional eighteen months and then severed his business relationship. One August evening, while we were watching television, Larry made his announcement.

"I've decided I'm going to play Santa Claus for Madison this year. My hair is shoulder length like Santa's and I won't trim my beard so it should be long by then. Do you think you can find a Santa suit for me?"

I gazed over at him and smiled. I suspected he'd make a great Santa with his rosy cheeks and his slight paunch of a belly.

"I've seen them in the JCP catalog. I'll check it out."

It was a simple task. I found a great one for a reasonable price and ordered it. As Christmas approached, I looked forward to taking some family photos with Larry in the center as Santa. On the designated night, I instructed Jake and Nikki and Jason to wear denim jeans and either a white or red shirt or sweater. I did the same. I invited a young friend of ours, Sonya and her daughter, Mercy to have their pictures taken too. I had always teased that Mercy was like my un-grandchild. I also called another friend of ours, who I considered talented with a camera, and asked if he would take the pictures. He agreed.

Santa and Madison, 1998

We had the best fun that night. Nikki had purchased a green, velvet Christmas dress for Madison, which coordinated well with the red Santa suit and the center of attention. My sons, who come by it honestly, were mischievous the entire time. They sneaked into the hall bath and came out wearing the Santa hats I had given them. They had stuffed the hats with paper, which made them look like dunce caps.

"What do you think, Mom?"

I was not to be undone by their humor. "I think you boys look quite natural."

We all shared a hardy laugh until I heard Larry call from our bedroom.

"Louise . . . I need some help."

"What else is new?"

I wondered at what age he would be able to dress himself without some

Jason and Jake, silly Santas, 1998

assistance or advice and headed into the bedroom. He was close to finished with the pants, padding and jacket on, but needed me to buckle his belt and tuck his pant legs into his boots. I stopped inside the threshold and stared. It was like magic. He was Santa Claus.

"Oh, Larry, you look wonderful. I think I believe in Santa Claus."

"Good, because I have a present I'd like to give you later."

I put my finger up to my lips and shushed him. "Quiet, the children will hear you."

"I don't think that will be a problem. They're twenty-six and twenty-two. I think they can handle it. Could you hurry, I'm already sweating in this get up."

I went to his side and assisted with his accessories. "Let me put a little blush on your cheeks to rosy them up even more."

He agreed. He exited our bedroom after me and I think everyone in the room did a double take. Larry had been transformed. Halfway through the picture taking and after Sonya and Mercy left, Larry had to take off his jacket to cool down. No one left in the room was a true believer so he didn't blow his cover. It was a sight to see him with his hair cascading down to his bare shoulders and with only his padding, pants and hat on. One of the boys handed him a beer to drink. He looked like bad Santa. It was, however, the beginning of a new career, albeit not a very lucrative one.

With the exception of 2002, when he was in the hospital, he has played Santa every year since. Because of his surgery, his engagements are short and have become fewer as he has a tendency to become dehydrated after thirty minutes in his suit. He has fun with the persona, however, and wears red suspenders, his hat and a red shirt of some sort wherever he goes during the Christmas season. One year, he and I were purchasing some last minute gifts at the department store near our house. We were in the garden center looking at miniature trees for decoration when two little boys hovered nearby.

I had seen them when I looked over Larry's shoulder and whispered to him that Santa had been caught. He turned around and with a gleeful HO, HO, HO, bent down to speak with the children.

"Hello boys. What are you doing here?"

They were curious, but apprehensive. They seemed to be about three and five. Their parents each picked up a child and held him, which gave the older one enough courage to talk.

"Hi, Santa, why are you at Target?"

"Ho, Ho, Ho. Mrs. Claus asked me to come here with her to buy a miniature tree for my elves."

The little boy was in awe. His eyes were big and he was barely able to respond. The sound came out of his mouth in an exhale.

"Wow."

Larry patted him on the shoulder.

"I hope you sent your letter in to me to let me know what you want. We get real busy at the North Pole this time of year."

That was my cue to move Santa along.

"Okay, dear, I think I know which one I want. I have one more thing to show you and we don't have much time."

"Ho, Ho, Ho . . . that Mrs. Claus keeps me busy too. You boys have a nice Christmas."

We left to get out of the boys' view. A few minutes later, I was looking at clothes for our grandchildren when the mother of the boys approached me.

"Your husband is wonderful. He looks like a real Santa with his natural beard. Which mall does he work in so I can take my children to get a picture?"

Larry, Maddy, Chloe, and Dylan 2005

I stopped my search, turned toward her and smiled. "He doesn't work in the mall. He works at the North Pole."

The lady's mouth dropped and I slipped away from her. It's rather fun to be Mrs. Claus. As each of our three grandchildren has become old enough to be intrigued with Santa, we have entrusted them with our family secret. Their Pap is Santa Claus.

❦ ❦ ❦

We flew home for the 1999 New Year's holiday. Larry and I and my siblings, Jack, Laura and Charlie and their spouses attended a traveling keg party in Charlie's neighborhood. After the turmoil of having to commute over the past several years it felt good to be home with them. It had been fourteen years since we had lived near family. We stayed with Jack and Andrea for the long weekend. The house directly behind them went up for sale while we were there. My intuition told me we should move back home. I couldn't tell if I longed for family or if I had a premonition they would need me. I think Larry missed the camaraderie as much as I did. We looked at the house the same day. While it needed considerable updating, it had potential and we bought it. My next work assignment was in

Denver for six months. Since I would have to commute home on weekends anyway, the flight to Arizona was shorter than to Georgia. Both of our sons were adults and engrossed in their own lives. Jason lived in Atlanta and was in a serious relationship. Jake and Nikki were married and had a baby. Leaving all of them behind was a difficult choice, but we needed the change.

We hired my nephew, Michael for the entire month of January. He and Larry made wonderful improvements on the new house. At the end of that time, Larry, my brother Jack and I flew to Georgia and rented a truck to move our belongings to Arizona. On the day we loaded the truck, Jake asked if they could come with us. I was elated. They sold their house and were in Arizona by the middle of March. We bought a condo within a few blocks of our new home and they moved into it until they could get established on their own. The following year, they bought the house across the street from us.

Chapter Fourteen

L arry and my brother, Jack rekindled their friendship after returning from our fourteen year hiatus in Georgia. Because Jack and I were close in age, we were only two grades apart in school. We had made several mutual friends when he was in grades ten through twelve and his current wife had been one of them. I looked forward to having them as back door neighbors.

The villas we lived in had a zero property line; therefore, part of the back wall of our house was Jack and Andrea's fence. To save us the short walk through the park to their street, we removed cement blocks on our mutual fence line and installed a gate. We went back and forth to each other's houses on a regular basis. We shared dinners, used our yards and houses for combined, large family gatherings and even vacationed together on occasion.

Larry and I planned to meet up with several of our riding partners from Georgia for a motorcycle trip to Sturgis, SD the following summer of 2000. Larry had expressed some concern about making the long trip to my brother, Jack, as our Harley was not operating well on a consistent basis. Larry didn't want to repeat another trip he'd taken when he drove from one Harley dealership to another as his motorcycle broke down in between. He and Jack discussed Larry's options for a different bike on a number of occasions. Larry had his mind set on a Harley Road King like Jack's. We had a year to make a decision, but Jack was vigilant in his search for the right bike for Larry. Jack was also looking forward to have a riding buddy of his own so his motivation was somewhat selfish. One day he walked through the gate into our yard with newspaper in hand and found Larry sitting by the side of the pool.

"I saw an ad in this paper for a Honda Gold Wing. It looks like a good deal."

Larry looked at Jack in a quizzical manner as if Jack had lost his marbles.

"I'm a Harley man. I can't buy a Gold Wing. I'd rather trade in the Ultra Classic for a bike like yours."

In spite of Jack's fondness of his own Harley, he continued with his sales pitch because he knew the Gold Wing would offer good performance. Jack was also a pushover for a good deal and it was fun to spend someone else's money.

"It can't hurt to see it."

When Jack read the ad to Larry's, it piqued his interest. Jack was a whiz at mechanics quite the opposite of Larry. Because of Jack's skill, Larry valued his opinion.

"I'll go check it out if you'll go with me."

Motorcycles, but in particular, their riders have morphed over the years. They are no longer bad guys, who live to ride and offend victims as they go. Instead, about the time we bought our first Harley, in 1993, the trend had changed. Professionals, lawyers, doctors, business men, etc caught the bug to spend their spare time riding the countryside on their Harleys with the wind in their faces. Larry and Jack were among the lucky ones. They both owned Harleys. It was a status symbol. It was cool to belong to a local chapter where in addition to the camaraderie one enjoyed certain benefits. For example, if a Harley owner were traveling to another state, Harley dealers would rent them a Harley. It was called fly/drive. Of course, experienced Harley owners knew the HD did not stand for Harley Davidson; rather it stood for hundred dollars as one could not leave a Harley store without spending at least that much.

When one started the engine of a Gold Wing, it went unnoticed, but when one started the engine of a Harley, it roared like a lion. The bottom line was a Gold Wing was not macho like a Harley, which was the reason for Larry's apprehension.

Nevertheless, they went together to see the bike. Larry took it for a trial jaunt. It was the best ride he'd experienced in a long time. The Gold Wing exceeded his expectations. It was a pale silvery, green with custom paint decorations on it. It came with the stock seat and a custom seat and two windshields. It was built for long road trips. Larry was sold.

"I'll take it."

He wrote the seller a check and rode it home. He put our Harley up for sale the same day. To practice riding the Gold Wing, Larry tagged along with Jack to the Laughlin, Nevada Motorcycle Rally, which was frequented by Harley people. Larry was embarrassed because he was in the minority on his Gold Wing. He hadn't come to terms yet with the great performance of his new bike versus the reputation of riding a Harley.

They made a pit stop in Oatman, Arizona located on Route 66. A weathered looking Harley rider walked over to Larry. He took off his sunglasses and stared at Larry's bike.

"Obviously, you're a Harley man or so it looks by the way you're dressed. What in the world are you doing riding a Honda?"

Larry, who was wearing his black leather jacket with an Atlanta Harley chapter patch on the back, looked at the Harley man square in the eye.

"Well, y'all can see I'm from Atlanta, Georgia. I figured I'd try one of them fly-drive deals. When I arrived at the dealer in Mesa, Arizona, I was told all of the Harleys were broke down. This here Gold Wing was all the dealership could offer me."

The old Harley rider walked away shaking his head. Larry felt proud of himself for coming up with a good story so quickly instead of explaining why he had purchased the Gold Wing.

Larry, Louise, Andrea and Jack near Ouray, Colorado

Practice time was over. Larry was ready for a long trip. So, in October 1999, we took a two-week motorcycle trip with Jack and Andrea, through Colorado and Wyoming. Our plan was to camp out at KOA Kabins whenever we could to save money. We had to provide our own bedding and towels, but we were never concerned about cleanliness. The cabins had one room with a queen sized bed frame and bunk beds, wooden pegs to hang clothes, enough floor space to house our gear, a mirror on the wall and a wooden porch swing. The campsite also had men and women's locker rooms that included showers, flush toilets and sinks with mirrors. In spite of the prospect of having helmet hair ever day, it was an opportunity to get refreshed at the end of the day.

We had three luggage compartments on our Honda. We used the side saddlebags for our wet weather gear, sleeping bags and towels. That left one compartment that measured approximately fourteen inches by twenty-four inches by eleven inches deep for our clothes for two weeks. Fortunately, my years of travel had taught me the art of packing. Needless to say, we had very few creature comforts; rather, we carried an extra pair of jeans, a couple of tee shirts each, clean underwear and clean socks.

Our first stop was in Cortez, Colorado. Our cousin, Nancy and her husband, Bucky Sparks lived in the little town. Jack and I have always had a close relationship with the cousins on our mother's side, therefore we took advantage of every opportunity to visit. After we had dined at a local town restaurant with Bucky and Nancy, Jack, Andrea, Larry and I headed to our campsite.

Early the next morning, our adventure began. We rode to Durango for breakfast, which was forty miles away. We planned to take our next break in Ouray, CO. We traveled north on Colorado State Highway 550, which is known as the Million Dollar Highway because it cost so much to construct. We had only gone about twenty miles when Jack's motorcycle quit. Breakdowns are the downside to motorcycle travel. We spent over an hour on the side of the road while Jack fixed his bike. We started out again and only went ten miles when it began to rain. We stopped again and put on our rain gear.

When we reached Ouray, it had stopped raining. So, we took our raingear off and walked around the town. We each ate an ice cream cone, but as usual, Larry's was hurrying me along. He wanted to get going. I noticed there were black clouds overhead, which warned us to don our raingear again.

"What a pain in the ass this is to put these boots on and take them off."

I huffed and puffed as the elevation was eight thousand feet high and I was unused to it. I struggled each time I had to dress in raingear and I was the last one dressed. Larry always had the same words to say.

"Hurry up. What's taking you so long? Everyone else is ready to go."

It aggravated me so I finally confronted Andrea. "How do you get your rubber boots over your leather boots so fast?"

Her response surprised me, it was so simple.

"I have plastic grocery bags in them. I pull them over my boots first and the rubber ones slip right on."

"No way. Do you have more?"

She didn't. I trudged half a block to the corner and went in the store and asked for a couple of plastic bags. Between the altitude and the heft of my apparel, I was worn out from the struggle. I offered to pay for them. When I told the clerk why I wanted them, she gave me several. I suspect I looked a sight with my helmet on, bright yellow rain pants and coat over my motorcycle jacket. I felt like the kid on *A Christmas Story* with his snowsuit on.

I went back to where the bikes were, leaned against the brick wall of the building and slipped my rubber boots over my plastic bag clad boots. They went on so fast; I nearly fell over as I yanked as hard as I had been without the bags. I was bent over and the momentum of my tug knocked me off balance.

"Geez, why didn't I ask sooner? This was so easy."

Larry stood by our motorcycle and tapped his gloved finger on the grips.

"Give me a break. I'm worn out from getting dressed."

It made the rest of my trip a breeze instead of drudgery as it rained nearly every day of our vacation.

We ate a quick lunch in Grand Junction and sped off for the Royal Gorge. We had planned to spend a couple of hours there, but all we had time to do was walk across the bridge, stop in the middle, see the river rush through the narrow canyon and over the huge boulders that created a rapids effect. We had to leave the spectacular view to reach our final destination for the day. It was about four in the afternoon and we still had miles to ride, which we hoped to accomplish before dark.

Cañon City was only a few miles down the road. When we arrived, we could see that it was coming up a bad cloud as we learned to say in Georgia so we stopped at a park and put on our rain gear, again. We still had about sixty miles to ride to the KOA south of Colorado Springs where we planned to spend the night. It was about five in the evening and we were tired. Our itinerary averaged about three hundred or more miles per day.

This part of the trip, in the daylight, would probably have been a pleasant ride. But, night falls quickly in the mountains; especially, when a huge rain cloud is overhead. It seemed to instantly turn from daylight to the black of night. We missed out on dusk. The fierce rain came down in sheets with fat drops that pelted us because we had to travel so slowly. Usually when we hit rain, it flew over us as we rode. This time, however, we had to slow down too much for that to happen because the road had been recently paved and the painted lines weren't completed. There was a middle line that we could barely see, but that was it. A rule of thumb in defensive motorcycle skills was to focus on a safe distance and to be prepared for what lies ahead. Between the rain and the darkness, we couldn't see two feet ahead of us. Larry yelled to me.

"I can't see Jack."

I stood on my pegs and directed him to move to the left a little bit. "I have on my glasses. Maybe, I can see better than you."

Even though, his vision was good, I felt I might have an advantage as the rain-spattered windshield hampered his view. Unlike a car, there are no wipers.

It was so dark, we didn't know if there was a shoulder to the road or if it was a drop off; consequently, we couldn't stop. Larry yelled again.

"I can't see Jack."

I yelled back to him. "You're okay, but don't go any farther to the left or you might cross the middle line."

This time he screamed.

"No. I mean I can't see your brother."

Larry looked for Jack's headlight, but it wasn't visible to him in his rearview mirror.

"Oh gosh, I thought you meant jack shit."

I felt like a dope. It hadn't occurred to me that he meant he couldn't see my brother. Call it a blonde moment, if that's any excuse, but the manner in which he said, Jack, I interpreted it with a different connotation. I stood up and tried to turn around to look, but with all my bulky gear on, I couldn't twist my body. Our only option was to keep driving forward. In spite of our slower than usual speed, we caught up to another motorcycle rider. He leaned into the turns with familiarity, which made Larry think he'd been on this road more than once. We stayed close behind him so that we could keep him in our sights.

What should have been an hour drive took three hours. We reached Interstate 25 at eight-thirty in the evening and pulled into the first gas station we saw. Both Larry and Jack were shaken from the tough ride and the responsibility of keeping their wives and themselves safe. Andrea and I both commiserated on how cold and hungry we were. My nerves were on edge from the ride.

"I thought we were driving into an abyss."

She agreed.

"I'm frazzled too."

The worst part was we had to get right back on the motorcycles as we still had twenty miles to travel to our camp. We had one hour until the registration office closed, which meant we couldn't stop at a restaurant on the way. It was after nine when we checked in. Typical of the KOA Kampsites, there was a small store adjacent to the registration desk.

Andrea and I grabbed some snack food while Larry and Jack rode to the cabin to unload our gear. She found some individual pizzas. There were two microwaves so we stood there and waited for our food to cook. We couldn't take off any of our outer garments because it was still raining outside. All I wanted to do was get out of my damp clothes. A nice glass of wine was in order, but they didn't sell any alcohol in the little store.

Our cabin was on the far side of the camp so the boys came back with the bikes to pick us up. I handed Larry my bag of food while I got on the bike. He looked haggard.

"It's going to be a long night."

"Why. We're here and safe. We'll have a roof over our head so we'll be dry. We can listen to the rain patter on our roof. It'll be nice."

He shrugged his shoulders and handed me the bag.

"You'll see."

When we reached our cabin and got off our bikes, the water was so deep that it lapped over the tops of our mid-calf high rain boots.

"What in the world?"

It was as noisy as if we were standing in the middle of Niagara Falls. We had to shout to be able to communicate with one another. The cabins were located on the bank of Fountain Creek.

"Told you it'd be a long night. The neighbors told us that three cabins have washed downstream."

"Which ones?"

"Ten, eleven and twelve. We're in cabin number thirteen."

I waded through the ground water and stepped up onto the porch to see the creek for myself. I thought Larry was making up a bad joke to scare me. The creek raged like an angry river. I flagged down a security guard on patrol. I couldn't believe our situation.

"Isn't there anywhere else we can go that's safer?"

"Aw, you don't need to worry. I'll be on patrol all night and will alert you of any impending danger."

I threw up my hands in disgust. "What if you're too late? Isn't this situation dangerous enough?"

KOA Kabin #12 floating down stream

His only alternative offer was to let us pitch a tent in another area. I was angry.

"Perhaps you didn't notice, but that creek is rising. It's pouring down rain. We're on motorcycles. We don't have room to carry tents."

"Well, you try to get some rest in your cabin. I'll come get you if you need to evacuate."

I started to object once more, but he ignored me and drove away. I don't know if he didn't care or couldn't hear me, but I was afraid. I went back to the porch and joined the others. We watched as chunks of ground broke away from the bank and crashed into the river. The family in the next cabin had a friend parked inland in a motor home so they had evacuated. We looked to Larry as our trip leader for his direction. Larry was exhausted, but volunteered to take guard duty.

"I'm not going to be able to sleep in this noise. I'll sit on the porch swing with my friend, Jack Daniels and keep watch."

Jack and Andrea and I went to bed. Because we were so tired, the volume of the noise didn't bother us. I did say my prayers that we'd be safe and placed all my trust in Larry. We arose early in the morning and perused the damage. Larry pointed to a little tree about ten feet from our cabin that was on the brink of being swallowed up by the river.

"See that tree? I decided if the water reached it, I would wake you guys up. By the way, I never saw the man on patrol come back here."

I made Larry stop at the office as we exited so I could complain. On the way, I saw a building with windows that looked like a rugged banquet hall. That really made me angry and I let the man and lady on duty know it.

"Last night, we didn't know if our lives were in peril or not, but that covered building was exactly what you people should have offered as shelter for every tent camper and those of us in cabins along the river."

Colorado Springs, Colorado —
"The tree goes, we go"

The lady looked startled by my remarks, but she offered no viable explanation. I don't remember specifically what she said, but it was something lame like they only used it for dining. I didn't have the patience to continue our conversation and left.

I went back outside to where Larry, Jack and Andrea were waiting. They were curious about my talk with the camp staff, but I told them we'd discuss it later. Larry had a better idea.

"I think we should skip Pike's Peak today. It's foggy and it will be cold up there. I suggest we drive up to Englewood, get a hotel room and relax."

Andrea cheered and Jack gave Larry a thumbs up. I climbed on the bike and patted Larry on the shoulder. "That's a great idea."

We rode the seventy miles north to a hotel where I had lived for six months while on an assignment near there. We were greeted in the lobby by several service people who were familiar faces to me. It was almost like coming home. We unpacked when we reached our respective rooms. All of our clothes were damp or dirty. I called Andrea and inquired on their clothing situation.

"Are you game for taking turns in the laundry room?"

"I am."

While one of us loaded the washer or dryer, the other one catered to our husbands, who spent the day in the warm Jacuzzi. They were our heroes. We were refreshed by the hotel stay. The next day was sunny and warm until we reached Wyoming. There, it was cold, but dry.

When we arrived in Daniel, where Andrea's daughter, Nan, lived, we went to the Green River Bar. It had a reputation for being the center of the universe for the small cowboy town; population one hundred and ten. In addition to the bar business, it served as a town meeting place for special events such as baby showers and wedding receptions.

The adjacent room to the actual bar also hosted the Joe Hausen, no rules, library. Joe was an avid reader; particularly, of Louis L'Amour. In 1976, after having read his collection, he asked if he could have some space to share his wealth. The owner agreed and installed bookshelves. The idea worked so well, more books were donated and shared on an honorary system. During Library Week, the local women celebrated with a proper high tea much like the county library boasted. This zany group dressed in hats and gloves of their choice; cowboy hats and leather gloves, perfectly acceptable. They sipped their first brew of tea in fine china teacups that they brought with them, but often refilled the containers at the bar.

Larry and Jack had been there two times before while on motorcycle jaunts when we lived in Georgia. They had met up with one another once in Sturgis and the other time in Colorado. Both times, they rode to Wyoming to see Nan. Larry had loved the atmosphere of the small town and even suggested we move there and buy the bar. The owners were originally from Georgia and had been considering moving back.

Larry told his tales to the patrons, who were eager to listen. They shared the bar's history with us. We learned it was the oldest building in Daniel dating back to 1899, when it had also been a store and post office. The town was named after the builder and first proprietor, Thomas Pixley Daniel. Around 1923, the store was turned into a pool hall and while alcohol could not be sold during prohibition, it was possible to buy a straight shot. A trap door was discovered in a 1980 renovation that revealed where the underground supply was kept. Rumor had it that it had also been a brothel, but we couldn't verify that one. It received its new bar name because of its close proximity to the Green River and was the location of the historic meeting place called the Rendezvous. In the 1820s and 1830s, trappers and Indians traded furs for goods in addition to swapping stories, drinking and competing in events. The nearby town of Pinedale celebrates a reenactment every summer.

I don't know if we were caught up in the moment, wanted to be a part of the history or exactly how it happened, but before we left town, we had bought the bar with Nan as our partner. A book entitled *Daniel, Wyoming, The First Hundred Years* was in the process of being authored. Our bar purchase, which occurred one hundred years and one month after Mr. Daniel filed for his homestead and three months prior to the anniversary of the one hundredth year, permitted us to be included in the heritage. We felt honored.

We traveled to Daniel several times a year for a few days each time and were treated like we were kinfolk because Nan was our step-niece. Nevertheless, bar ownership with its trial and tribulations was difficult. We were part owners for nearly four years before we sold our share to Nan. I've heard people say that the best day of your life is when you buy a bar. The next best day is the day you sell it. We found the hearsay to be true.

Jack, Andrea, Larry and Nan McKeough in front of
the Green River Bar in Daniel, Wyoming

My intuition to move home had been a good one. Our need to live near family again had, indeed, been mutual. Not only had we developed close friendships with our family, but we also discovered the next spring in 2000 that my younger sister, Laura had two lumps growing in her lower abdomen. She had surgery to remove them, but that was only the beginning of her ordeal. She had contracted colon cancer at forty-two years of age. Larry and I were thankful that we could be near Laura during this difficult time. She spent a total of two grueling weeks in the hospital on a twenty-four hour chemotherapy drip. Afterward, she had to have daily radiation for two months. But she won her battle and remained in remission for two years.

Larry's and my relationship with family was special. Our siblings, his and mine, were also friends. It created an environment where it was difficult to distinguish which family member belonged to whom. Because of this, whenever one of our family members had health issues, we both felt the hurtfulness of it.

We had long planned a motorcycle trip for the summer of 2000 and the time had finally arrived. Larry had been to the Sturgis Bike Rally, aka Harley Heaven, many times before, but always on a Harley. We both looked forward to seeing our friends from Georgia. This, however, was my first trip to Sturgis. I had a love/hate relationship with the long trips we had taken. I loved the close up view of the sights and smells of the countryside. There was a certain indifference to the outside world when traveling in a car. On a motorcycle, the shear exposure made me with one with the environment. The hate side was the lack of protection that the metal of a car offered, but I trusted Larry's riding skills to get us to our destination and tried not to think of the vulnerability.

With all the power the Honda offered, we bought a trailer and loaded it with camping gear, including a cooler with evening refreshments. We purchased new helmets and headsets so that we could communicate with each other. We were ready for anything the two weeks on the road had to offer.

We still wore our Harley labeled clothes. We weren't old enough or committed enough to rid ourselves of our Harley fashions. On the way to Sturgis, we stopped at a KOA campsite and met a member of the Gold Wing Club. He saw us pull up to our cabin and rushed over to meet us. He wore plaid Bermudas, a different plaid shirt, long black socks and sandals. He was friendly enough, but introduced himself as a "wing dinger." I didn't know which was worse; to be called a "Harley HOG" or a "Wing Dinger." Neither was too appealing to my way of thinking.

Two days later, we arrived in Lead, SD; a small town built on the side of a hill.

Larry's vest was emblazoned with an Atlanta Harley H.O.G. (Harley Owners Group) patch. My leather coat had a Ladies of Atlanta Harley patch on it. We pulled into a gas station. Larry struggled to manage the Gold Wing's 1200 pounds, on the tilt of the ground. The extra weight of the trailer and the passenger; namely, me, along with the stares from a hundred Harley people put Larry a bit on edge. As we drove up to the pump, one of the Harley men yelled at Larry.

"What the hell are you doing here with a Honda?"

Without looking directly at the heckler, Larry yelled back over his shoulder.

"Kiss my ass."

As Larry put down his kickstand and shut off his bike, he peered in his rearview mirror and spotted the biggest man he had ever seen, bare from the waist up, making his way toward us. Larry whispered to me through our headphones.

"I think I'm about to get my ass kicked. Don't say anything foolish."

Right. He was the one who had mouthed off. I hadn't uttered a word. I hoped his wisecrack wasn't going to get us in trouble. As the man approached, Larry sat frozen to his seat. I think he stayed on the bike in case he needed to make a quick getaway. The man stood beside Larry with his arms crossed. He had muscles everywhere; which had not gone unnoticed by my fifty-three year old eyes. Larry turned toward him. All he could see was the guy's belly button. Larry slowly raised his head to look at the man's face, following the contour of the man's huge chest as he went.

"Hey, you don't need to kiss my ass right now."

The guy burst out laughing.

"I was just funning about the Honda."

I heard Larry's heavy sigh of relief in my headset. It turned out that the man had joined the Atlanta Harley chapter, after we moved to Arizona.

"I saw your Harley patch and thought you had lost your mind."

Then he introduced himself.

"The name is Goldberg."

His occupation was professional wrestler and he was a former Atlanta Falcon defensive player. He was about 6'8" and we guessed his weight to be over 300 pounds. He was there with a few of his little buddies. I use that the term little very loosely here because every one of his friends was taller than six feet.

Larry climbed off his bike and chatted with him while he pumped gas. When he was finished, Larry shook Mr. Goldberg's hand.

"It was great to meet you. I sure am glad you have a good sense of humor."

Mr. Goldberg laughed and walked back to where his friends stood.

We caught up with our friends at the hotel later that evening. Larry was anxious to share our day's events.

"You will never guess who we met today."

Larry relayed the story of our earlier experience. They all laughed, but were not surprised because only Larry would have encountered Goldberg.

"That's really funny, Larry, but we have to tell you that we've voted and since you're on a Gold Wing, you'll have to ride in the back."

Larry was not intimidated by the comments or the group's decision. He didn't even care that they were embarrassed that we weren't riding a Harley. He stood up straight and lifted his chin.

"I don't know if I can drive that slowly, but I'll try."

After we spent a couple of days in Deadwood and Sturgis, we hit the road for the Black Hills. By that time, no one cared that we were on a Honda and we often led the pack.

Chapter Fifteen

Larry and I received a telephone call early in the morning on Friday, September 7, 2001 from, our son, Jason, whose usual clear voice sounded weak and difficult to understand. He was living in Atlanta with his fiancée, Jean. There was a three-hour time difference when daylight savings time was in effect; therefore, we were still in bed asleep.

"Jean and I were in a motorcycle accident last night. A drunk driver turned left in front of us."

I remember sitting bolt upright in bed. My heart began to race with fear, but I tried to sound calm for his sake. My first concern was for both of them.

"Are you okay? Are you hurt?"

"I have to have surgery this morning on my ankle and Jean's foot is broken. We could use some help. Jean can't drive and I'm going to be here for a couple of days."

He was heavily medicated and unable to communicate much on the telephone. No matter; they needed us or he wouldn't have called.

"Dad and I will figure something out today. Don't worry."

I hung up the phone and shared the content of the conversation with Larry, who had rolled over toward me trying to hear what Jason was saying. Larry and I decided the best course of action was for me to go and take care of them for a few days.

When I arrived in Atlanta, I discovered that the accident had caused a significant injury to Jason. He had dislocated and fractured his Talus bone, which carries the blood supply to the foot, and this would be a physical challenge to him for an indefinite period of time. Jean's broken bones would heal, thankfully. We had become quite fond of her and I didn't want her to be in pain either.

Jason had to stay in the hospital for a couple of days, but once I had both invalids home and settled in their chairs, I made us some supper. When I came out from the kitchen with our dinner, which I had planned to serve on trays to Jason and Jean, I was amazed when I saw Bailey, their German shepherd. Jason was reclined in his chair and Bailey, who usually liked to jump up on Jason, was sitting quietly in front of the chair with his head lying on the footrest. He looked at Jason with big, brown, sad eyes. He knew the master he loved was hurt. Jason continually leaned forward all night and scratched Bailey behind the ears to reassure him.

"It's okay, Bailey. I'm going to be fine."

Every now and then, Bailey lifted his head and turned to look at me and I swear he'd smile. He was glad I was there. He also would get up and go over by Jean to let her know he cared about her too. By Monday, Jason and Jean were maneuvering around their condo enough to care for themselves and I flew back home. The next day, Tuesday, was September 11, 2001; a day every American will remember.

Chapter Sixteen

In February 2002, my younger sister Laura began having some severe sciatic nerve issues. Her blood screening for cancer was clear so that didn't seem to be a concern. She started physical therapy sessions hoping to ease her pain, but it didn't help.

The same month, my brother, Jack's thirty-seven year old son, Jeff, was in Tucson at a weeklong church evangelical function. Late one evening after the service, he and a friend left to walk to their hotel. When they crossed the street, a car turned the corner from the other direction and collided with them. They were both killed by the hit and run driver. The loss of this sweet, kind young man was tough for our family. At Jeff's funeral, Larry and I watched Laura. We could see the grief in her pale face. She drew in deep breaths as she grimaced from her own pain. We whispered to one another and worried that perhaps she felt vulnerable.

In May 2002, Larry and I moved to Daniel, Wyoming for three months. Our goal was to help our partner get our ailing bar business back in shape. She also needed a break as she owned a tee shirt shop across the street, which was monopolizing her time. Since my job allowed me to work from home most of the time, I just had to get internet service and a telephone line set up to perform the duties required of me. Larry's responsibilities were to manage the bar, work bartending shifts, perform janitorial duties and pay the bills.

We owned an eight foot by twenty-seven foot, circa 1950 trailer that came with the bar. There was a small wood paneled living room open to the kitchen, complete with the original turquoise appliances and Formica table. The bathroom had a tub and shower combination, a very small sink and toilet stool. It was a one person at a time room. The bedroom was next on the path of the inside of the trailer. We had brought a queen size bed with us that fit into the room, but one had to walk sideways on either side of the bed to crawl into it. The small hall that led to the bedroom had closets on both sides with plenty of storage room and drawers at the bottom for our clothes. This was great since we had no room for a dresser. As much fun as I thought our vintage art deco kitchen was, it wasn't much space. I decided on my first day that I was not a candidate for permanent mobile or motor home living.

The end of the kitchen table by our sliding glass door became my office. I spent all day and night in the trailer, which caused plenty of cabin fever so being able to look outside helped. Fortunately, there was a screen there so that I could open the heavy glass door on sunny days. The mosquitoes enjoyed the balmy weather too, so I needed protection from them. While I worked my regular job, Larry performed his duties in the bar. We served fast food, but Larry couldn't get the knack of serving drinks and cooking at the same time as our female bartenders managed to do. When the lunch crowd arrived, he'd holler out the back door.

"Louise . . . come and help me . . . I'm swamped."

I didn't mind this break in my day even if my lunch breaks were spent as chef. It gave me an opportunity to stretch my legs. I cooked hamburgers, hot dogs and pizza in quick fashion. Then I cleaned up, restocked and went back to my real job, which paid me a salary.

On my days off, I usually worked one shift tending bar or both of us would work in the evening if the hired help called in sick. Our routine ran smoothly and gave us the opportunity to meet our patrons, who were primarily ranch owners and ranch hands in the area. The town boasted of a population of one hundred and ten, but for three months, it was one hundred and twelve with us in town.

Larry enjoyed special camaraderie with cowboys and he had a new audience to hear his stories that he loved to tell. When we first arrived, it was hay season. The ranchers helped one another bring in the hay, farm by farm. Several of them were related, which was another reason for the teamwork. It didn't take long to become acquainted with the townspeople, which was nice. While I had my reservations about a long-term commitment, I had an appreciation for a simpler life. It was enough that Larry and I purchased a five-acre property in the event we did decide to stay permanently at some point.

One night Larry and I were tending bar when a tall, broad shouldered, rugged looking cowboy with a heavy five o'clock shadow strutted into the bar and sat down on a stool. He introduced himself to us and told us he was a manager of a ranch. He was handsome and looked like he could have been the Marlboro man on a commercial. Typical of our teamwork, Larry shot the bull with his new friend while I waited tables and cooked. At one point I heard the cowboy burst into hysterics. He laughed until he had tears streaming down his face at the joke Larry told him.

"That's priceless. I can't wait to tell someone else. Tell me again so I'll remember it."

He laughed just as hard the second time as the first. The very next night he came back to the bar. We were at home so he came around the building to our trailer and pounded on the door. Larry answered his call.

"Hey Gary. What's up?"

"I need you to come bar hopping with me. I told that joke you told me last night and no one laughed. I can't get it right. "

Larry had worked all day and was tired and didn't want to go, but promised he'd do it another night. I thought it was a hoot that Gary needed to take my husband along. I couldn't blame him; Larry was a great storyteller. He fit into the crowd with ease.

When it was branding time, one of the ranchers invited us over to watch. When we arrived, we saw many of our customers, some of whom weren't regular ranch hands, on horses helping to herd the mama cows and their calves into a holding pen. I was quite impressed with the skill these folks had; especially, the smaller women. Once the animals were safely corralled, we watched two cowboys on horses take turns separating the calves from their mothers. There were two teams of people waiting at a second fenced in area where they would brand, castrate the boys, remove horns and administer health shots and vitamins.

Standing on the outside of the fence wasn't good enough for Larry so he asked if he could help. I was satisfied with taking movies of him with my video camera. The two-month-old babies were wailing and the mothers were mooing so loud, it sounded like an elk bugle to me. My heart ached for both. I felt the pain those mothers experienced for their tortured calves. On those occasions when my children were injured, like the day Jason rode his bicycle too close to a mailbox and ripped off his finger nail, I had sympathy pains so bad I could hardly administer first aid.

As I watched and videoed this process, my eyes misted. I knew this was no piece of cake for the calf. Larry was the back end guy, which meant that when the front-end guy wrestled the calf to the ground and held him down, Larry had to put his boot over the calf's butt hole to keep from getting covered with shit. At the same time, he had to hold on tight to the back legs of the calf. Larry was horizontal on the ground with his legs stretched forward and used all his strength to perform his job. A third person branded the calf with a red-hot iron, while another cut off the testicles of the males. He'd throw them into a bucket held by a waiting child. The kids would throw them onto the barbecue and cook them. They ate those baby mountain oysters like popcorn. Even then the poor little calf wasn't done. Someone else would be at the ready to dig out the horns with an instrument like a miniature post-hole digger. And the last two team members administered the shot and shoved a huge vitamin down the calf's throat. When this was completed, every one jumped back from their positions while the calf up righted itself and bawled for his mother.

Blood dripped down its cute little face and legs and steam rose from its side as a result of the hot iron. The mother responded to her baby with a loud, shriek-like moo. The baby took off running toward her and the cowboys on the horses would usher them into the finish pen. I couldn't watch the process from start to finish. I needed breaks in between to keep from throwing up.

I was sickened by the sight, but knew this was just another day of ranching for these people. The main purpose of the castration and horn removal was so that the calves would all look the same. Buyers paid more money for steers without horns as they looked nicer. It was all about a higher rate of return on investment not to mention a mechanism to prevent the calves from hurting one another.

At the end of the day, the cowboys congratulated Larry with high fives and pats on the back. They were so impressed with how quickly he caught on to the process; they invited him to the rest of the team ranch brandings. After each event, the host rancher threw a beer and barbecue bash for the workers, and they bought all their beer from our bar. It was a way of life in that town. However the jury was still out on my ability to become a fellow citizen.

Not too long before our three months were nearing the end, one of the ranchers asked Larry if he'd like to help him herd cattle up the Wind River Mountain Range. They drove cattle up where it was cooler and at the end of the summer; they would drift down into a fenced area alongside the road into a funnel where they were separated by brand. When Larry told me about it, he was ecstatic.

"It'll be like the movie *City Slickers* only I'll come home most nights."

I shook my head back and forth. "You're like a little kid, but I have to admit, it should be a good experience."

When he told the rancher he'd help out, the rancher was a bit surprised Larry had accepted.

"How long has it been since you've ridden a horse?"

Larry had to think about that for a while and advised him it had probably been more than twenty years. With that information, the family of ranchers who had invited him powwowed about which horse would be best for Larry to ride and decided on Strawberry. She was a good cutting horse, but not too wild. The first morning of the drive, Larry met them at the ranch. They worked all day herding the cattle, but only went about ten miles. A couple of the ranch hands were left to tend to the cows while everyone went home for the night. Larry had done so well riding, the rancher put Strawberry out to pasture and brought another spunkier horse for Larry. This was another pat on the back for him and he felt quite proud. I was impressed he was so adaptable and capable of being a real cowboy.

The second day, an owner of a dude ranch brought his guests to ride along. Now, this was really the *City Slicker* gang. He pointed them in Larry's direction. When they reached him, they sounded out practically in unison.

"Where do you want us to ride, boss?"

Larry stifled a snicker as he felt as green as they were, but that didn't stop him from barking out orders.

"You two go over to the far side of the herd and you three stay on this side. Give them a whoop or a yell and wave your arm in an upward and forward motion. They'll move."

They rode to their designated locations and yelled, "Yippee Kiyay" as they went.

By the third day, Larry asked one of the younger cow hands how he'd rate Larry's skills on a scale from one to ten.

"Hell, that's easy. You're a ten."

Larry sat up straighter on his horse and put his chin higher in the air.

"Really? I didn't think I was that good."

"Well, you brought the Jack Daniels and that's what counts. We can handle the rest."

Larry was a bit deflated, but not too much as he knew he had pulled his weight. A few weeks later, we moved back home. I think Larry could have stayed forever, but we sold our share of the Green River Bar back to our partner. She had enjoyed a good vacation from the business and was ready and able to get back to it. I, on the other hand, was ready to go home. It was a nice place to visit, but I didn't want to live there permanently

ༀ ༀ ༀ

That June, my younger brother, Charlie and his wife, Rhonda invited Jack and Andrea, my oldest brother, Jim, my sister, Laura and Larry and me to spend a week on a houseboat time share on Lake Powell. Charlie's children, Tyler, Kristen and Andy were each allowed to bring a friend since it was their family vacation. Tyler, their eldest had invited his best friend Ryan, who happened to be Laura's son. Altogether, there were eight adults, six children and a dog.

Kristen and her friend organized a weeklong Survivor game fashioned after the popular television show. We were all fans of the program, thus were more than willing participants. The first night, we picked three teams, were assigned names of Indian Tribes from the area and issued colorful team bandanas. To signify her universal membership, Shera, Charlie and Rhonda's dog, wore a bandana from each team. Shera, who was named after a cartoon heroine, was a twelve year old, docile mixed breed golden retriever.

Shera, the Wonder Dog

We played competitive games such as horseshoes, who could hit a golf ball the farthest, and checkers or card tournaments. The two teams with the lowest

Larry plays Survivor   *Louise loses brim of hat at the lake*

score had to vote out one member each per night. We only had five nights so had to speed up the process. My brother, Jim, was the only man on the red team and voted himself out on the first night. He figured the women would vote him out anyway so why not make it unanimous. My next oldest brother, Jack, was also voted out the first night and complained about it.

"I can't believe I was beat out by a dog."

Someone from his team had written down Shera's name on one of the ballots.

We changed camping spots each day so that we could see many areas of Lake Powell. Kristen and her friend would set up the tribal council near the boat. At dusk, Tyler would play the Survivor theme music and the fourteen of us would march single file carrying our torches to the council area. I went armed with my video camera to capture the hysterical moments we shared. Shera always brought up the rear.

One memorable event was when, my mild mannered, sister, Laura, intentionally picked a fight with our equally kind, jovial, sister-in-law, Rhonda and re-enacted a scene from the first *Survivor* TV series.

"If you were dying on the side of the road, I wouldn't stop to give you water."

Undeterred, Rhonda faced Laura.

"Right here. Right now. Bring it on."

It was great fun to watch later on the video. I also taped the private comments from the team member after they had voted at tribal council as they do on the television show.

On the third day, Laura and I had a real belly laugh when we walked to Rainbow Bridge with our siblings. Charlie wore, with pride, the immunity necklace he had won in a competition the previous night. It was long, with wooden beads and multi-colored brown feathers wrapped around a turkey wishbone and a tassel at the bottom. He walked ahead of Laura and me. A young man, who walked toward us, did a double take. He looked at his friend.

"Was that guy wearing a dead chicken around his neck?"

We burst out in laughter. I can still hear her infectious chuckle. Laura shared the lower level sleeping area of the boat with Larry and me, but after the first night, Larry moved to the top deck and slept in the open air. It was simply too hot for him where we were.

After a few days, our little cubby hole was beginning to smell like a gym locker room. We complained to our boat companions to quit throwing their dirty socks and shoes down there. On the last day, when we were cleaning up, Laura lifted her Murphy bed to its upright position. Larry was helping me strip the sheets from my bed in the corner. All of a sudden, Laura shrieked.

"Yow. There's a dead mouse under my bed."

Larry and I collapsed on the bed overcome with laughter.

"No wonder it stinks in here. Guess it wasn't the sneakers."

The best part of our vacation was that Laura felt quite well and without pain. We were all encouraged.

Chapter Seventeen

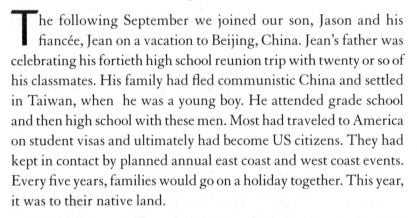

The following September we joined our son, Jason and his fiancée, Jean on a vacation to Beijing, China. Jean's father was celebrating his fortieth high school reunion trip with twenty or so of his classmates. His family had fled communistic China and settled in Taiwan, when he was a young boy. He attended grade school and then high school with these men. Most had traveled to America on student visas and ultimately had become US citizens. They had kept in contact by planned annual east coast and west coast events. Every five years, families would go on a holiday together. This year, it was to their native land.

After Jason and Jean told us about the fantastic trip they had planned with her parents and friends, I asked if we could tag along. His future mother-in-law, Lily was delighted that we were interested in joining them.

"We would love to have you come along. It will be a great opportunity to get acquainted with the future in-laws. I'll talk to the trip organizer and have all of the information sent to you."

Robert, Jean's dad, and Lily arrived in China the evening after we did. Since we were flying on frequent flyer air miles, we had to adjust our dates somewhat. Lily worked for Delta and flew standby. They had made special arrangements to be our tour guides. They didn't want us roaming around China, unable to speak the language.

The night we arrived, we were swarmed with people wanting to haul our luggage for us and provide taxi service. Lily was right to think we were out of our element. We followed a man to the awaiting taxi mostly because he had grabbed our bags from us. We told him our destination and were immediately swept away. He seemed in a great hurry to escape from the airport. My friend whom I had shared an apartment in California with, Kathy Federoff, couldn't pass up the opportunity and had accompanied us on the trip. When we had been in the car over an hour, the three of us exchanged concerned glances and rode along in silence. She leaned toward me and whispered.

"Do you think he's kidnapping us?"

"I hope not. But, Larry's much bigger than the cab driver, he can protect us."

When we arrived at our hotel, the cab driver parked across and down the street about a half block. We piled out of the small car. The bell captain of the hotel walked out the front door and saw us. He called to us in English.

"Are you guests of our hotel?"

Practically in unison, we yelled back. "Yes."

He then spoke in Chinese to the cab driver in an admonishing tone. The cab driver obviously didn't like what he was hearing, but got back into the car and drove across the street to the front door of the hotel. I took money from my wallet when the bell captain intervened once more.

"How much has he charged you?"

I told him the amount.

"That's too much."

He spoke, again, in Chinese to the cabbie, who argued with him. He turned to me.

"Give him thirty-five dollars. No more. He's over charged you."

I obeyed. The cab driver glared at me, but left with no additional argument. When we got inside the hotel, the bell captain explained the man wasn't a legal cab driver. He went on to tell us how to recognize a legitimate taxi. Our first night in the country and already we had already messed up.

"Thank you so much for taking care of us."

He smiled and bowed.

"My pleasure."

The next day when we ventured out of the hotel, we were more careful in our transportation selections. When Robert and Lily arrived that night, we relayed our first night's story. Lily shook her finger at us.

"I knew we needed to be here to protect you."

Delightful hosts, Robert and Lily made our trip memorable as tour guides for famous sites. Having translators fluent in Chinese and English was of special benefit. We appreciated their efforts and became friends right away.

When the actual reunion tour began, we moved to another hotel with the rest of the two busloads of tourists. The classmates rode in one bus where the conductor spoke Chinese the entire time. Larry, Kathy and I rode on the bus with the adult children, where the tour was conducted in English. Larry's story telling skills provided the comic relief during the entire trip. For example, he'd challenge everyone on the bus.

"I'll give twenty bucks to anyone who sees a dog or a cat."

Another time, he initiated a song of limericks. He sang the chorus to them.

"Aye, yai, yai, yai, in China they do it for chili. So sing me another verse that's worse than the other verse and waltz me around won't you Willy."

It didn't take long before he had everyone on the bus joining him.

For the first dinner the three of us sat with our bus mates. We all had difficulty understanding the menu selections. Robert came to check on us and when he heard of our dilemma, took over and ordered our meal. Our dining companions were entertained by

Larry's eagerness to eat the local fare. Jean's sister David watched in amazement.

"Hey, Larry, how do you like those sea cucumbers?"

"They're a little squishy."

The whole table of people giggled because they knew it was a food one must learn to like and many of them still did not. Larry explained his ability to try new food.

"When I grew up, there were six kids at our table. When my mother would serve dinner, my dad would say that he who eats the fastest, eats the mostest."

He told the group that sometimes they didn't know what they were eating; he once took a bite of some strange tasting meat. When he asked his dad what it was, Whitey told him it was rabbit. It took a moment for that to sink in.

"Peter? You mean I'm eating my pet rabbit, Peter Cottontail?"

This time, our tablemates howled. He told them he dropped his fork and left the table.

"It took me a while to forgive my dad, but I did."

Other delicacies that Larry and Kathy ate while on the trip included camel tendons and duck blood soup. I did try one spoonful of soup, but was a bit fussier. Every place we went, food was served onto a lazy Susan and we spun it around to select our choices to eat. The last night, I was determined to use only chopsticks, but every time I thought I had positioned my sticks correctly, I couldn't pick up any food. Rather, I stabbed it until it became mush and uneatable.

"I'll just have some of that nasty red wine."

It was from an in-country winery and named Dynasty Wine, but from my vantage point, I couldn't see the DY as it was on the opposite of the table. My name for it was more appropriate, but after a couple of glasses it didn't matter. Larry and Kathy both had mastered chop sticks, but I was clumsy and challenged and often succumbed to eating with my fingers. A few places had forks, but the often mystery cuisine killed my appetite.

One day, we went shopping at the silk alley. It was a maze of rows of tiny stores, which were cement cubicles with metal doors that slid down in front to close the shops. There were three carloads of women and a few of the boys, who escorted us much like bodyguards. The classmen were all attending a function on their own. Larry had stayed at the hotel to rest, as shopping is his least favorite thing to do. Jason and Jean took off to search for gifts for their bridesmaids and groomsmen for their wedding the following year. Kathy and I decided to head to the far end and work our way back. There was so much we wanted to see and touch and buy that it was like eye candy. Two of the young men followed and stayed near us.

Halfway through our shopping spree, armed guards showed up. They were at the same end of the alley as we and were there to inspect stores for knock offs. This was an occasional, but unplanned inspection. The owners of the shop we were in pushed us outside and slammed their door shut. The boys tried to hustle us up toward the front of the alley, but we took a turn to the adjacent side full of stores to look at some watches. They hovered over us and hurried us along. As we moved, there were doors slamming to the ground so we knew the guards were close behind. We weren't afraid as they weren't after us, but they were sure putting the kibosh on our shopping. When we reached the front, there was a store that sold luggage; something we had to buy to carry our new goods home. Kathy was having a difficult time selecting which suitcase she wanted. The guards turned the corner and the shop owner tapped Kathy on the shoulder and then pointed to the outside to get her to leave. She shook her head no so he closed the door with her in it. The boys and I stood there dumbfounded. I was frightened.

"What was she thinking? Is she nuts?"

Our bodyguards stood on either side of me. One put his arm around me.

"Don't be worried. As soon as the guards leave, they'll open the doors."

"Really? How soon will they be out of here?"

That's when they explained to me it was standard operating procedure to keep the merchants on their toes. Sure enough, about five minutes later, the door opened. I ran toward Kathy.

"Are you okay?"

"Yes, but that was a dumb thing I did. It was pitch black in there after the door closed. I was wishing I had stepped outside. It seemed much longer than it was."

She bought a suitcase and we went to join the rest of the group. We had all agreed to meet at a specific time and go back to the hotel together. That way no one would be left behind. Our protectors explained that as soon as they were teenagers, it was their duty to protect their "aunties" as they called them. They referred to one another as cousins. Their frequent vacations together had created a close-knit family. Jason and Jean showed up with several bags. They were talking excitedly and I was relieved to see them.

"Did you see those guards?"

Jean was the first to respond.

"I saw them all right. Jason was inside this store and hadn't finished paying for his purchase. I was standing in the alley and the door closed. The last thing I saw was the cast on Jason's foot."

I punched Jason playfully. "What's the matter with you?"

He shrugged his shoulders.

"I had spent so much time picking out what I wanted, I wasn't about to abandon my purchase."

I could tell Jean was still a bit shaken from her body language. When she was upset, she tilted her head down, her shoulders moved slightly forward and her arms closed over her body. I put my arm around her to comfort her. That brought tears to her eyes.

"Are you all right?"

"Yes, but I was worried about him."

Jason gave her a hug.

"I was fine."

With everyone accounted for, we hailed our cabs and went back to the hotel. We shared our adventure story of the afternoon with Larry on our arrival. I couldn't wait to tell him.

"You missed out on the most exciting shopping trip I've ever been on."

While he chuckled at the antics as he knew we were safe, Larry shook his finger at Jason and then at Kathy.

"You'd better be more careful."

The next day, we went to a park. Kathy and I had to use the rest room so Larry sat on a bench to wait for us. When we returned, Larry had a small child on his lap. Her father was taking a picture of them. To the side was a line of about ten families waiting on their turn. After they took a picture, they would nod their head.

"*Shie-shei*, (which means thank you), Mr. Christmas."

We couldn't believe it. Larry was Santa at home during the Christmas season, but his beard was still quite short. He was having great fun, though, so we stayed to let all of the children get their picture taken.

During the trip, Larry walked with Carl Fang, one of the men from the class, on our way from the bus to a tourist attraction.

"Carl, did you used to be a movie star? I swear there's a guy in an old war movie, who looks just like you."

Carl blushed and chuckled.

"I didn't know I was that handsome, but thanks for the compliment."

Before we parted, Carl gave Larry a battered business card from his wallet.

"My son, Kenith, is a fine doctor in Phoenix. If you ever need heart surgery, call him. He'll take good care of you."

It seemed all spectacular sites in China included long walks; especially The Great Wall. With my inability to eat much with chopsticks, I actually lost a couple of pounds on that trip. Larry and I endeared ourselves to the entire group by the end of the five days; both busloads of them. At dinner on the last night of the tour, the entire group stood, and invited us to join them. They held up their glasses high. One of Robert's classmates provided the toast.

"Here's to the newest members of our family."

We were honored at the warmth and recognition they showed us. They were fun, friendly and smart people. Larry and I were happy to become part of their extended family.

Our attitude toward China changed on that vacation. I think our expectations of the country were that it was foreboding. What we found were spectacular gardens, where landscapes were cared for with precision, friendly people willing to stop and practice their English in conversations and reverent, ancient monuments. We were amazed at the numbers of people on bicycles. They slipped in and out of traffic as if they had a ton of steel around them instead of the vulnerability of no protection. We saw a man, who had loaded a box springs and mattress on a platform, which was attached to the

back of his bike. There was a toddler on top of the load. I don't think OSHA exists in China.

Most of all, we were thankful that the group allowed us to crash their party.

Louise and Larry — Beijing, China 2002

Chapter Eighteen

A few days after we returned from China, on September 24, 2002, our granddaughter Chloe was born. Larry and I competed to hold her soft new body that still cuddled so close, a habit from being in her mother's womb. New babies have a special smell about them that's sweet like a flower. On our second visit to the hospital, my sister, Laura, went with us. I don't know which one of us cherished children more. I took a picture of Laura with Chloe in her arms. You see could the delight in her smile as she stroked the baby's warm cheeks. Laura's pain had returned with a vengeance, but her stress abated as she gazed upon this cherub. It was so good to share this small bundle joy with her.

On the way home, Laura told us that she was scheduled for an MRI the following week. Since the physical therapy hadn't worked, the doctor was stumped as to what had been causing her pain. Because the screening earlier in the year had shown no indication of cancer, it was not a major concern. At the end of the first week in October, she asked me to go with her and her husband, Randy. I think she already knew the results. She was in such excruciating pain that she couldn't even sit in the examining room. When the doctor entered, he greeted Laura and nodded to Randy and me. He had a grim look on his face.

"Part of your sciatic nerve is encapsulated with a cancerous tumor."

At hearing the news, Laura's knees buckled. I jumped up from my chair as I thought she was going to collapse. She extended her arm toward me. I held her hand. I remember wishing that Larry

Laura Walters Woods

had come along. He loved Laura and his strength in difficult times would have been a comfort to all of us.

The doctor explained that she could not have radiation because of the amount she had had two years earlier. He also didn't consider this tumor operable as it would definitely leave her disabled. The last blow was that the type of cancer she had was not curable. It would continue to attack her organs; perhaps one at a time.

"It's possible to keep the cancer at bay. You responded well to the chemotherapy treatment the last time."

I watched as Laura tried to stand tall and brave.

"I feel like you've handed me a death sentence."

The doctor reached over and patted her arm.

"Miracles do happen."

The three of us walked to the car without speaking. I was there to support them, but my heart ached for her. Laura was eleven years my junior and I felt almost as motherly to her as I did sisterly. I started up the car. Laura was in the front seat with me. When I turned around to see behind me to back out of our parking space, we made eye contact. I didn't have to say anything as she all ready knew what was on my mind.

"I promise to give it my best shot. But, if the doctor is right about this coming back over and over, I don't know how many times I can battle it."

"I love you, Laura. We will all support you however you need us to."

We drove the rest of the way to their home in silence.

The next day, Larry told me that he had been experiencing extreme discomfort for over a month with what he self-diagnosed as heartburn. Even though he wasn't scheduled for his diagnostic procedure to check on the Barrett's Esophagus that he suffered from until the following spring, I heard the concern and urgency in his voice.

"Will you make me an appointment for me for an endoscopy? I don't feel well. I don't know how to explain it, but I can't remember ever having heartburn this often."

I didn't hesitate. I called the doctor's office right away as it took six weeks to get booked. I felt frightened that Larry had cancer too because I had noticed on several occasions in the previous weeks that his breath smelled like rotten eggs. It hurt his feelings when I told him he should go gargle or something. He'd get grouchy and defensive.

"I can't help it. My stomach and esophagus are a mess and this reflux probably causes it."

I couldn't tell him what my real suspicions were. The appointment date was November 22, 2002. Laura's first week in the hospital on the twenty-four hour chemo drip went well. She didn't lose her hair, which was one of her bigger concerns and she felt well; although tired. After a one-week rest, her second week of chemo was administered. On Wednesday, Larry went up to the hospital to sit and visit with Laura. Her nurse was late for work that day and had failed to order her chemo drip when she arrived. She told Laura, it would be a couple of hours wait. It was nine-thirty in the morning.

"Larry, I love chatting with you, but if you don't mind, I'm going to take advantage of no IV hookups to get in the shower and wash my hair before she comes in with the poison."

Larry understood. He kissed her goodbye and reminded her that I would be there on my lunch break from work. When I arrived three hours later, she still did not have her chemo drip. She was aggravated.

"I was glad for the break this morning, but I expected to have my IV over an hour ago. Now, this means that on Saturday, instead of leaving about noon, I won't get finished with the medication until late afternoon."

I consoled her with words, but her best friend arrived with a cheese crisp from Laura's favorite Mexican food restaurant. That helped lift her spirits.

"Yum. Thank you so much."

"I wish I could do more."

Laura and her friend had been best pals for over twenty-five years. The gesture of kindness felt insufficient, but we were all at a loss of what we could do. When Saturday came, and the bag of chemo was delivered, Laura remarked it was the biggest bag she had seen. She didn't finish her therapy until seven o'clock that evening. She was exhausted and annoyed. When the nurse told her it would be another forty-five minutes before they could find an available wheelchair to take her to the car, she blew up.

"I'm not staying here another minute. My husband will get me to the car."

Randy stood and put his arm around Laura's waist. She put her arm around his neck and shoulders for support and they left.

The following Tuesday, Larry went to their house to visit with Laura. I was in Seattle on business. He stayed a short time as Laura's strength had diminished and she needed to sleep. I called on Friday night when I arrived home, but I was told she was sleeping. Every time I called over the weekend, I received the same answer. On Sunday, November 17, 2002, after church, I insisted on stopping somewhere to get Laura a strawberry milkshake. It was one of the few things that didn't taste like metal to her. Larry didn't hesitate to accommodate me. When we reached Laura's house, her oldest son, Ike, answered the door.

"Mom's sleeping. She is so worn out that we hate to disturb her."

I was disappointed, but understood. "Please put this in the refrigerator for her. When she wakes up, tell her I love her."

A few hours later, her husband, Randy called me.

"I'm worried about Laura. She's listless."

"Call her doctor and take her to the hospital emergency room."

When he called the doctor's office, the instruction he was given was to stay home unless her temperature reached one hundred one degrees. He followed their advice. The next time we talked, Randy told me her temperature had not elevated so he was going to let her rest.

That night, at nine-fifteen, Randy called me. There was terror in his voice as he shouted into the phone.

"I think Laura's dead. Please come now."

Larry and I raced to the car. I don't know how fast he was going, but our usual twenty-five minute trip took less than fifteen. We ran into the house and back to her bedroom. There was my precious, sister, lying on her bed . . . dead. Larry covered her up. With him there as my support, I took over the role of the person in charge. Randy was sobbing. He hadn't called 911 or his children, who were both at girlfriends' houses. I went in and called the paramedics first. Then, I called my siblings. I knew my mother would be sleeping and didn't want to deliver this news over the phone. She lived north of Phoenix about seventy miles and wouldn't be able to do anything that night anyway. I asked my oldest brother, Jim, who lived near her to tell her in the morning. My brothers, Jack and Charlie and their wives came to Laura and Randy's house.

Ike happened to come home to see the emergency vehicles outside with lights flashing. His eyes were wide and his mouth looked like he had inhaled a deep breath and held it revealing the panic he felt. He entered the house knowing what the commotion outside probably meant. Family comforted him while I called Laura's youngest son, Ryan. When he came to the phone, I had only spoken his name when he interrupted me.

"Mom?"

"No, honey, it's your Aunt Louise. I need for you to come home now. Your mother has passed away."

"I'll be there as fast as I can."

Ryan still didn't drive, even though he was eighteen. At that moment, it was a blessing as I knew a friend would drive him and be there for him when he arrived. As promised, Laura had given it her best shot, but she did not rally this time as she had before. It was difficult to bear.

When Larry's appointment day arrived, it fell on the same day as visitation hours at the funeral home for Laura. Larry wanted to cancel his appointment and try to get it rescheduled in December. I disagreed.

"No, you're not going to cancel the EGD. If you're having problems, we need to know why."

He argued that he could wait until a better time.

"You know how the anesthesia makes me feel worn out for hours afterward. How am I going to go the funeral home tonight?"

I was sympathetic to his plight and knew he was glued to his chair for twelve hours or more after the procedures.

"If you don't feel well, stay home. I'll go to the funeral home without you. Everyone will understand."

But he loved Laura too and felt the same need as I to share the evening with family and friends. I convinced him that his health had to take priority.

"If Laura were here with us, she'd agree."

I took him to his appointment as scheduled. After he was wheeled off to have the umpteenth EGD, I settled in an uncomfortable worn out chair in the small, poorly lit outpatient surgery waiting room. I realized it was the first quiet moment I had had to reflect on all that had happened in the days since Laura died. I had assumed the task of dragging Randy around with me to make funeral arrangements. He was like a zombie, but I understood he was devastated. My brain was cluttered with so many thoughts. I made mental notes of my list of undone tasks before going to the funeral home that night. There had been no time to grieve.

I looked up from my book and stared at the old, drab blue walls. I wondered when the last time this room, lined with chairs, had been renovated and decided probably never. There were a few other people present, who perused the outdated magazines piled on the corner table.

Tears streaked my cheeks. As they cascaded from my eyes, I knew people were looking at me, but I didn't care. I tried to discreetly wipe away the wetness. I missed Laura already. Dr. Saperstein came out from the recovery room and sat next to me.

"Larry had another polyp, but this time it was only the size of a pea. He's had them quarter size before so I'm not too concerned. Nonetheless, we biopsied it and sent it to the lab. You know the drill. I should know the results in ten days and my office will call you."

I nodded my head, but looked at the floor and not at him. I was so grief stricken about Laura that I was numb to his news. Needless to say, I was not my usual cheerful self.

"Louise, what's wrong?"

I looked up at him revealing my red, swollen eyes. "My sister died this past Sunday from cancer. I'm not coping very well."

He put his hand on mine and patted it.

"I am so sorry."

He was kind to understand my state of mind.

"Don't worry about Larry. This is the smallest polyp we've ever found."

I was grateful for his words of assurance. I took Larry home to rest. Larry was always so zoned out from anesthesia, I'd have to tell him whatever the doctor told me two or three times. This time was no different. After he inquired as to his state of health for the third time, my response was abrupt.

"You're going to be fine. Please try to get some rest before we have to leave for the funeral home."

Worn out, he complied without question. That night we put on our happy faces as best we could and greeted the people at the funeral home. It warmed my heart to know how many people loved my sister. I was especially touched by her many fellow workers at America West, who came to pay their respects. I knew a few of them as I had worked with them at a Republic Airlines.

Chapter Nineteen

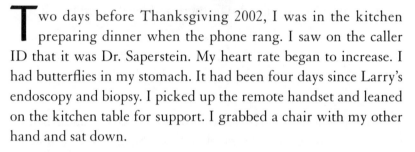

Two days before Thanksgiving 2002, I was in the kitchen preparing dinner when the phone rang. I saw on the caller ID that it was Dr. Saperstein. My heart rate began to increase. I had butterflies in my stomach. It had been four days since Larry's endoscopy and biopsy. I picked up the remote handset and leaned on the kitchen table for support. I grabbed a chair with my other hand and sat down.

"This isn't good news or you wouldn't be calling so soon."

Larry heard my comments, muted the television and came into the kitchen. I pointed to a chair for him to sit down and scooted mine next to him so that we could share the phone receiver.

"I'm afraid I do have bad news. The polyp was malignant. Larry needs to have his esophagus removed before Christmas. There's a doctor next door to my office, who specializes in this surgery. I don't know Dr. Runfola, personally, but I think you should call him first thing in the morning and make an appointment."

Larry and I looked at each other. I'm not certain whose eyes misted over first . . . his or mine. My voice cracked as I try to mutter a response to Larry's doctor.

"Thanks for calling. I'll contact Dr. Runfola first thing in the morning."

I pushed the off button on the phone and put it on the table. Larry and I sat in a stupor for a few moments. Then we put our arms around each other. I rubbed Larry's back. I remember feeling his muscles tighten up and his body convulse as he cried.

"We'll get through this. We always have. You're like a cat with nine lives and though you've been threatened before, you've not used them all up yet."

We sat and talked about what to do next. If our doctor didn't know the one he had referred us to, then we needed to determine what other alternatives were available. Jason and Jean were in New York to celebrate the Thanksgiving holiday with her family. We knew Jean's parents, Robert and Lily Lin, with whom we had traveled to China, would also be there and we decided to call.

"Jason, I have some bad news. Dad has to have surgery within the next three weeks. He has cancer. Please ask Robert or Lily if one of them would call Carl Fang. His son might be able to recommend a good doctor."

I could tell he covered the mouthpiece of the phone while he explained to those around him what the problem was. Lily grabbed the phone from him to talk to me.

"We are so sorry to hear about Larry. We don't have Carl's phone number with us in New York, but we're flying home to Atlanta on Saturday and will call him as soon as we get there."

We chatted awhile about how we had come to know of Larry's illness and said our goodbyes. Jason got back on the phone.

"Do I need to come to Arizona right now?"

"No. There's nothing you can do."

Jason and Jean had planned to spend Christmas with us. They lived in Atlanta, and it would be costly for them to make the trip twice.

"Stick to your plans and come home for Christmas. I'm not certain when Dad will have to have surgery. Right now, we don't know much of anything."

We hoped that if Robert and Lily called their friend Carl, whose son, Kenith practiced medicine in Phoenix, that he could guide us to the best doctor. The next day, Wednesday, I called to make the appointment with Dr. Runfola. He wasn't on my health plan, but we needed to know information. It would be another three days before the Lins would be back in Atlanta. We knew it would be the following Monday before we could take alternative action.

Our Thanksgiving Day dinner was not the usual maddening crowd of adults and children frolicking about. Rather, it was subdued. We did share it with Jack and Andrea and our son, Jake and his family, but the pain of losing Laura and the fear of what Larry had to face caused us to reflect more than celebrate.

On the Saturday evening that followed Thanksgiving, as promised, Robert and Lily contacted Carl, who in turn phoned his son, Kenith. At nine-thirty the same evening, we received a call.

"Hello, this is Dr. Kenith Fang. Please forgive the late hour, but my father called me about your husband. Could you please explain the problem he's experiencing to me?"

I told him the facts as I knew them, and admitted there was so much we didn't know.

"Well, I've actually performed that surgery myself, but I'm not an expert. I believe the real expert is Richard Perry. If you don't mind, I will call some of my colleagues to see if they agree."

I couldn't believe he admitted that someone else was better than he for this particular surgery. I thought he was credible beyond words. The special attention he paid us impressed us as well.

"We're honored you've taken the time to help us."

"I promise. I'll call you back tonight."

An hour later, he called back and reported that four of his colleagues had, indeed, recommended Dr. Perry.

"I'll call his office for you first thing on Monday morning. I want you also to call to make an appointment with him. Take care."

Before he hung up, Dr. Fang gave me his office number, his home number and his cell phone number in case I needed to reach him again. We were amazed and encouraged at the quick, caring response from Dr. Fang and his colleagues during their holiday time. Monday morning, we called to make the appointment and discovered the earliest available date was December 12, 2002. We found that Dr. Perry was a revered general surgeon in Phoenix; consequently, the lead-time for an appointment was six weeks. Because of Dr. Fang's intervention, it was shortened to only ten days. But, Larry was still frantic.

"I don't think I can wait that long to find out more about the surgery. Dr. Saperstein said I'd need to have my esophagus out before Christmas. That's only three weeks away."

I was filled with anxiety myself, but I didn't want to let Larry know it. One of us had to be calm.

"I've already made an appointment for Tuesday with the original specialist, Dr. Runfola. We'll keep that appointment so that we can understand what we can expect."

On the first appointment day, the doctor was kind and took special care to explain what the surgery entailed, such as it would require a ten to fourteen day hospital stay and recovery time. I wrote notes furiously in my journal that I had brought with me as I knew this was more information than I could remember after we left. The five percent chance of risks was daunting. The list included a heart attack, fibrillation, pneumonia, fluid buildup around the lungs, leakage from sutures, hoarseness and sometimes temporary or permanent loss of voice from the nerves being cut in the neck. Other internal problems could occur as well and a feeding tube would be required in the stomach for a period of one to six months. Last, he mentioned that one in three patients have stricture in their throat. I was glad I had a pen. He took the time to answer all of our questions.

At the end of the doctor's consultation, he recommended we call Dr. Richard Perry, the most skilled surgeon for this surgery. Dr. Runfola went on to explain that Dr. Perry had trained him. He ended the conversation by advising us he wouldn't be approved to perform the surgery as he wasn't a provider on our insurance plan.

"I knew that was the case, but we needed to understand what to expect. You've been wonderful to take this time with us."

Of course, we paid him for his consulting, but he never hurried us though the discussion.

"I have booked an appointment already with Dr. Perry. A family friend referred him. It's good to know that you recommend him as well."

He assured us that we were in good hands and advised us what CT Scan Larry would need to be prepared for our meeting with Dr. Perry. We promptly called our primary care physician, Dr. Lofgreen, to have him order it. It was Tuesday, December 3, 2002.

Larry had the CT scan on Thursday, December 5. We were told it would take at least three days for the results, but that afternoon, Dr. Lofgreen called. This concerned me as Dr. Lofgreen didn't have office hours on Thursday afternoons. It could only be more bad news. I felt the dread of answering another bad news telephone call.

"We have the results of Larry's test. He had a hepatoma (an unidentified spot) on his liver, which the radiologist thought could be cancer. It's possible the cancer has spread, but I'm not the expert you need to determine that."

I called Dr. Perry's office as soon as I hung up with our primary care physician and pleaded for an earlier office visit. His office moved Larry's appointment to four days earlier. We still, however, had the long weekend to wait and worry.

On Monday, December 8, 2002, Dr. Perry told us that Larry's esophageal cancer had not spread as Larry's type grows upward; not outward.

"The hepatoma, you can see here as we viewed the x-ray is either liver cancer or a benign mass of blood vessels. If the former, it would require a separate surgery."

We explained to Dr. Perry that Larry had contracted aggressive hepatitis in 1976.

"All right, let's get it biopsied and find out what it is."

He ordered the procedure on Larry's liver the following Friday, the 13th.

Larry was admitted for outpatient surgery at Good Samaritan Hospital. They wheeled him away and I sat in the surgery waiting room. The longer I waited, the more anxious I became. Four hours later, a doctor came to talk to me. He explained that to perform a biopsy on the liver was invasive and no easy task. It required going through his lung to get to where the mass was located.

"Because of this, I consulted with three other radiologists on the MRI results we took this morning. We all agree that the hepatoma is not cancer; therefore, we decided the biopsy wasn't warranted."

That was the best news I'd heard in two weeks.

We spent the week before Larry's surgery making certain our business was in order, which was difficult to do as it felt like we were preparing for Larry's demise. We updated our will, including our burial preferences, signing a living will, and assigning me medical power of attorney. Larry crossed all his t's and dotted his i's.

"I want to go to confession. I'm not certain what I'll say, but it can't hurt."

This act of our religion had always filled me with anxiety until it was over; especially when I entered the confessional. The booth had a certain foreboding for me. I preferred to speak to the priest face to face as then it was more like talking to a friend. When Larry was a child, it was a weekly ritual for him. When I became a Catholic thirty-four years earlier, the Church had relaxed its rule. Neither of us had been to confession for almost sixteen years. Larry was frightened he would not survive his surgery and wanted to get everything that bothered him off his chest. I decided it couldn't hurt to join him.

"I'll go with you."

It wasn't something I was excited to do, but it was good moral support for my husband. When we arrived, there was a line. The waiting made me nervous and my palms were sweating. The confessional was built so that one could kneel in front of the draped window or walk around the wall and sit down in a chair to engage in a private conversation with the priest. Larry and I each did the latter. Afterward, we knelt to pray in the front row. Another older priest was nearby and we asked him to anoint Larry in a prayer for the sick.

On the way home, I shared my confession experience with Larry.

"I told the priest, I wasn't exactly certain what to say as it had been so long. He asked me if I had committed a mortal sin. That made me at ease since I would never do that. I shared how I was sad about Laura and frightened about you. I also said to him that I didn't know what confession was all about anymore since we asked God to forgive us every week before communion. I told him I prayed every day. He was very nice and advised me I didn't need to come to confession unless I had sinned big time or if it made me feel better."

Larry laughed at me.

"You are some Catholic."

He had teased me many times before when I questioned Church rulings or rituals, but it certainly did not diminish my belief in God or my faith in God's promise. With our house in order and our faith professed, we were ready to tackle the next step.

The week before Larry's surgery, our good friends, Carol and Dan May, came to see us and presented Larry with a Sacred Heart badge to wear during surgery. On it was a picture of Jesus with His heart exposed. As a symbol of love and faith, it was a reminder to turn over all of our fear to God and let him take control. Dan's mother had asked her priest to bless it, which was meaningful to Larry. The next day, we attended a bowling match with our nephew's church youth group. Larry was too nervous to bowl, although, it would probably have helped him release the stress. Instead, he sat and watched. He had his Sacred Heart in his pocket.

He'd take it out, say a prayer and put it back. A couple of hours later, we left and went home. As we walked into the house, Larry reached into his pocket to feel the Sacred Heart and it wasn't there. He panicked.

"I've lost the badge. I'm going to die."

Larry has never been one to look at the bright side of any situation.

"Don't worry. We can get another one."

"No. I need that one."

We called the bowling alley and requested they look for it. They said the area had been cleaned up and the trash dumped. Larry walked across the street to our son's house and asked if Jake would go with him to search the trash. Jake understood his dad's urgency and agreed. When they came back from dumpster diving, Larry had a forlorn expression on his face. His eyes were widened from fear and his mouth turned down in a frown.

"We couldn't find it."

I called my sister-in-law, Rhonda, to ask her to check with other adults, who had chaperoned the group that afternoon in case one had found it. I also called Carol to see if we could get another and received a positive reply. I went in to report the good news to Larry.

"Carol and Dan are going to get another Sacred Heart from his mother so you can stop worrying."

"It won't be the same."

I hugged him and told him he would be fine. Fortunately, all of that concern was put to rest the next day. Rhonda called with even better news.

"I have your badge. One of the ladies found it. I'll bring it right over."

I watched Larry's mouth turn up in a smile. His shoulders broadened as if he had relaxed the tension in his body and he stood more erect as his confidence increased.

"What a relief. I feel much better. I know I probably overreacted, but I wanted the original gift."

I understood his feelings. We had been married thirty-four years and it didn't take too much body language or words to understand his plight. With that obstacle hurdled, he was prepared for the challenge.

Larry's surgery called THE or Trans Hiatal Esophagectomy was performed on December 19, 2002. Larry and I went to the hospital around four in the afternoon. Since this was an emergency surgery, he couldn't get it scheduled early in the day. Dr. Perry had to perform it after his usual hours. That meant, Larry couldn't eat or drink anything all day. The anticipation of the surgery made him feel ill at ease, but his dry mouth and growling stomach made him a little grouchy. I didn't blame him. I'd be thirsty too. We completed the admission process and were escorted to the surgery waiting room until the anesthesiologist arrived, which was thirty minutes later. We were taken into a draped area, where Larry disrobed and donned his hospital issue gown and took a seat on a gurney.

The doctor came in and introduced himself and explained why he was injecting a needle in Larry's back. He told us it was a procedure used for surgeries that would last several hours. The nurse came in and I told her about the Sacred Heart and asked where we could put it.

"I know exactly what to do."

She put the badge on the inside of Larry's arm and wrapped paper tape around it. Then she took a sharpie and wrote the words, Sacred Heart, on the tape.

"That's a safe guard in case someone needs to remove the tape."

Larry thanked her. As the nurse took a position behind the gurney to help push, the doctor instructed Larry to lie down and gave him the first shot of anesthetic.

"It's time to say goodbye."

I leaned over Larry and kissed him. "Everything will be fine."

I watched as they wheeled the gurney with Larry down the hall and prayed my bravado had convinced him. I walked slowly to the waiting room, sat down in a chair against the wall, and opened a book to read. After reading the same paragraph three times because I couldn't concentrate, I closed my book. I looked around the room at different people; some alone, some with family. I wondered if their reasons for being there was as critical as mine or perhaps worse. I noticed a young Asian doctor walk toward me and sit down next to an elderly lady at a table nearby. He spoke softly to her. Her arms were outstretched with her hands folded resting on the table. He patted her arm as he chatted. Their facial expressions were not grim, which indicated to me that whatever surgery he had performed had been successful.

As he rose to leave, he looked around the room as if searching for someone. I thought that must be Dr. Fang and stood up. When we made eye contact, I extended my hand to shake his.

"Are you Dr. Fang?"

As soon as I said it, I saw his name embroidered on his white coat.

"Yes, are you Louise?"

We sat down next to each other.

"I was looking for a white woman with an Asian girl."

I laughed. "And, I assumed you were the only Asian doctor here."

We both enjoyed how ridiculous we were in our assumptions.

"My son and his fiancée won't be here for a couple of more days. I'm pleased, though, that it was you and that we could meet in person."

"I promised my father that I would look after Larry as if he were family. In fact, I stopped in his operating room before I came out here. Everything is going fine. Dr. Perry is an excellent surgeon."

I thanked him again, for his kindness and the special attention he'd given us.

"It's my pleasure. I'm glad I could help. Are any family members joining you tonight?"

"My son is coming here right after work."

I had the impression he would have stayed and kept me company if I was going to be alone.

He left to go home. It was about six-thirty in the evening. I expected my son, Jake, and Larry's sister, Stephanie and her husband, Jim, at any time. Stephanie and Jim were visiting from Ohio. The room where I sat had thinned out considerably since I had arrived. In fact, there were only two families still there.

One was a Mexican family and the other a man and his young son, who I guessed to be about ten. In the following days when I passed through the waiting room to see Larry, I saw the Mexican family there every day. Sometimes there were several members and other times a young woman, her husband and their baby. They told me that their mother, father, grandfather, who was not expected to live and four other family members had been in a terrible truck accident. We pledged to pray for one another. The other man and son I had seen had reason to celebrate. A gentleman he worked with, but hardly knew, had donated a kidney to his wife. Both surgeries were a success. It was reason for all of us consumed with our own grief to cheer.

By the time, Jake and the others arrived, we were the only ones left in the waiting room. My brothers joined us a few minutes later. It was around seven-thirty and I didn't expect Larry's surgery to be completed for several more hours. We were at a loss for conversation so we played cards. No one would have known by watching us that we were stressed out. Our game lightened the load and initiated plenty of laughter. By eleven, Jake and I were the only two still there. We exchanged minimal conversation with the exception of Jake expressing his fear about Larry's survival.

"Will he be okay, Mom? Why is it taking so long?"

We were both concerned and tired. We were startled when the telephone on the unmanned volunteer's desk rang at eleven-thirty and broke the eerie silence. I raced to answer it. It was Dr. Perry.

"I have good news. Everything went well. I'll be out there in a few minutes to explain what we've accomplished."

I hung up the phone and gave Jake a thumbs up sign. He exhaled a huge sigh of relief. Dr. Perry joined us about fifteen minutes later.

"I've removed ninety percent of his esophagus. Fortunately, I found no cancer cells in the margins. Because of previous surgery Larry had years ago, we really had to stretch his stomach to reach where we stapled it to his throat. Now, his stomach will be like a tube from about where his Adam's apple is to his intestines. I've also disabled the acidic glands at the bottom of his stomach. From now on, he will not have a normal digestive process. The saliva in his mouth will act as the sole agent in digestion. That means he'll need to chew until his food is pulverized. We can talk more about this tomorrow. For now, go see Larry. The recovery room will call you soon to visit him."

This was good news. How blessed we felt. A nurse came out to fetch us and took us into the recovery room. She explained a few things on the way.

"Larry is awake, but not for long. He needs to rest. There are no rooms in ICU available so we're keeping watch over him in the recovery room over night. He's on a ventilator as a precautionary measure, which is typical for this surgery so don't be alarmed by it. It'll be gone in the morning when you come to visit."

Larry was alert when Jake and I arrived at his bedside. His eyes widened when he saw us. He tried to talk, but couldn't because of the breathing device. I leaned in close to kiss his cheek.

"Your surgery was successful. You have no more cancer."

Tears formed in Larry's eyes, which spoke of his thankfulness. He grunted a few times trying to form words, but I couldn't understand him. It sounded as if he had asked how long so I explained it was close to midnight and we were only allowed to stay a few minutes.

"You have to rest now. I'll be back tomorrow."

As choked up as he was, Jake, in his bravest voice, told his dad he loved him.

After we left the recovery room, Jake put his arm around me.

"He looks terrible. He has blue stuff in his hair."

"I know. The nurse told me it was a sterilization solution of some sort that had spilled in his hair. What bothered me was the ventilator and how they had it taped to his mouth. Did you see how it forced his mouth open and exposed his teeth? It made him look like a wild animal. I wonder if he's uncomfortable. I'd be gagging."

Jake agreed with me.

"Sure isn't like the movies where people look so peaceful."

Jake and I were certain the worst was behind us, however, so we accepted the temporary conditions. We knew we should be able to take him home in ten to fifteen days barring any complications. The chance of risk factors had been explained in our quest for information before the surgery. Dr. Perry didn't know, however, he was treating Larry "Murphy" Laughlin. What could go wrong, did. With the exception of not permanently losing his voice or dying, he experienced the rest of the risk factors one at a time.

Early the next morning, I arrived in time to see his nurse washing Larry's hair. She was using a nifty contraption similar to a shampoo bowl in a salon with the exception that it jutted out sideways instead of down. As she poured water on his head to rinse his hair, the water and suds flowed along the side depression and into a bucket placed on the floor. I was intrigued.

"Good morning. Some clever person had a great idea."

The nurse turned and smiled at me.

"We couldn't have Larry hanging out here with turquoise hair."

I stood by Larry's side until she was finished and then relieved her chore and dried and combed his hair. The ventilator had been removed and he looked calm and well.

"You look great. How do you feel?"

His voice was strained and shaky, but at least he could talk.

"I'm okay."

The painkillers took care of the discomfort from the surgery. We had only chatted a few minutes when Dr. Fang arrived. I was amazed by his dedication.

"Well, look who's here. Larry, I'd like you to meet Dr. Fang."

The doctor came over and shook Larry's hand. Tears streaked down Larry's cheeks as he acknowledged our new friend.

"I don't know how to thank you."

"None is needed. I'm happy for you that things worked out well. I'll come by and check on you while you're here so if you need anything, please do not hesitate to ask."

He left us and moments later Dr. Perry came in. It was like a parade of doctors. He examined Larry and was pleased with what he saw.

"We're going to keep Larry here in the recovery room in the capable hands of this staff until I can get him a room in ICU."

He updated his chart and waved goodbye. Larry's nurse brought me a stool and told me I could stay as long as I chose. The room was so crowded that Larry's gurney was in the middle of it. By the end of the day, he was moved to ICU, which became his home for the following thirty-nine days.

Chapter Twenty

The area of the sutures had to have time to heal. Saliva contains bacteria and in order to avoid infection in the area where his stomach was joined to his throat, Larry was not permitted to swallow any fluids. Unfortunately, on Saturday, December 21, 2002, two days after his initial surgery, Dr. Perry discovered a small leak where he had stapled Larry's stomach to what was left of his throat.

"I'm sending Larry to radiology to have an NG tube inserted in his nose to drain his thoracic region to reduce the chance of infection. Larry is also experiencing some pulmonary problems; therefore, I've engaged a specialist to examine him. He starts respiratory therapy today."

Though I wanted to stay with him that morning, I had to go home. When Larry first discovered he had cancer, he had asked Jake and Nikki to have our two granddaughters baptized and he wanted me to be there. The ceremony had been scheduled for that same Saturday after his surgery. They had been unaware when it had first been planned that Larry would be in the hospital. They had considered postponing the event when they discovered Larry would be unable to attend, but before he had his surgery, he had told them not to change the schedule.

"In case something happens to me, I want to know my grandchildren have been baptized. Please don't change your plans."

It was a lovely ceremony. My family members took turns filming the whole affair with my video camera so Larry could view it later. Usually, our family would spend the rest of the afternoon in celebration. Instead, we grabbed a quick sandwich and piece of cake and caravanned to the hospital. I escorted our children and Larry's siblings into his room two at a time. Larry was pleased to see them, but the highlight of his day was watching the movies of the baptism. I went home satisfied that Larry was improving based on his cheerful attitude throughout the rest of the day. After midnight, however, Larry insisted the nurse call me at home.

"Call my wife, right now. I'm thirsty. Why can't I have some water? I need her to be here."

Hearing my voice put him at ease. By the next morning, he had forgotten the explanation. This request for water began after only three days and would ultimately last for thirty-eight days.

"I love you. You're going to get well. I'll be there first thing in the morning. I'll spend the night with you tomorrow night."

The next day, Larry's nurse, Mary Catalana, who became his favorite, and I helped him get into the recliner. He became disoriented.

"How do we get this baby?"

Mary and I looked at each other, our eyes wide with surprise. We had no clue where that remark came from. He wasn't in the chair long, when his heart rate soared. Mary called the nurse practitioner, who ordered medication and we moved Larry to his bed. While the medication worked to slow down his heart rate, a cardiologist was consulted.

Because of Larry's stress and paranoia, I stayed overnight with him as promised. It took a long time for Larry to get calm enough to rest. His confusion caused him to pull on the tubes in his body. I sat next to his bed and held his hand until he fell asleep. I moved to a recliner and covered up with a comforter I had brought from home. When I closed my eyes I became aware of the offensive sounds that permeated Larry's room. I heard a clanging noise much like a slot machine spitting out coins to a winner. I rose from my chair and walked out into the large circular room that was the nucleus of the ICU. I saw a machine discharging labels that were used for identification on orders for work performed for the patients. I questioned the ward receptionist why it ran at night.

"Wouldn't that machine be less invasive to run in the daytime?"

"Honey, that machine runs all the time. We are all used to it and tune it out."

I turned around, went back into Larry's room, and closed the door to reduce as much noise as I could. It was odd I hadn't noticed it before, but I suspected it was because there was more people and commotion in the daylight hours. I shut my eyes only to have my ears tune into Larry's monitors above my head and the pinging noise they emitted as Larry's vital statistics wavered. Add that to the nurse's hourly check on Larry or medication administration and I understood Larry's fear of the nighttime. At three o'clock in the morning, Dr. Morgan, Larry's cardiologist, who had been added to the list of specialists, arrived.

I sat upright. "Good grief. Why are you here in the middle of the night? Is something wrong?"

"No, no. I had to check on another patient and thought I'd see how Larry was doing while I was here. I should ask you the same question . . . why are you here?"

I explained Larry's concern for being alone at night.

"I'm sure he appreciates your dedication, but you should be home and getting your own rest. However, since you're here, I did want to talk to you about a procedure I'd like to do."

I sighed heavily wondering what else could go wrong.

"I want to jump start his heart. I think the procedure will help to get his heart back on track."

"Isn't that dangerous?"

I immediately recollected my father dying of congestive heart failure a couple of days after the same procedure, but he had suffered from emphysema for thirty years and he was twenty years Larry's senior when it happened.

"Not for Larry. I'll do it around eight o'clock in the morning while you're at breakfast."

When Dr. Perry discovered I had spent the night, he told me to go home every night as he didn't want to see me suffer from ICU psychosis.

"It's not unusual for a patient to become confused and disoriented with the interruptions of people and sounds while they're here, but they forget everything once they've recovered. The same could happen to you without the proper rest away from here."

I accepted his word without question. Of course, after having spent a miserable night, it didn't take much. Dr. Fang arrived to check on Larry as promised. It became part of his routine during Larry's entire ordeal.

It was difficult to observe Larry struggle with survival. He had always been strong and vibrant, but I watched his stamina diminish. In the four days since his surgery, his cheeks had become sunken and his eyes looked vacant as though he searched for something, other than me, that was familiar. I wasn't certain how much weight he had lost at that point, but by the end of his stay, it was sixty-five pounds.

I found courage and strength from my faith, but I kept my sanity by keeping a daily journal beginning with Larry's first doctor visit after we were advised of the cancer. There was no way I could have remembered everything I was told about Larry's procedures or his state of health or what needed to be done next if I hadn't written it down. When I'd go home at night, there were always messages waiting on our answering machine; too many to return. I decided that sending out a daily email to advise family and friends was more efficient and provided an avenue for me to vent at the end of the day. My own stress was building because my heart ached watching the man I loved suffer. The journal helped to bring my emotions in check. Months later, as I looked back on the string of emails I sent, I realized how tired I must have been at the end of those long twelve to fourteen hour days. In some of them, I rambled and in others I made grammatical errors; definitely, not my style, but I knew our well-wishers saw beyond my mistakes.

Larry's fifth day in the hospital was difficult for him, his caretakers and me. Larry's nurse was one of the team leads, but had not cared specifically for Larry. Because he was so restless and kept touching the NG tube in his nose, she had tied down his hands. He didn't like it. When I was at his side, I wiped the sweat off his forehead, but if I took a restroom break, Larry couldn't perform this simple task on his own. It frustrated him. He asked me over and over what was in his nose, but would forget the answer minutes after I told him.

Journal entry, December 23, 2002:

Today, Larry had to have his catheter changed as there were signs of a bladder infection. While the nurse was getting a container for a urine sample, Larry succeeded in pulling his NG tube from his nose. He did this with his hands tied down. I had walked down the hall to the rest room and returned to see every nurse in ICU trying to hold Larry down to get the catheter reinserted. My job was to hold down his head and try to talk to him. He was like a cornered dog showing his teeth only he was yelling; not growling.

"Get out of here. Leave me alone. YOU! You, get them out of here. Help me."

Once the catheter was inserted and body fluids flowing, he calmed right down and slept. Later, he had to go to radiology to have his NG tube reinserted. The good news is that they have removed his epidural.

His distress that day was due to his lack of understanding of what was bothering him. It was his inability to relieve himself. Further, the NG tube was uncomfortable and since he couldn't remember why he had it, he continued to try to rid himself of the annoyance. I was disturbed and cried that day when he screamed at me. He must have thought I was aiding and abetting his discomfort.

Once his catheter was replaced and his bodily functions were back to normal, he forgot the pain he had experienced moments before. However it took me until the next day to sort out my emotions.

The day before Christmas, my children took turns visiting Larry in the hospital. Jason and Jean were in Arizona to spend Christmas with us. We didn't know when we had pre-planned our holiday, months earlier that the circumstances would be dramatically different. Instead of our family together playing games, eating great food and making merry, we sat in gloom by Larry's sick bed. Our family wasn't the only one to have a changed agenda. Dr. Perry's family suffered as well.

Journal Entry, December 24, 2002:

Christmas Eve: At 5pm tonight, Larry pulled out his NG tube for the second time. Dr. Perry, a radiologist, an anesthesiologist and a pulmonary specialist took him to radiology to reinsert the tube and put a second tube from his back into his right lung to drain it. The original surgery scars on his neck and stomach are now healing well, but the other complications are causing him so much difficulty. In addition to the fluid in his lung, there is an infection in his neck . . . away from the surgical area, but nonetheless needs to be treated immediately. They have changed his antibiotics and hope to clear up that problem. If not, the only option is to open his chest and clean it out . . . not a desirable alternative.

Late on Christmas Eve, I thanked Dr. Perry for his dedication and attentiveness to Larry. He never showed his discontent at being away from his family so as not to make me feel guilty.

"It's all in a days' work. I'm going home now. We still have time to celebrate."

I went home too and tried to salvage some quality time with my children. On Christmas morning, Jason, Jean and I went to Jake's house to watch his children open gifts. Afterward, we all went to the hospital to see Larry. I felt reenergized from seeing the delight on the faces of my granddaughters with their new toys.

That changed, however, when we arrived at the hospital. Larry didn't recognize any of us. I think Jason was the most disturbed.

"Why doesn't he know who we are? What's going on? Is he okay?"

I comforted him as best I could and tried to explain Larry's roller coaster of lucidity. By the afternoon, Larry, was back in the real world. This relieved all of us, but especially, Jason. He and Jean had to fly back to Atlanta Christmas night. He continued to worry something drastic would happen to Larry after he left. As visitors came and went all afternoon, Larry asked each of them for a drink of water or expressed his desire to go home. Many were in tears from their inability to help him or grant his requests.

On Thursday, a week after Larry's surgery, his confusion often turned into disorientation. Dr. Perry ordered a CT scan and conferred with Dr. Fang and three radiologists on the results. The fluid and infection in Larry's body cavity had increased and needed to be drained through a non-invasive procedure. However, to ensure Larry's immobility during the process, they were going to administer a general anesthesia. An orderly pushed his bed out of his room and transported him to an operating room. Larry's nurse accompanied him. I waited in his empty room, which was eerily quiet with the monitors off and Larry gone. I sat in the silence for over an hour. The doctors returned and advised me Larry would have to undergo more surgery as the problem had worsened. The surgery was scheduled for the next morning.

On December 27, 2002, Larry had a Thoracotomy, which was performed by Dr. Fang. Ironically, he came to our rescue once more. His daily interaction with Larry proved invaluable in understanding the seriousness of the infection. Dr. Fang hoped to release the infection by making four small incisions in his chest and using a scope. The fluid and infection were so bad, though, that Dr. Fang had to open up Larry from the middle of his back all the way around to the front. I was grateful for Dr. Fang's involvement, but this procedure added four more tubes to Larry's body. He had more drains in him than he had ports. In addition, he had to be on a ventilator again for twenty-four hours. I knew when he awoke from the anesthetic, he'd be unhappy as he wouldn't be able to talk with the life support in his mouth. I felt so sorry for him. He looked uncomfortable as the drainage tubes in his back were about a half-inch in diameter. His nurse and I propped pillows under Larry to force him to lean to one side and not lie directly on the tubes.

As I looked over Larry's body to see the additional drains, I noticed the Sacred Heart was missing from his arm. I felt a bit of panic that it was lost again and worried what Larry would think when he was conscious enough to notice. While he rested, I raced to a phone to call Carol and Dan to ask for yet for another one. I made arrangements to stop by Dan's mother's house to pick it up on my way home from the hospital that night. With that resolved, I turned my full attention to Larry.

Jack, Andrea, Charlie and Rhonda came to the hospital later that day. Andrea had brought him a white board with a pen so Larry could communicate with us. She thought it would relieve the stress of being on the ventilator. She explained what it was and he took it from her. He drew a barely legible map to Hannagan's Meadow near Alpine, Arizona. The clearest word on the drawing was "ashes." Rhonda grabbed the board and erased it.

"Stop that. Right now. You are not going to die."

I wasn't as convinced. That night, I knelt down to pray at my bedside. I pleaded with God for His help as Larry seemed to be losing his will to live. I reminded God that His promise to us was to not give us more than we could handle. I was at the point where I didn't know how much more I could watch him suffer. I still hadn't had time to grieve for my dear sister and now I faced losing Larry. My body shook as I wept. "Please make Larry well. Jason and Jean are getting married next October. I need him to hold me in his arms when we dance at their wedding. Don't allow him to leave me now. I want to grow old with Larry."

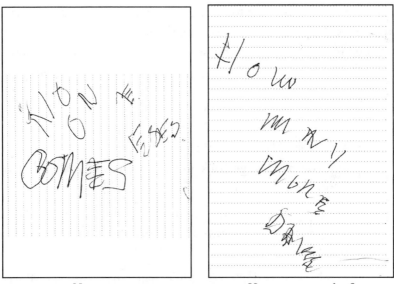

No one comes   How many more days?

Notes Larry wrote to Louise in the hospital.

On Friday, I taped the new Sacred Heart to Larry's arm determined not to alarm him that the first one had gone missing. That night I helped his nurse bathe him. When we leaned him forward to try to wash the area around his back and to apply some lotion, I saw the original Sacred Heart taped to his left shoulder blade. I chuckled and took it off.

"I don't believe it."

The nurse saw what I had retrieved and knew I had searched for it the day before.

"I bet they had to remove it from his arm because they needed a new IV location."

Whatever the reason, I swapped the original for the new one. Larry would never know. Later that night after I had gone home, Jason called the hospital from Atlanta to check on his dad. There weren't telephones in the individual rooms so he had to first talk to the ICU receptionist at the nurses' station. She laid the phone receiver down while she took the phone patients used into Larry's room. As she plugged in the phone, she let Larry know that Jason wanted to speak to him. Larry screamed an unexpected reaction.

"Jason, call your mother, call the cops. It's a conspiracy. They're trying to kill me."

This really shook Jason. As soon as he finished talking to Larry; all the while trying to calm him down, he called me.

"Mom, you need to go back to the hospital. Dad said they're trying to kill him. What are they doing to him?"

I knew it was all Larry's imagination run amuck. "Honey, don't worry. They're not hurting him. His medication makes him think crazy thoughts."

Jason felt helpless that he couldn't be at Larry's side, but Larry wouldn't have remembered that Jason had been there anyway.

On January 4, 2003, another Thoracotomy had to be performed as the infection was threatening Larry's life. Several good friends and family members had come to see Larry. In fact, we were in the healing garden when they called us back inside for the surgery. Larry was holding Madison and Chloe and was reluctant to let go. Our friends and family, who were visiting, stayed with me until the surgery was over. We all went upstairs to the surgery waiting room. We prayed and cried together. Bless our son, Jake, for his gift to lighten the load.

"Mom, I have a great idea. I think the doctors should inject fix a flat and seal up the leak."

As ridiculous as it was, it initiated a crescendo of laughter; medicine we needed. When the doctors reported back to us, they were confident that this surgery did the trick. I mentioned the fix a flat idea to Dr. Perry, but he didn't find it quite as funny as I did. His mind was still on the seriousness of Larry's condition.

Other than being on the ventilator again for twenty-four hours, Larry's spirits seemed to improve. I raised my eyes to Heaven and said a silent thank you. To date, Larry had suffered pulmonary problems requiring respiratory therapy and oxygen, heart problems, which required his heart to be jump started, three surgeries, CT scans nearly every day, chest x-rays every day, no food, no water, medication crushed and inserted in a tube in his stomach, delirium and depression. It seemed he'd take two steps forward and one step back without ever having learned how to do the two-step. Each time he had a surgery, he was required to be on a ventilator for a twenty-four hour period afterward. It confused and frustrated him and it reduced me to tears on a number of occasions.

When I was twenty-two years old, I made a vow that Larry would be my life-long partner. I believed the pledge I made, but I had no real concept of 'til death do us part' at that age. It was for old people. I wasn't prepared to let go of him. This state of mind and prayer motivated me to help Larry to fight harder. I spent long hours whispering words of encouragement to Larry to fight. I asked one of Larry's former college football buddies and close friend, Dan Dunn, whom we considered courageous because of the life obstacles he had overcome, to visit Larry and help rekindle the motivation for life Larry had once had. Larry perked up when his friend was there. Another former football player , Ron Pritchard, came by and prayed with Larry. Frank Kush, Larry's coach at ASU stopped by to visit and as usual had words of advice.

"Larry, you survived Camp Tontozona. You can survive this too."

We received support from friends we had made from all over the nation. Perhaps it was part of God's plan that I was transferred so many times, which broadened the scope of our acquaintances. One of Larry's former motorcycle riding partners belonged to a Christian motorcycle club called the Moo Cows. It was founded by the owner of Chick Fil-A and was comprised of over two hundred members. Larry was on their prayer list.

Chapter Twenty-One

In spite of all of this positive support, Dr. Perry and Dr. Fang pulled me aside one evening to explain the next steps if Larry didn't begin healing. They described how they might have to undo Larry's surgery by detaching his stomach and directing it to another drain, wait ninety days for him to heal and then send him to UCLA Medical Center for a more invasive surgery. I knew Larry could not tolerate his current condition without water and food for the extended time period they were talking about. I mustered up some courage and gave them a simple answer.

"It's won't be necessary. Larry will survive this ordeal."

They looked at each other and then me. I knew they weren't as convinced as I, but I depended on a higher power. The day after my plea with God, Larry told me he had met God the night before.

"It was strange. There we were, God and I, flying above Hannagan's Meadow. I couldn't see Him, but I could hear Him and I knew he was right next to me. I told him I was ready to let go. He told me it wasn't my time."

As frightening as this all was, I was certain God was working to answer my prayer. We needed a little more time. My feelings were confirmed that Sunday, January 5, 2004. I went to church and prayed my heart out. I tried to join in as the congregation sang, but my throat constricted as I choked on tears. A lady, who stood next to me, dressed in a wispy, flowing black dress, reached out to me and asked why I was crying. I told her I feared my husband was dying. She told me to stop crying.

"He'll be okay. I'll pray for him and so will my mother."

She pointed to the lady, who stood next to her.

"She is close to God."

I asked the lady her name.

"It's Mary."

I felt calm and knew what I had given over to God would be a positive outcome. I truly believe I had met one of God's angels, who was sent to comfort me.

By January 8, Larry was taken off oxygen. His temperature was normal for the first time since his surgery, which was a good indication the infection was gone or at least significantly reduced. I was witnessing a miracle.

On the twenty-second day after Larry's surgery, his physical therapy was increased to a walk outside his room instead of bedside exercise. There were loud cheers, applause and smiles from the nurses as we passed each patient's room. It took four of us to escort Larry around the nurses' station. I walked behind him with a wheel chair ready in case he became tired. Two physical therapists walked at Larry's sides and held the straps that clipped to the sides of the canvas belt that surrounded his torso. He looked like a dog on a leash. Mary, his nurse, carried the hoses that were attached to his body and the containers they emptied into. The nurses' station was like the hub of a wheel while the eight rooms surrounding it were the spokes. It took Larry about fifteen minutes to walk a quarter of the short distance.

"I want to go back."

We granted his request and turned around. It's hard to imagine what a struggle and a triumph it was for him to make it that far. A healthy person could walk all the way around in fifteen seconds.

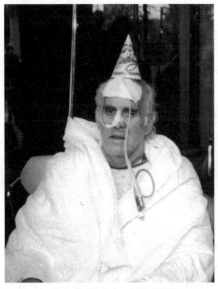

Larry's birthday 1/12/2003

We celebrated his birthday, January 12, 2003, with a big party in the healing garden. Larry eyes had dark circles around them and appeared lifeless, but his spirits were good. His forehead and nose were covered in adhesive tape to hold his NG tube in place. There was a small plastic bag on the drain from his neck, a container that caught fluid from the drains in his back and a container hooked to his catheter that hung on his wheelchair. His hands shook involuntarily from the medication. There was no way to prepare someone who hadn't seen him frequently for what to expect.

Our friend, Sonya, came from Georgia with her children, to see Larry. I tried to tell her to wait until he was home again, but I knew she worried that day wouldn't come. She thought of Larry and me as family. She was so startled when she first saw Larry, her face reddened and she began to weep. She had to step away and gather her composure so that Larry wouldn't see her reaction.

Larry continued to improve slowly, but on January 16, he had a painful mishap. He had been sitting up in the chair in his room, but was ready to get back in bed. Ralph, his nurse, dropped the footrest on the recliner. Even though Ralph had checked to see if Larry's many tubes were free of the chair, he hadn't noticed Larry's catheter line had fallen behind the foot rest. When Ralph reached for Larry's hands to help him to stand up, Larry's catheter was yanked out. Larry bent over and expelled a gulp of air.

"What's wrong, buddy?"

Larry wasn't quite sure what had caused the pain. Ralph noticed blood on the floor and investigated its origin. When he realized what had happened, Ralph told me his knees buckled. He couldn't even imagine how it really felt to Larry. I shared the story in my journal that night:

> *. . . So, Larry has another tube removed! (Reference: catheter removal.) There's a silver lining to every day. Oh my goodness, what a way to rid oneself of a tube. The good news is he is able to continue bodily functions on his own so he won't have to have the catheter reinserted. Thank God each day for these small miracles.*

It wasn't until January 21, that the doctors felt Larry was ready to have his leak tested. The reason was that it consisted of drinking Barium and then having an x-ray to see if anything leaked. It was the first liquid Larry had swallowed in thirty-five days. The results were good. He was rewarded with a few ice chips. Even though he enjoyed them, they didn't equal the treat he'd had during this tribulation, when, Mary, his nurse and I felt especially sorry for him. He had begged us for something to drink often. The only relief Larry was permitted was for one of us to swab his mouth. The instrument was a six-inch long stick with a hunk of moistened sponge at the end of it. I tried it on myself once and found it less than satisfactory. Larry was sitting on the side of his bed and had posed the usual question. His tongue had peeled it was so dry. It looked like it belonged to a lizard.

"I want some water, please. I won't drink much."

As I consoled him, Mary said she had an idea. She mixed Listerine, water and ice in a cup and stood in front of him with strict instructions.

"I'm going to let you swish this special cocktail around in your mouth for a couple of seconds, but do not swallow it."

To emphasize her directions, she handed me a container for him to spit into.

"Now, take a small sip."

She and I cried out in unison. "Don't swallow, swish, don't swallow."

He swished and spit in the dish. We cheered. He grinned.

"That was the best cocktail I've ever tasted."

A few days after his Barium test, he had his first real drink in thirty-eight days. It was cause for celebration. Our daughter-in-law, Nikki, and our two granddaughters came to visit Larry. His nurse and I wheeled him to the Healing Garden for the visit. Nikki had made crowns for the girls and Larry. He wore his crown with pride. We put baby Chloe, who was four months old in his lap. He rubbed her chubby little hand like it was satin; a trait he'd demonstrated with all babies. He had his other arm around five year old Madison. He cherished these little children. I was so grateful his healing process had progressed enough that he could appreciate their presence.

When we returned to his room, he took a rest and right at shift change, he decided to go for a stroll.

"I want to show off my crown to the nurses. Let's go for a walk."

King Larry with Princess Chloe and Princess Madison in the hospital healing garden

This time, he pushed his wheelchair around the entire perimeter of the nurses' station. He looked so regal with the crown on his head. He was King for a day in ICU. It took him twenty minutes, but he did it. It was a triumph and a new beginning in his quest for wellness.

He had become a well-known resident of the intensive care ward. His miraculous recovery earned him pats on the back as he circled the room. In addition to the cheers, there were also tears of joy on the cheeks of those wonderful nurses who had so patiently seen to his every need.

When we returned to his room, his nurse had changed his bed linens. We helped him to bed, hooked up his monitors and arranged pillows around him to relieve the pressure of the drains in his back. The nurse bathed the sweat from his brow, changed his bandages and left the room. Larry asked me to lower his bed, which I did. I heard a crunching noise and walked around his bed to see what caused it. I discovered the plastic container that caught the fluid from his chest tube was stuck under a rail. Instead of raising the bed again to free it, I tried to pull it out. It fell and made a loud crash. Every nurse in the ICU, plus one who was off duty and on her way out the door, was in his room in seconds. I turned around, holding the evidence and blushed.

"Oops. All y'all sure came in here fast. Sorry."

His nurse stayed to help me hook the container back up while the others left. They weren't upset with me. I had been there every day for so long; they trusted me to perform certain tasks. I had just handled this one like a klutz. They're main concern was that the king hadn't fallen out of bed.

Chapter Twenty-Two

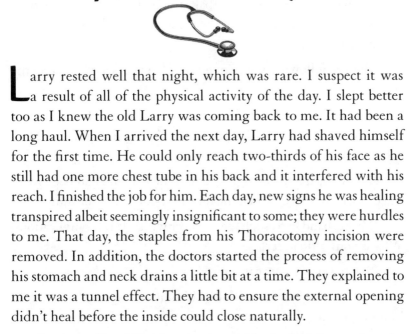

Larry rested well that night, which was rare. I suspect it was a result of all of the physical activity of the day. I slept better too as I knew the old Larry was coming back to me. It had been a long haul. When I arrived the next day, Larry had shaved himself for the first time. He could only reach two-thirds of his face as he still had one more chest tube in his back and it interfered with his reach. I finished the job for him. Each day, new signs he was healing transpired albeit seemingly insignificant to some; they were hurdles to me. That day, the staples from his Thoracotomy incision were removed. In addition, the doctors started the process of removing his stomach and neck drains a little bit at a time. They explained to me it was a tunnel effect. They had to ensure the external opening didn't heal before the inside could close naturally.

On Super Bowl Sunday, Larry said he looked forward to the football game, which was a surprise to me. Every time I had turned on his TV before, he had asked me to turn it off. What I learned, but not until after they removed his NG tube, was that it had caused him double vision. He didn't even know who was playing, but he didn't care.

"Did you bring me beer or chips and dip?"

"Funny boy. I'm sure they won't let you go from sips of water to beer."

We had intended to watch the game together, but by the time it started, he was too tired to enjoy it much. When he seemed relaxed enough to sleep, I left to go home. His nurse told me she'd watch the game with him if he awoke.

On my way out to my car, which was a long hike down a dark sidewalk adjacent to where the new parking structure was under construction, I heard footsteps close behind me. I hastened my pace, but the sounds of the steps increased to match mine. Even though I was afraid, I turned around to see how close the pursuer was. Larry had always told me that in football, the best offense was a strong defense so I looked right at the man, who walked up behind me. He smiled at me.

"I'm not following you. I'm going to the parking lot across the street too."

I slowed down to allow him to walk beside me. "It's a far jaunt after a long day. I'm on day thirty-nine visiting my husband. How about you?"

He breathed a heavy sigh and told me his wife had been there since Christmas Eve, which meant thirty-four days for him.

"My husband had esophageal cancer with several complications. Why is your wife here?"

"She has pancreatic cancer."

I felt so badly for him. I asked him her name and his and told him I'd pray for them and ask my friends to do the same.

"I send out an email journal every night to a growing distribution list. There's even a two hundred person strong Christian Harley motorcycle club praying for my husband. I'll be happy to share the network."

He was quite grateful. I'm not certain why I invaded his privacy, but I think it was because I could feel his pain. His face looked worn and tired from worry.

"Any chance you're a Catholic?"

"No, but my wife is."

My thoughts went immediately to the second Sacred Heart I had procured from my friend Carol's mother. I happened to have it in my pocket because of the fiasco of losing the original.

"Take this Sacred Heart and tape it on your wife's arm. There's no place to permanently pin them. Then say a prayer with her. Perhaps it will bring her comfort."

He looked directly at me. I could see his eyes fill with tears and I knew he understood my sincere sentiment.

"God bless you. I'll do it tomorrow."

We reached our cars and waved goodbye. I drove home and thought about how sad he must have been. As promised, I included him and his wife in my email journal to our friends and asked for their prayers. I never learned the outcome for his wife, but I hope our prayers gave him courage.

On day forty, Larry sipped some chicken broth. There was a small slippage in his quest for good health. His blood count was low, which required a couple of pints of blood. It seemed insignificant after all he had been through. He was winning his battle as I knew he would. God answered all of our prayers.

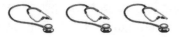

Larry was finally able to come home on February 1, 2003. During the months of recovery at home, Larry asked me lots of questions about his hospital stay as most of it was a blur to him. The doctor had warned me that he would forget. I think it was God's way of not forcing him to remember the struggle. One day, Larry told me that he remembered his CT scan the night that the registry nurse was in charge. I knew what night he meant as I had seen the CT scan technician myself and some of Larry's recollections were true. He remembered they had wheeled him into this dark room and this tall, bulky, dark-bearded man with long hair and lots of chains around his neck said he was going to take care of him.

"What the man really did was take a mama cat that was in a pillowcase and place it between my legs. He wanted to x-ray it to count how many babies there were."

I howled with laughter.

"I get it. CAT SCAN."

After I had wiped the tears from my eyes, I explained that the description of the technician was pretty accurate as I had met him when I signed papers for the scan, but that I was quite certain that they hadn't x-rayed a cat.

Another of his recollections from his hospital stay was the day Nurse Mary took him to have an x-ray by wheelchair instead of in his hospital bed. She said she had a treat for him and instead of going to the x-ray department where, by the way, they still knew him by first name six months later, she took him outside to enjoy the sunny day. The hospital is near the airport and he could see planes flying low to land from his hospital bed. In addition, there were frequent helicopters landing on the helipad on top of the hospital bringing in accident victims. Larry remembered that day this way.

"Mary took me by helicopter to get to the x-ray department. There wasn't much room in the helicopter so they had to shove me down on the floor under the feet of the co-pilot."

I knew the day he referenced as Mary and I had gone together to take Larry to the radiology department. It was bright, sunny and warm for a January day so we stopped at the back patio along the way. While we were there, a helicopter landed on the helipad not far from where we stood. Larry's medication caused him to hallucinate on occasion. Based on his view of the day, this was one of those occasions.

Mary Catalana's care went way beyond the rudimentary tasks required. She was interested in his quality of life and felt certain that trips away from ICU were important. It was one of the reasons she packed up his equipment so that Larry could make visits to the Healing Garden. It was serene and more visitors could surround Larry at one time. It was no wonder Larry chose her as his favorite.

Even when Larry was out of it, his witty side shone. During his third week in the hospital when our prim and proper neighbor stopped in to see him, she asked Larry how he was doing. He sat up at straight as he could and put his shoulders back in a gesture of bravado.

"I made a turd."

She did a double take.

"What?"

He repeated it. I needed that laugh, desperately. Sandy still couldn't understand him so I finally translated. I think she was too shocked to respond with anything other than a "that's nice."

Larry's strength, stamina, sense of humor and faith carried him through this traumatic experience. My love for him, support from family and friends and my faith in God carried me.

Chapter Twenty-Three

Wh)en Larry returned home from the hospital after a forty-three day stay; most of which was in ICU, he was fragile. I was his primary caretaker during this recovery period. Fortunately for us, I worked from home, which permitted me to handle my job responsibilities and check on Larry frequently. One wall of my office, which was a few steps down the hall from the living room, had an open archway, which allowed me to hear Larry without difficulty. He sat in his recliner and like a newborn baby, slept most of the time for the first month. He had a few regular visitors, who'd come once or twice a week to keep him company. It was a relief for me because then I wasn't taking anything away from my employer or feeling any guilt for not giving Larry my undivided attention.

While Larry was able to eat soft foods, he had to supplement his diet through enteral nutrition. Each day, I poured liquid nourishment in an IV bag, and attached the end of the line to a feeding tube that had been surgically inserted into an area above Larry's waist. The tubing from the IV bag wrapped through and around a contraption, which hung on the IV pole. It was similar to feeding film through a projector or threading a sewing machine. I had to check to make certain that the drip was released at a certain speed before I turned it on. The feeding process took about forty-five minutes to complete.

Three days after he came home, I served him his lunch and a glass of water. He took one drink of the water and choked. He spit it out and tried again with a smaller sip. He choked again. It frightened both of us. I grabbed the phone and called Dr. Perry's office.

"Larry cannot swallow any liquid without choking. What do I do?"

The receptionist put Dr. Perry on the phone right away. I could hear the concern in his voice, which exacerbated my own fear.

"How fast can you get to the hospital?"

"I can be there in forty minutes. It's a thirty-five mile drive."

With no hesitation he gave me instructions on what part of the hospital to go to and where to park. He wanted us to meet a doctor he was going to call at the outpatient surgery department. Larry and I left immediately as instructed. The entire ride, Larry spat his saliva into a glass so that he wouldn't choke on it. When we arrived, the receptionist sent us upstairs to the endoscopy floor, where we met with Dr. Wadas. He greeted us with a warm encouraging grin. I was impressed and appreciative of his quick response to Larry's problem.

"Wow. I can't believe you were available so fast."

He shrugged his shoulders as if it was no big deal.

"I skipped my lunch. It was good timing. Dr. Perry and I have worked together a long time. He shared Larry's situation with me. We're going to put him under anesthesia and insert what is called a French wire with a balloon. When the balloon is inflated, it will stretch Larry's throat. I'll take good care of him."

An hour later, Dr. Wadas returned to the waiting room.

"I'm glad you brought him in when you did. His throat had constricted to the size of the tip of a ballpoint pen."

In order to demonstrate his explanation, he took a pen out of his pocket as he talked and pointed to the end of the pen.

"Like this."

I received his message loud and clear.

"I want you to bring him back in a week and we'll do it again. If you prefer, you can call my office and schedule an appointment at our endoscopy center. It's more personal than the hospital."

I thanked him for his quick response to Dr. Perry's call. He patted my shoulder and left. As it turned out, we followed this procedure every week for a month. The next month, it was every other week and then monthly for three more months. Dr. Wadas was a tall man with cheerful, bright blue eyes. He had an air of confidence; yet a kindness about him that helped us to accept these visits without as much fear. He wanted Larry to get weaned from the procedure, however, so that his throat would be taught to stay open and not become dependent on the manual stretching.

ૐ ૐ ૐ

Our routine of caretaker and patient was similar to the situation when my father-in-law, Whitey, had a stroke in May 1975. His ability

to speak was severely impaired. My mother-in-law, Helen, was his home nurse for several months. She told me the time they shared that summer was the best of their marriage. Whitey was appreciative of everything she did to care for him. Because of his speech impairment,

Helen and Whitey Laughlin with Jason—1973

he spoke little, therefore, never criticized what she was doing or how she was doing it.

Helen was a soft-spoken person, but Whitey was quite the opposite. Before this time, his gruff voice and quick speech pattern had sounded demanding even in normal conversation. I think a part of me enjoyed Larry's convalescent period for the same reason as Helen. While I'm hardly mild mannered, Larry, like his father, unintentionally spoke in commanding tones. During those six months, Larry did not protest any of the treatment I provided; rather he was grateful. I understood the quiet respite Helen had enjoyed while she cared for Whitey. Larry's weakened condition left him unable to argue; verbally or otherwise. It was contrary to his once robust spirit and vigor.

I had to crush his medication in a jar designed for that purpose, add a bit of water and pour it into a plastic syringe which was about ten inches long and half an inch in diameter. The bottom of the instrument narrowed so that its contents could be injected into his feeding tube. There were moments of tenderness between us when I performed this process three times per day. He watched me prepare the mixture and would pat my arm as I administered the medication.

"Thank you. I love you."

I would touch his cheek softly and look into his tired sunken eyes.

"I love you too."

🍂 🍂 🍂

At the point where he began giving me instructions on how to execute these duties I had done for several months without complaint from him, I knew he had improved and regained his dominant personality. It was time to stop responding to his beck and call. Further, he needed to learn to swallow pills. He was still fearful they would get stuck in his throat in spite of the doctor's assurance to the contrary. He began with small ones and worked up to a half of a large pill. He kept up the progression until he was able to swallow a whole pill with confidence. It was difficult to watch his trepidation with such a simple task. I wondered how long his sick period would last or indeed was it, in fact, life-long.

Larry and I had always had a close relationship. Not only were we lovers, but we were also good friends. Larry's cancer survival had been an answer to my prayers, but I was unprepared to handle the next phase of our married life. There were plenty of good times that kept us going, but a dark side had crept into our lives and it invaded our happiness. It took awhile to learn how to cope with it, but we learned that because his digestive system had been dramatically changed, he could no longer accommodate food, or alcohol, in the same way.

With food, he had to chew until he pulverized it. The saliva in his mouth was the only method he had to digest food. All of his glands that excreted acidic juices had been disabled during his surgery. There were times when he would eat a meal as he had always done, but within an hour, he would sweat profusely and his body would shake. This was not a slight reaction; rather, it was profound. We talked to our general practitioner about it, who had him tested for hyperglycemia. Larry was normal. A year later, his surgeon explained that Larry could not drink liquid and eat solids at the same time in the morning. Since his body had been at rest all night, it wouldn't know which to digest first and would signal its confusion through this reaction. From that point forward, Larry drank coffee when he awoke and waited for thirty minutes before he ate food.

Larry had always been a social drinker, but after his surgery, his behavior changed dramatically when he drank. He'd have a couple of drinks and be fine, but when he drank a third one, he was blitzed. In this state of inebriation, he became belligerent. This phenomenon took a couple of years to understand, but basically, alcohol did not go through a digestive process like food. It went right to his blood stream. He learned that his tolerance for alcohol was slim to none. Because of this, he has had to change his social habits to accommodate his new internal plumbing.

Our thirty-fifth anniversary was in August; six months after Larry was discharged from the hospital. He was still somewhat unsteady on his feet. The long months of bed rest and trauma had taken a significant toll on his body. Larry used to tease me and say that unless our anniversary fell on a Saturday, the same day we were married, it wasn't really cause for celebration. Since, the twenty-fourth fell on a Sunday in 2003, it didn't count. Whether it was his joking or that we didn't require the special acknowledgement of the day to be assured we had made a good decision; we had never been advanced planners for celebrating our marriage.

❦ ❦ ❦

In spite of his big talk, that year, Larry had managed to buy me a beautiful silver bracelet from Tiffany's. He gave me the bracelet Saturday morning and told me the story of how difficult it had been to get it. It had not been a simple task for him.

"I took advantage of a day last June when you were away from home at a customer's site."

It had only been a month since his feeding tube had been removed and he was still frail. He explained he had driven to Tiffany's in Scottsdale, which was about fifteen miles from our house, while I was at a business meeting with a customer that afternoon. He remembered I had mentioned I wanted a silver bracelet with a heart.

"I wanted to buy you something special for our anniversary to thank you for all of the years by my side, but especially for the care you provided while I was ill."

He was so weary from the impact of his illness, however, that he found it difficult to explain to the sales clerk what he wanted to buy. Instead of purchasing the bracelet I had requested, which cost about a hundred and fifty dollars, he bought a bracelet with no heart that cost over four hundred dollars.

"I was exhausted from my forty-five minutes of shopping and headed back to the car. I realized I didn't remember where I had parked."

He was so disoriented, he had to sit down on a bench and think hard about what direction he had come from. This took about an hour. He took a chance by following his instincts and located his car. By the time he reached home, he had to take a three-hour nap to regain his strength. He never mentioned this to me until he gave me the present the day before our anniversary.

"I'm sorry I bought the wrong one, but I hope you like it anyway."

I kissed him.

"I love it and I love you. I don't care if it doesn't have a heart."

I was so touched by his effort that I didn't mind at all that it wasn't the one I had described. I still wear it on a regular basis, but even so, he eventually went back to buy a heart for it. When he discovered an attachment was not designed for my bracelet, he bought another bracelet with a heart and had my initials and the date of our wedding engraved on it. I cherish that one as well.

Chapter Twenty-Four

On October 11, 2003, the day of Jason and Jean's wedding, members of both families traveled across the nation to be in Las Vegas and share this special time with them and us. While I was in the bathroom taking a shower, I prayed a word of thanks to God for this day and for His blessing that Larry was alive to share it with me. It had been ten months since his cancer surgery and because God had answered my prayers, Larry and I would have the privilege of dancing at our son's wedding.

I stopped my day dreaming, rinsed my hair and stepped out of the shower. It was nearly time for the bridal party, which included Jean's mother, my mother and me, to be picked up at our hotel and taken

Larry's Family Left to Right
Joann Wiener, Larry, Marlene Ellis, Kenny Laughlin,
Stephanie Miller, Tom Laughlin

by mini-bus to the hall. I put on my casual clothes, grabbed my dress, accessories and make-up and kissed Larry goodbye. I stopped by my mother's room, tried to make certain she had all she needed and we headed down to the designated location for our transportation. When we arrived at the meeting site, we joined in their lively conversation. It sounded like we were near a beehive as there was so much chatter and buzz. We were downright giddy with excitement. The driver arrived and we boarded the bus. The ride there was joyful. Jean, who had planned her entire wedding via the Internet, had our chauffer stop at a bagel shop on the way. She had left no detail undone.

When we arrived at the banquet hall, they provided a room large enough to house a crowd of fifty for us to don our gowns and have our hair done. Jean's mother scurried over to the walk-in closet where I was hanging my garment bag.

"Let me see what you're wearing."

I unzipped the bag and showed her my black dress. "You'd think we were going to a fancy funeral, but since the bridesmaids' gowns are black, I bought one too. Besides, it' more slimming . . . if that's possible."

Lily grabbed two garment bags from the closet where she had hung them.

"I'm so glad I asked. I brought two dresses. One is flowery for the outside wedding, but in case you were more dressed up than I, there's a second, more formal one. It will look better for us to match."

We hugged and proceeded to finish getting ready. The chatter in the room developed into louder conversation. Some of the girls shrieked with laughter as they became acquainted with one another. I don't remember what was so hysterical, but I recall we had plenty of fun. There was also a professional make-up artist, who applied the bride's make-up. Jean looked like a China doll. The fact that she was first generation American Chinese helped.

Madison, our five-year-old granddaughter, was the flower girl. She wore a beautiful, long white dress. She looked like a miniature

Maddy gets her hair fixed —
Jean and Madison

Cinderella. She watched in awe as we each received the glamour treatment. The hair stylist noticed how interested she was.

"Would you like some French braids in your hair and perhaps some little flowers?"

Madison's eyes lit up as she grinned a big toothy smile.

"Yes."

I thanked the kind lady for the unsolicited attention she paid to Madison and offered to pay for her services.

"Oh, that's not necessary. I have a little girl and I know how special she'd feel."

We all applauded when the stylist was finished. Madison glowed with pride.

The photographer knocked on the door and was offered entry. He concentrated his efforts on capturing great photos of the bride, but he also took snapshots of Madison with Jean. They were both too cute for words.

While we were having our fun, the groomsmen and fathers were chauffeured from the hotel in the mini-bus to the hall and ushered into a smaller, but suitable room for them to get ready for the big event. They had their own special fun, some of which wasn't revealed until the pictures were developed. It seems they thought it would be fun to stand in a line, drop their pants and shoot a moon at the camera. Jean's father, Robert, must have taken the picture as he wasn't in the photo and I'm certain he did not want to participate. He's too much of a gentleman. When they were finished dressing, the photographer took them all outside for some fun photos . . . with their pants on.

Jean and Jason had hired more buses to bring guests without transportation from the hotel to the reception hall, as it was twelve miles out of the city. On arrival, the guests were directed to the location of the outside ceremony. There were planters filled with flowers and colorful plants on both sides of the aisle.

White, wooden, folding chairs were set up on the far side of the planters. The aisle had a slatted patio covering, which blocked out the direct sunlight and created a shady, serene ambiance. The minister stood under a gazebo at the front of the aisle.

Inside, the wedding party with the exception of Jean, was led downstairs from our respective dressing rooms. Jean was kept out of view until Jason had exited the building. Larry and I were supposed to walk down the aisle with Chloe, our one-year-old granddaughter as her parents, Jake, Nikki and her sister, Madison were all part of the wedding party. At the last minute, Chloe started running a fever. A tired, sick baby masked her usual cheerful demeanor. She stood with her arms outstretched toward us. Her white dress was pleated all around. She looked like a little lampshade with the light beneath it turned on low.

The little lampshade —
Chloe

"Up."

She didn't cry, but we could tell, she felt terrible. I picked her up and held her in my arms. I was thrilled to have her small body cuddled against my bosom. When it was our turn to proceed, Jason gently grabbed my arm at the elbow to stop me and showed me a single, white rose.

"I'm putting this on the first chair in the front row in memory of Aunt Laura."

Tears filled my eyes and I had to catch a breath as I felt an uninvited sob creep up from my chest. "You should have given me more notice about this."

"Sorry, Mom, but we wanted her to be acknowledged and thought this would be a good way to do it."

My heart ached that Laura would not be at this happy occasion in person. I knew, though, that she watched from Heaven. "I'm so proud of you and Jean to pay tribute to Aunt Laura."

Larry and I proceeded with our promenade down the aisle. You could hear the audible "Ohs and Ahs" from the crowd as we walked. Chloe had her head on my shoulder with both arms wrapped around

Larry, Louise and baby Chloe

my neck. When we reached our seats, I laid Chloe in her reclined stroller. I gave her a bottle, which she suckled greedily. Without so much as a whimper, she fell asleep.

After Jean's mother, Lily, was escorted down the aisle by her two sons, Jason was next. He was still on crutches as he had had his ankle fused six weeks earlier. His issue was a residual defect from his motorcycle accident the year before. The whole purpose of the surgery was to avoid the crutches, but his ankle had not healed as planned. He hobbled to the start and pitched his crutches to the side. Determined to walk down the aisle to deliver the rose, he limped the rest of the way. He received applause for his effort. He stopped to place the rose on the chair reserved for my sister. I was in the next chair so he leaned toward me and kissed my cheek. What a thoughtful son! My eyes misted again. The minister announced the purpose of the white rose to the guests and requested a moment of silence in memory of Laura.

I turned to watch my family, who were seated behind us. Their heads were bowed, but I could see tears roll down the cheeks of some and others grabbed for tissues from their pockets. I don't think there was a dry eye among us. Murmurs of condolences from the bride's guests on the other side of the aisle added to the emotion of the scene.

The rest of the ceremony was typical of most weddings with a couple of exceptions. When Jean and her father reached the altar, Robert touched his cheek against Jean's in what seem liked a mock hug.

Jason limps down the aisle with a white rose in memory of his Aunt Laura

Her mother, Lily, was much more demonstrative than her husband, and hollered something at him. Their family members joined in her communication He turned toward them with his arms outstretched and his palms up.

"What?"

"Kiss her."

"Oh."

He turned to Jean, again, and gave her a peck on the cheek. This small gesture caused giggles among the guests. It was obvious that big hugs were not commonplace between Jean and her dad. She would have an awakening in ours as we were quite the opposite. At the end of the ceremony, the minister nodded his head toward Jason.

"You may kiss your bride."

Jason, like Jean's father, gave her a peck; only on the lips. The minister gave a hardy laugh.

"That's not a kiss. Mr. Best Man, step over here. Do you have a watch on?"

"Yes sir."

He showed him the timepiece on his arm for proof.

"Great, now time them. The next one needs to last at least a minute. Okay, Jason, now kiss your bride."

Cheers erupted from the crowd. I believe I shouted my own "woohoo" for the minister. This time Jason threw his arms around Jean, bent her backwards and kissed her.

They were introduced to the crowd, who gave them a standing ovation. They went down the aisle and slipped around the corner of the building instead of going inside. The minister invited the guests to proceed indoors for the reception while the photographs were taken of the wedding party outside. Larry's sister, Marlene, took charge of Chloe, who slept through the whole ordeal. To entertain the guests while we were busy with the photographer, a video was played that Jason and Jean had created and narrated weeks earlier. It included pictures of their families and each of them throughout their growing up years to their adult life together. The banquet hall coordinators helped everyone find their seats and started the movie, which was displayed on a ten foot screen on the wall. At the beginning of the movie, Jason addressed the guests.

"Jean and I have created this little film for your viewing pleasure while we have our pictures taken. The bar is open. Please have a beverage and watch our video."

This was a great crowd pleaser. I heard later how wonderful the video was, but I didn't get to see it until we were home in Arizona and had a chance to watch our copy.

After our pictures were completed, the entire wedding party was ushered around the building to the second story area where we began our day. When the movie ended, the disc jockey kicked up the

Jason and Jean's wedding — October 11, 2003

music and announced each couple as the wedding party descended the stairs into the reception hall. Jean's parents were first, Larry and I second and then Madison, who glided like a princess and had a smile stretched across her face. There was a landing half-way down. Before we descended, we had been instructed to do something fun and spontaneous when we reached it. Jean's parents gave a little bow. Larry twirled me around and Madison curtsied. Each entrance was a little different. It was quite fun.

Flashes from cameras, sounds from the upbeat music and cheers and applause from the crowd made me feel like I was walking the red carpet at the Oscar Awards. This continued until all of us were standing on the dance floor, taking our bows. Jason, as the host raised his hands.

"Let the party begin."

When Larry and I danced our first dance, I held him tight. I closed my eyes and prayed "Thank you God for this moment. It is one I will treasure forever."

About an hour later, the toasts began. Larry left our table and walked over to Jason and Jean and raised his glass. He began what he intended to be a simple toast that they have a life-long friendship as he and I had enjoyed. Instead, he included how I had stayed by his side at the hospital and helped him get well. He had the crowd's undivided attention. He introduced Dr. Fang, the son of close friends of Jean's parents, who were also in attendance.

"I want you to meet the man, who saved my life . . . Dr. Kenith Fang."

Larry walked over to Dr. Fang, who stood to greet him and gave him a hug. Kenith, who was crying, hugged him, patted him on the back and whispered a plea to Larry.

"Don't let go. Don't let them see me. Doctors aren't supposed to cry."

The crowd cheered. My cousin walked over to me.

"This is the most perfect wedding I have ever attended. The only thing missing was the tissue on the tables."

Later, I danced with my grandchildren until I became too hot. I stopped at one of the tables and picked up a cocktail napkin to dab at my face to keep my make up from dripping. Carl Fang, the doctor's father, walked over to me. He was weeping.

"Oh, that was a beautiful thing Larry said about my son. I am so proud. That night I called him to help you; he said he would treat Larry like family. In fact, Kenith said I will help him like he was my father."

I put my hands on Carl's arms. "Your son did indeed treat us like family. He checked on Larry every day even before he actually became his doctor. We are proud to know him and thankful to you for calling him. Larry meant every word he said."

He grabbed the damp napkin from my hands and blew his nose. I hugged him. He walked away from me nodding his head in agreement.

Promptly at three o'clock, the proprietors thanked us for coming. It was their tactful way of telling us to get the heck out of there as they had another party to host.

Chapter Twenty-Five

Part of Larry's healing process was to engage in fun activities to achieve a healthy attitude. A college friend of Larry's, Ron Pritchard, was inducted into the National Football Foundation's College Football Hall of Fame in December, 2003. Ron had spent a great deal of time with Larry while he was in the hospital and during his recovery period at home. We appreciated Ron's support and prayers and wanted to reciprocate by flying to New York City to attend the gala and celebration.

I had enough hotel points from my own travel to stay at the Waldorf Astoria, where the black tie affair was held, for the several days we were in New York. Larry and I watch *Good Morning America* every morning together and I thought it would be fun to go in person. Somehow that had more appeal than Christmas shopping in the beautifully decorated stores on Fifth Avenue, which is rather ironic for me the shopaholic.

I went online and secured enough tickets so that our group of ten could attend. As it turned out, Larry was the only one of the men who was willing to rise at o' dark thirty to go to the show. Before we had left our home in Arizona, I set the television to record the show. I also purchased a long red and white stripped scarf with fringe on the ends in addition to bringing a red Santa hat for Larry to wear. His beard was full and curly and ready for his winter alter ego, Santa. I even made a few signs to hold up for the TV cameras and carried them with me.

We had planned to walk to Times Square, but as soon as we exited the hotel at five o' clock in the morning, we changed our minds. The winter morning seemed bitter cold to us Arizonans. My eyes watered so much that tears dripped down my cheeks and froze there. My nose was just as bad, but that was gross. We hailed a cab and rode to ABC Studios.

We were surprised to learn on arrival that we weren't the first people there, but we joined the other souls who braved the cold in line. Since we had tickets, we were more fortunate than some and were granted entry into the studio after only fifteen minutes outdoors.

Once inside, the five of us from our group were positioned at the back of the audience. The producer was giving us instructions on when to be quiet and when we could talk. I held up my pitiful signs and realized the printing was not bold enough to be seen on camera. I turned to look at Larry and he was jumping up and down and waving a dollar bill. The guest weatherman started laughing at him. The producer called out to Larry.

"Hey Santa. Why are you waving the dollar bill?

The people in front of Larry parted like the Red Sea.

"I want to sit on Diane's lap."

What a gimmick . . . the production crew loved it.

"It'll take more than a buck to make that happen."

It had done the trick, however. To make the temporary weatherman's appearance more fun, he instructed Larry to wave more money every time they broke for the weather report. Once the show began taping, Larry did as he was told.

On cue, the weatherman, Mike, pointed Larry out to the camera.

"Santa has flown in with the storm and is trying to pay his way to the front of the crowd. We'll have to see about that."

The second set, Larry waived a ten dollar bill and we all moved closer. By the time Charlie Gibson came down to the studio where we were, Larry was in the front row and was holding up five twenties and his gold card. Charlie Gibson took the money out of his hand.

"For this much money, you can replace Diane."

Laughter erupted from the spectators and Larry had his fifteen minutes of fame, but it didn't stop there. Charlie handed Larry his money back off camera. When the red light came on, Mike, the weatherman, gave Larry the microphone and invited him to hand the show back off to Diane. Larry didn't hesitate.

"Ho, ho, ho. Back up to Diane we go."

Diane, in her usual jovial manner, chuckled.

"Ho, ho ho . . . back at ya, Santa."

After the show finished taping, Diane, Charlie and Robin came downstairs where we were and met us. They were gracious enough to take turns getting their pictures taken with us. What a fun morning. We left and after stopping for breakfast, we walked back in the sunny, brisk air to our hotel. On the way, a couple of people came out of their stores and hollered to Larry that they had seen him on TV.

"Hey, Santa, you looked great."

When we reached Rockefeller Center, there were thousands of school children on a field trip. They grabbed Larry's sleeve or patted him as he passed them. One little boy held on tight.

"Santa, will you please bring me a sled?"

Larry has learned not to promise anything so always responds the same.

"We'll do our best. Have to check with the head elf to see what he has in store. Merry Christmas."

When we returned to Arizona, we had messages on our answering machine from friends, who had seen the show. Instead of looking pleased, Larry looked glum.

"What's the matter with you?"

"I wish I could have seen myself on television."

I walked toward the television set and turned it on, while I rewound the tape.

"Here you go, Santa."

Larry was so pleased with himself that we had to show that tape to every guest who visited us for months following his debut appearance. What a ham he is.

In the months following his discharge from the hospital, Larry's health steadily improved. He would never regain the stamina he had once had before his surgery, however, and he continued to have episodes of tiredness and weakness. It was as if his body gave out on occasion without warning. To get reenergized, he takes a nap every day as he learned to do in kindergarten. He takes powdered formula vitamins to supply what he might lose in digestion, goes on walks to maintain his strength and eats healthy foods.

As he achieved relative wellness, Larry began to question why God turned him away when he said he was ready to die. God told him when they met during Larry's toughest week in the hospital that it wasn't his time to go. It had been the turning point in Larry's survival. As he pondered what he had experienced the previous ten months, Larry questioned his mission on earth. I've often thought it was his reward for selfless acts of heroism. The additional time granted provided more years on earth for him to enjoy his family and watch his grandchildren grow. Viet Nam was a soldier's story. He was recognized for his heroism, but Larry had considered it part of his job.

The first time I witnessed his quick response to a crisis was April 1, 1970 the month after he returned from Viet Nam. We were driving to California to visit his high school buddy, Jim Grywalski and his wife and to see my high school friend, Linda Brady and her husband. We were ten miles east of Desert Center on Interstate Ten. There was nothing but desert landscape fifty miles in one direction and forty miles in the other. Our car broke down. It simply stopped working. Larry got out of the car and kicked the tires, which was the extent of his mechanical ability. We were only there a few minutes when two young men in a big one-ton truck full of slate they had gathered and a trailer in tow with a small motorcycle on it stopped to offer help. One of our rescuers restored VWs as a hobby so he opened the hood and examined the motor.

"Your car has thrown a rod. You aren't going anywhere. We'll tow you to the gas station at Desert Center, but it's a small operation. I don't know if they can fix it or not."

The men retrieved a rope from their vehicle and tied one end to the front bumper of our car and the other end to their trailer. As the owner of the truck stood back to look at the makeshift arrangement, he put one hand on his hip and scratched his head with the other.

"This is going to be tricky and not real safe, but if we go slow enough, you should be able to see around our trailer."

Larry and I were amazed at their kindness. Larry rode in our Volkswagen to steer as they pulled us. We agreed that I would ride in the cab with them. It didn't occur to me that I would be in peril with the strangers, but Larry had some trepidation. Larry was a deputy sheriff at the time and had his gun in our car. He pulled me aside for a private conversation before I climbed up into their big truck.

"If I see clothes flying out the window, I'll shoot out their tires."

Now that he planted a seed in my brain that I could be in a danger, my heart skipped a beat. I concentrated on positive thoughts instead. "Don't be silly. They're nice men."

Larry raised his eyebrows and shrugged his shoulders.

"We'll see."

His concerns were unnecessary. They were the kindest Good Samaritans we had ever met. As we rode the ten miles, the guys and I discussed alternatives if there wasn't a mechanic at the oasis in the desert with the parts to fix our car.

When we arrived, as we anticipated, there weren't facilities for repair. These nice men offered to tow us all the way to Riverside; close to our original destination of Anaheim. They disassembled the trailer and Larry and the two men hoisted it onto the bed of the truck on top of the rock. They also squeezed in the motorcycle between the slate and the tailgate.

"You guys are incredible to do all of this. We'll be forever grateful."

The driver blushed. He was the quiet one of the two. His passenger waved his hand in a downward motion.

"This is nothing. We're going your way. We can't leave you stranded in the desert. Perhaps you can return the favor someday by helping out a stranger in a jam."

While we were at the station renting a tow bar, we heard a helicopter that sounded much too close to the ground. Larry looked up at it as it became entangled in high-tension wires and flipped over. He and another customer, whom we had not met, jumped in the man's car and took off for the crash scene. The rest of us joined him after we had the tow bar set up completed and our car attached to it. The gas station attendant had called an ambulance, but it had to come fifty miles from Indio, which at the time took nearly an hour.

The Arizona Air National Guard pilot had been ejected and suffered an obvious compound fracture in one of his legs plus he was in shock. No one was qualified to determine the extent of any other injuries. Nonetheless, Larry put his first aid training to work and treated the man until the emergency team was at the scene. The paramedics praised Larry for his efforts in keeping the pilot alive. I was proud of Larry's quick thinking and skilled action.

Our rescuers stood silently by during this entire ordeal without one utterance that we should be getting on our way. With the situation being handled by the experts, we continued on our trip with the same travel arrangements; namely, I rode in the front of the truck and Larry rode in our car. The truck had dual tires on the back of it and an inside tire blew out with two more miles to go to Indio. The driver was calm as though this was an everyday occurrence. Larry would have had a temper tantrum.

"I know we'll be able to make it to the gas station, but don't know if that town is big enough to carry the tire I'll need."

He was right. While the truck owner hitchhiked to the next town to buy a tire and thumbed a ride back, his passenger, Larry and I ate supper at the diner. We bought our driver a meal to go. Our guardian angel's time was shortened significantly as a highway patrolman picked him up on his outbound and inbound tire purchase trip. Nevertheless, it took at least three hours to complete the task. By the time we reached Riverside, it was after midnight. We had spent over twelve hours on the road and had experienced very unusual events. We were all exhausted but we had made friends with our rescuers in the process. The passenger offered the best suggestion.

"Why don't the two of you stay in our guest room tonight? Tomorrow, I can check in with the Volkswagen service center. I know several of those folks. Besides, Anaheim, where your friends live is thirty miles farther than my house. No sense in waking them up now."

Their offer of hospitality overwhelmed us. We accepted. In the morning, we met the man's wife before she left for work. She thought the whole situation was bazaar, but she should have been with us the day before. As promised, our host called the dealership, who promised our car would be fixed by Saturday night. We kept in touch with our roadside Samaritan for several years, but as our paths took different directions, we eventually lost track of one another.

The rest of our weekend was also filled with April fool's surprises. On our return from picking up our repaired car, we passed a station wagon stopped alongside the highway. The motor was on fire. We screeched to a halt to help them. The man had thrown dirt from the ground on the shoulder of the road onto the ignited motor without much success.

Jim Grywalski, Larry's friend whom we were visiting, followed our lead. There was a church across the way so Larry and Jim ran over there to try to get a fire extinguisher. It wasn't open, but their yard was full of water from irrigation. They ran back over to where we were to get a container to carry water back and forth. All that was available was a motorcycle helmet in the trunk of our car, which proved to be ineffective. Fortunately, a semi-truck driver stopped and put out the fire with his extinguisher.

Jim and his wife, and my friend from high school, Linda and her husband and Larry and I spent the next day at the beach, where we could relax. We discussed the comedy of events and decided there was nothing left to go wrong. That night, we gathered around the table for our first fondue party. After a day on the beach, we were ravenous. The slow process of cooking a hunk of meat at the end of a long fork in bubbling oil frustrated Larry. He was anxious to savor the flavor of the steak. He picked up his fork out of the pot, glanced at the meat and stuck it in his mouth. The rest of us responded in similar fashion to one another. There were gasps of breath and hands in the air in attempt to stop Larry's forward progress, but we were too slow. Larry's lips hit the hot fork.

"Yow."

Larry spit out the meat on his plate, but the damage was done. His lips puffed up in an immediate full blister from corner to corner. At first he was stunned, but he quickly shoved his puckered lips into his glass of ice. We all stared at him for about ten seconds and then broke out in a fit of laughter. I was the first one to compose myself.

"What's the matter with you? You watched that fork in the hot oil. You're supposed to put the meat on your plate not use your cooking fork to eat it."

Larry tried to mumble a reply, but his swollen lips got in the way. I laughed too hard to be truly sympathetic.

"I think you're going to have to sip your dinner through a straw."

After soaking his injury for an hour, he was able to eat a few bites of meat that I cooked for him and let cool down on his plate. It was the last time we ate a fondue meal.

On our way home from our weekend of mishaps, we stopped at the hospital in Indio to see the pilot Larry had helped on the first day. He was still in a coma and not expected to survive his injuries, but his wife thanked Larry for the help he had provided.

"Had it not been for you, I may not have been able to spend this precious time with him. I am so grateful."

Larry was embarrassed by her kind words as he felt he had not done enough to deserve them. He had been hopeful his actions would have prevented the injured pilot's death.

ও ও ও

Another heroic event was in the fall of 1987 when Larry was an assistant coach for Jake's team on the city football league. We were at the post-season playoffs also known as the Junior Super Bowl hosted in Daytona Beach that year. Teams from all over the Southeast and Midwest came to compete. We had the afternoon off from games so we relaxed on our second floor veranda and drank margaritas with our good friends, Howard, the head coach, and his wife, Gloria.

Actually, Gloria was on the other side of the nearly three-foot cement wall, which separated their porch from ours. I heard someone knock on the front door of our motel room so left to welcome the visitor. It was the father of one of our team players, who was an executive from Japan assigned to manage one of the Japanese businesses in Peachtree City where we lived. He bowed in a gesture of greeting.

"I thought I saw Coach here. May I speak to him, please?

I returned the courtesy bow and called back toward the veranda door.

"Hey Howard, Mr. Osawa wants you."

The three of us talked for a few minutes.

"Mr. Osawa, won't you please join us on the veranda?"

We headed outside. Larry was not there. We looked over the sidewall at Howard's porch as Gloria walked outside from refreshing her drink.

"Is Larry over there?"

"No, how would he do that . . . jump over the three foot wall?"

That was our first clue. Howard and I looked at each other and then peered over the cement wall toward the ground. It was the only other direction he could have gone. Larry was climbing out of the swimming pool. Mrs. Osawa was also out on her second floor patio several rooms down toward the end of the building shrieking in a high-pitched voice a mile a minute at her husband.

The young daughter of the Japanese couple had just gotten her cast removed from a broken leg injury. She had been playing in the shallow end of the pool, but had drifted into the deep end. Her recovering leg was weak from having had the cast on for months, and was ineffective when she tried to kick. Furthermore, she couldn't swim. Larry observed her struggle and without a second thought jumped over the three-foot cement wall onto the concrete patio one story below. He dove into the pool and saved the little girl. I hollered at him at he exited the pool.

"How did you get down there?"

He looked up at me and shrugged his shoulders.

"I jumped."

We were amazed that he hadn't broken every bone in his body from the James Bond like leap to the first level.

"I saw that she was in trouble. I couldn't let her drowned."

By the time Larry had come back upstairs to our room, Mr. Osawa understood what Larry had done. He bowed and bowed.

"Thank you, thank you Mister Larry. You are so brave."

Larry escorted Mr. Osawa to the door so that he could check on his daughter.

"I'm glad I could help."

When Larry returned to the balcony, Howard and I saluted him with our drinks. Howard had a typical reaction to Larry's stunt.

"Here's another story for the book."

This was Howard's usual comment for what he considered to be Larry's mind-boggling tricks.

෨ ෨ ෨

A few years later, Larry and I were in the international terminal at the Atlanta airport waiting for a flight. We saw Mr. Osawa at a gate near ours greeting new executives, one of whom was his replacement. Their company recycled the executives every five years. I think it was to prevent the families from becoming too Americanized. When he came toward us, he immediately recognized Larry. He explained in Japanese to his fellow business associates what Larry had done and they all bowed in respect for Larry. He nodded his head to acknowledge their gratitude.

"You're welcome. It was nothing."

I think Larry rather enjoyed the attention. I was proud of him. When they left, I grabbed Larry's hand and leaned my head on his shoulder.

"You're my hero, too."

That became our catch phrase; one he would often use to announce himself on a call to me.

"This is your hero."

෨ ෨ ෨

In 1999, right after we moved home to Arizona. Larry was on a Home Depot run for materials to fix up the house we had purchased. He was behind a cement truck that was making a right hand turn at a busy intersection. The driver cut the turn too short. The wheels on the right side went up, over the curb and the weight of the truck caused it to tip over on its left side. Gasoline spilled out onto the pavement. Larry immediately pulled over, hurried out of his car and ran over to the cement truck. He climbed up onto it, struggled, but opened the passenger side door and pulled the driver to safety.

Then Larry left. The paramedics and fire trucks were arriving so he determined he was no longer needed. He didn't bother to hang around and receive any special recognition for saving the man's life. Larry told me it was the right thing to do. His heroics never ceased to amaze me.

Ironically, it was not the last time he handled a crisis situation. Six years later, he was driving through Payson on his way to our property in Forest Lakes east of there. An elderly lady was crossing the street and was hit by a car. The female driver, who had panicked, sat frozen behind the steering wheel. Her car had stalled and she couldn't restart it. The victim's legs were pinned under the wheel of the car. The accident victim screamed from the pain. Larry stopped and rushed over to the driver's side of the car.

"Get out. Let me handle it."

The driver stumbled out of her car. Larry reached over the steering column and put the gear in neutral. He sprinted over to the front of the car and with his back leaned against the vehicle; he put his hands under the bumper. With all his strength, he lifted up and pushed back at the same to free the woman's legs. He put the car down and knelt down beside the injured woman.

"You're going to be okay. The paramedics are on their way."

Another bystander had called 911. Again, Larry left when the emergency help arrived without acknowledgement for his quick efforts. He is the kind of man who will unselfishly pull someone out of harm's way without a second thought to his own safety or recognition.

Chapter Twenty-Six

&

or Valentine's Day, 2004, Larry and I bought each other four-wheelers. His was a used Polaris 700, 4-wheel drive and mine was a Yamaha 350. I questioned the judgment of these purchases, as we were fifty-eight years old at the time. While Larry could manage practically anything he tried to ride, I had already proved myself as a ground magnet on two wheel motorcycles.

We planned a ride with my brother Charlie and his wife, Rhonda to Crown King, AZ, which is located in the middle of nowhere at the top of a six thousand foot mountain. Charlie charted the course with his GPS. We had a choice of two routes to get there. This was my first time on a four-wheeler, or rather what experienced riders call a quad. The ride was thirty miles in each direction beginning from the desert floor and climbing to the top of the mountain. The carrot on the end of the stick was a steak and a beer at the saloon in Crown King. I hadn't given much thought to the ride back. My naiveté protected me from fear and my mild adventurous spirit enhanced the urge to join the pack.

Larry on his quad,
Fourth of July

We started out at seven in the morning on a dirt road. I felt comfortable riding the quad. Larry had given me instructions on the art of leaning to compensate for the terrain. I knew some of this from a short-lived experience riding dirt bikes.

About three miles into our adventure, we realized we had taken a wrong turn. The primitive roads do not have names; therefore, are not marked. After we had ridden through a really rough, dry riverbed with huge boulders in it, we thought we had found the path once more. The trail, which was on the side of a mountain, was created for mules; not people. The incline became steeper as we traveled. As we progressed through the wilderness, the track was washed out in some places, had deep ruts in others and started a downhill slant, which required we lean uphill to keep from tipping over. My nerves were on edge. I was relieved when we stopped for a break.

"Charlie, how much farther do we have now?"

"Let me check the map against the GPS."

He studied the topology map for about ten minutes. He'd look up at the terrain around us and back at the map and compare it to the GPS until he pinpointed our position.

"There's where we should be. He pointed to a place that was literally off the map. Here's where we are. We could go back or we can try to make it over to that spot and pick up the road again."

My body was tense from the miles we had just ridden. It had frightened me some, but I tried to be brave. Besides, there was nowhere else to go. I was the only one among us who whined.

"I do not want to go back the way we came. It was too scary."

Everyone agreed that forward progress was the best solution. Rhonda didn't seem to be bothered. If she was apprehensive or challenged beyond her experience, she didn't show it. Of course, she was about sixteen years junior to me. I think I had more bravado when I was her age. Charlie and Larry were fearless. This is what they considered a fun adventure.

We had to backtrack about a quarter mile and then make a couple of turns. Each change of direction was a worse road. We were on such steep, rocky paths that I couldn't figure out what was best; lean forward, uphill (mountainside), lean back, or sit upright. I concentrated on the directions Larry had given me in order to stay seated on my quad. I didn't think the trail could get more treacherous, but it did. There was no guardrail. I was miserable and wished I were at home.

I did discover that riding uphill was easier than going downhill. I couldn't see what I was in for on the upward slant. I stood up, leaned forward and gave it all the gas I could. I bounced around, but figured if I could keep my balance I'd be okay. Larry followed me so I decided he would pick up the pieces. There was no way to quit anyway because we were too far from civilization. I was committed; like it or not. I kept up my forward momentum.

All of a sudden, we were on the downward side of a mountain. I aimed for what I thought was the best side of the ruts. I was wrong. I maneuvered okay until I hit a washed out place in the path. I bounced so hard that my hands were jarred loose from the handles and I went airborne. I said a quick prayer that I wouldn't roll down the mountain too far with the four-wheeler right behind me. God answered as quickly as I prayed. I only did one revolution and landed in yet another rut. Larry watched my entire circus act.

"Louise, are you okay? Talk to me."

"I'm fine, I think."

I felt fortunate I was wearing a helmet because it had a deep scratch in it. I was relieved it wasn't my head. Besides a couple of bruises and scratches, I was fine. I noticed the four-wheeler up-righted itself after I fell off and still moved toward the side of the mountain. Larry, who was slightly uphill from me and on his quad, was over his apprehension for me. His concern now was my ATV. He wasn't in a position to help me as he had to hold onto his brake to keep from rolling.

"Hurry up and grab your four-wheeler before it hits the side of the mountain and rolls down."

I jumped up and caught my quad and stopped it; although I don't think it would have gone anywhere else. Before I climbed back on, I turned to look at Larry.

"You're one sympathetic guy."

I stared down the terrible path I still had to travel and saw that Rhonda had successfully reached another flat surface thirty feet below me. Charlie had seen me fly in the air and had started to ride back up to see if I was okay. He had come halfway when he saw me standing at the top. Since he had no place to turn around, he had to back down the mountain. I was fearful going forward. I couldn't believe he didn't mind going backward. I took a deep breath and began my trek down. When we took a break at the bottom, Larry sensed my uneasiness.

"Here, drive my quad until we get to the road. The four-wheel drive will help you manage the terrain."

I wasn't certain if riding his bigger quad was a good thing or not. I shook so much that it was all I could do to hang on. This was our first ride on these machines. He hadn't bought me a four-wheel drive, because he thought the size and type he chose for me would be the easiest to manage. This experience taught us otherwise. We finally reached another dry riverbed. This time I blessed the boulders. I now had experience to maneuver around, over and through them. My mood improved as soon as I spotted a parked vehicle.

"Hey look. There's a Toyota Land-cruiser. We must be near people."

My cheers were short lived as the vehicle was stuck and there was no driver around. Not far down the riverbed, we connected with the primitive road. We took another break. I saw a man driving a truck toward us.

"Let's stop him and ask for directions."

Rhonda agreed with me, but Charlie and Larry, typical males, wouldn't consider that a possibility. I have never figured out why men are reluctant to ask for directions.

"Charlie has a GPS. We don't need to ask for directions. He's finding our location right now."

I wasn't impressed. "That didn't help much the last time. I'm not too embarrassed to say I'm lost."

I flagged the guy down and asked where we were and how to get home.

"You're on the road to Crown King. It's about twenty-four miles up the road."

I watched Larry and Charlie turn their backs to us, but their tilted heads gave them away. I knew they were listening to my conversation. We had been riding since seven in the morning and it was now three-thirty in the afternoon. We should have been on our way home instead of having miles to go toward our original destination. We had only traveled six miles toward Crown King.

"I can't believe we are still so far away. We've been riding for hours."

I told the man the area where we had parked our trucks. He gave us directions to get back to them. He also gave us tips on how to locate the real road for our next attempt.

"It's real easy to get lost out here if you're not familiar with the road."

We said our thanks and goodbyes. Even though they wouldn't admit it, I think Charlie and Larry were glad I had stopped the man. I know Rhonda was thankful. I also knew there was no way I was still going to go to Crown King as it would probably take us another four hours on this terrain. The drive back in the dark would be treacherous. I was prepared to head back to the truck on my own if the others had plans to continue. There was no issue, though. All of us were tired and agreed to head home. Larry did have one suggestion.

"Let's ride up the road for a couple of miles to get our bearings and look for landmarks so we don't get lost next time."

Charlie and Rhonda agreed. I was ready to head back to the truck, but went along with the crowd. The road was bumpy for the short distance we traveled. Had I not experienced the challenge we had just completed, I would have thought the road to Crown King was undoable. As primitive as it was, it was a piece of cake compared to the route we had taken. Larry was excited. This was exactly the kind of adventure he loved.

"Let's come back tomorrow and try again."

I glared at him. "I don't think so. Maybe next year."

The next day, he took our six-year-old granddaughter for a ride. She was smiling when they left. As for me, I enrolled in an ATV safety class before I made my next attempt on the road to Crown King. The next time the four of us tried, we reached the town successfully. We had a great lunch and turned around for home.

We had almost arrived at our trucks before dark, but not quite. We were on the last five-mile stretch when the sun went down. We had headlights so that seemed like no big deal until I ran out of gas with a couple of miles to go. My former Boy Scout husband was prepared, however. He had a flat gas can tied to his quad with two gallons of gas in it. We poured it in my tank and took off. I was like a rental horse heading back to the barn. My speed increased the closer I was to the truck. Fifteen minutes later we were loading our quads on the trailer.

Chapter Twenty-Seven

I t is tragic when a family experiences the devastation of losing a beloved member. I believe our family has had more than its share. In spite of our losses, we have remained grounded in our faith as it has brought us all the courage to move forward with life. It also helps us to value what is important.

The first difficult loss to bear was my sister-in-law, Sandy, my oldest brother, Jim's wife. In the spring of 1979, Sandy, who looked in good health began experiencing excruciating headaches. She went to three doctors; only one had a CT scan performed. The results did not reveal the cause. Sandy was a member of the Arizona Senior Women's Swim club, where she held records in her thirty-five to forty year age group. She thought the headaches she was having might be due to swimming in a cold pool or to a head bump. The third doctor, a neurologist talked to her, gave her a prescription for pain and told her to call him in two weeks if the headaches persisted. She died five days later, a week before she was scheduled to swim in her next race.

She was at home watching Johnny Carson as she had heard a high school friend was going to be on the show. She was drinking a cup of coffee when she was struck with one of her paralyzing headaches. This caused her to choke on the coffee, which suffocated her. Her sister found her the next evening when she came to visit. She called me.

"Louise, this is Connie. I'm at Sandy's house and she's gone."

Her voice cracked in the middle of the sentence, which made me think something was wrong, but ever the positive thinker, I discarded the notion.

"She's probably on her way up north to meet up with Jim. He's at the new house. I heard he was getting the ground ready for a garden."

Connie was quiet a moment.

"No, I mean she's gone. Crusher (her dog) was outside lying by the front door when we arrived."

I was quiet a moment before I responded. Crusher was an inside dog. Sandy wouldn't have left him out overnight.

"I don't understand."

Now, she sounded frustrated.

"Is Larry there?"

I handed the phone to Larry. I watched as the color drained from his face.

"I'll be right there."

*Louise's sister-in-law,
Sandy Walters
and her dad, Buster Walters*

He hung up the phone and put his arms around me in an embrace.

"Sandy died."

I thought I was going to collapse. Besides her sister Connie, and a much older sister she had in Detroit, we were Sandy's family. Her parents had both died when she was a teenager. She was an integral part of our family.

"I'm going there to help Connie talk to the police when they come. She's a basket case and someone needs to explain Sandy's state of health to them. I need for you to go to your parents' house and tell them what happened."

My mom and dad had purchased a home a couple of miles from ours and did not yet have a phone. I called the neighbor girl to come over and watch the boys, who were seven and three. I dreaded going to my parents' house as I didn't know what I was going to say. I knew they had company; a couple I had known most of my life was visiting with them. When I arrived, I heard their voices drift into the house from the back patio. When I walked to the door, my cheerful mother greeted me.

"Well, look who is here, Louise, our little ray of sunshine."

I swallowed hard to get the lump out of my throat. "Mom, I'm not here to spread sunshine. I'm so sorry."

I started to cry, which invoked an immediate response from my mother, who stood to console me.

"What's the matter?"

I gently pushed her away from me and back toward her chair. "You're going to need to sit down. Connie called and found Sandy. She must have died late last night."

My mother stumbled as she sat down, but managed to make it to the seat of the chair.

"Oh my God. I can't stand it."

In addition to her beloved daughter-in-law, Sandy was her secretary at her real estate office and her dear friend.

"We have to get word to Jim. Larry is at their house now to see what he can do. Why don't you all come to our house where we have a phone and can call the rest of the family?"

My ever stoic, father, took charge of my mother from there and brought her to our house. Their friends stayed behind. As soon as I arrived home, I started making calls to the rest of my siblings. Everyone, including Jim, who had been up north an hour and a half away, gathered at our house. He brought his young sons, Jimmy, who was sixteen, and Michael, who was thirteen, with him.

Because she was alone when she died and because the coffee had spilled on her, which at first glance looked like dried blood, she was taken to the coroner's office where an autopsy was performed. It revealed an operable edema on the front of her brain. She was thirty-eight years old.

Jim took his sons into our bedroom to console them. Our son, Jason, age seven, joined them for a little while. He listened as his uncle counseled with his children, but finally spoke up.

"Uncle Jim. I have a question."

Jim loved little kids and considered this not to be an intrusion.

"What is it Jason?"

"Who gets all the money?"

This innocent question from a child, whose father was in the insurance claims business and must have been paying attention to some conversations, broke the ice of a horrific night. Jim put his arms around Jason.

"I don't know buddy. I guess we'll have to figure that out in time."

Three years later, in 1982, my brother Jack's oldest son, Jackson, age eighteen, and some friends were going to float the Salt River on inner tubes. Jackson rode in the back of the truck with the tubes. The driver hit a bump in the road and Jackson flew out of the pick-up. He skidded one hundred and fifty feet on his face. It cracked open his skull. Our family gathered at the hospital and waited for the hours to pass while Jackson was in surgery. The doctor finally came into the waiting room. My brother stood to greet him. The doctor put his hand on Jack's shoulder.

"I've managed to save his life, but I cannot guarantee his quality of life."

Jack's first wife, Judy, sobbed. We hugged one another happy for the news that he was alive unaware of what the quality of life actually meant. For the next six months, he was in a comatose state. When we visited, we all talked to him as if he were awake. He had begun to move around in his bed a lot so the hospital created a playpen effect on the floor. His friends would crawl in with him and hold him and talk to him and sing to him. One day he woke up. He was with his friends when it happened. He knew who his friends were. It took a while for him to verbalize words, but he tried. The first time he spoke one of their names they screamed with excitement and pushed the call button. The nurse answered immediately.

"Is something wrong?"

She could barely understand them as they were laughing and crying at the same time.

"Jackson woke up."

The nurse ran into his room. When she saw him, she cheered. He didn't remember her. He had intensive physical and language therapy for months thereafter.

The long-term effects have been difficult, however. He has no short-term memory and is legally blind. He can remember parts of his life before the accident; especially songs and numbers enough to count. He cannot, however, take care of himself, therefore, lives with a caretaker. He is proud that he can work for a company that caters to impaired employees. He counts out pieces of a product and packs them. Though his life is the same every day, he's satisfied with his contribution. He doesn't understand enough to be unhappy. His caretaker, a music lover like Jackson, takes him to the summer outdoor concerts in the town where they live. When the singers belt out their classic rock and roll songs, Jackson sings along with them remembering every word.

Andrea Walters

The day after Christmas in 2004 Larry, our son, Jason and I were at Charlie and Rhonda's cabin in Forest Lakes. Jack and Andrea were also there. We all went out for breakfast. While dining, we decided to go for a ride down the Young Road to the fish hatchery on our four wheelers. By the time we arrived back at the cabin, Jack had decided he was too tired to go for a ride. Jack suffers from narcolepsy, which is a sleep disorder. After downing such a big breakfast, he felt he needed to rest.

"I'll stay home and watch a football game on TV with Jason."

Andrea, who was supposed to ride with Jack, really wanted to go. She loved the out of doors. The crisp air and patches of snow here and there heightened her decision. She had experience riding a motorcycle, but had only ridden a four-wheeler on one occasion. She didn't consider that a deterrent. We had to drive three trucks with trailers to the entrance of Young Road eight miles away as we had an ATV for each of the five of us and each trailer held two. Jack expressed concern that Andrea wasn't experienced enough to drive his truck hauling a trailer and discussed it with her before we left. I think he would have preferred that she stay home with him.

"Are you certain you handle this?"

Andrea was an independent woman and already a bit miffed that her husband chose to rest and watch TV over spending the afternoon in the out of doors, but she understood. If too tired, he could fall asleep behind the wheel because of his illness.

"If I can drive the truck, I can pull a trailer too. I'm sure it doesn't require too much skill for the additional load. I'll be fine."

We drove in a caravan down Highway 260 to the turn off and parked our trucks. Larry and I unloaded our quads off our trailer and then helped Andrea. Charlie and Rhonda unloaded their off road vehicles and headed on down the dirt road. As they left, Rhonda waived and Charlie hollered his goodbye.

"See you at the fish hatchery. Do you know the way?"

Larry acknowledged him by raising his arm and moved his hand in a downward motion as if to shoo them away. We were all anxious to get going. In spite of the nippy weather, the sun was shining and it seemed like the perfect day for a fun ride.

"Y'all go on ahead. I want to make certain Andrea knows how to drive her ATV."

I was proud of Larry, who took time to show Andrea where all of the controls were, how to stop, how to shift into reverse and gave advice on how to drive smart. He even instructed her to practice forward motion, backward motion, shifting gears, pushing the gas and stopping with the hand brake. In spite of the automatic transmission, one has to step on a pedal on the right side of the ATV to change gears from Low to High, neutral and reverse. Further, he showed her how to engage four-wheel drive, although he didn't expect her to need it for the ride that we were taking. I watched and even inserted my own two cents when there was a break in the conversation. I appreciated the time he took even if we would be far behind Charlie and Rhonda. I liked riding on the dirt roads, but for whatever reason had a fear in my gut whenever I rode. It was probably because of the not so pleasant experience on my first ride to Crown King. I knew this ride would be a piece of cake. I wanted Andrea to feel that comfort too.

We left and tried to catch up with Rhonda and Charlie, though we didn't have high expectations of success. We made our turn about a mile down the road. The ground was rough as we drove over the mud holes left from the melting snow and vehicles that had ridden there before us. When we reached the dead end, we realized we had made a wrong turn. It was a good opportunity for Andrea to practice reverse and turning around. She jerked a bit when she hit the gas going backward, but hit the brake as instructed. She sounded a bit nervous as she chuckled.

"Well, that was fun."

Dennis Lloyd, Andrea, Rhonda, and Larry hike Mount Rainier

I giggled with her because I knew how I felt the first time I rode a four-wheeler. "You okay? Ready to go back the right way?"

She shook her head in agreement and smiled that big grin of hers.

"I'm fine. Let's go. I'll race you."

I turned around and got along side of her. "I don't think it'll be much of a race at ten miles per hour. I don't know about you, but I don't have plans to be covered with mud."

We nodded at each other in agreement and took off to catch up with Larry, who was about fifty feet ahead of us. When we reached the hard packed dirt road again, we turned left and drove about three miles before we reached the correct turn. Andrea had no difficulty keeping up. I'm a slow driver, so it wasn't much of a challenge for her. My top speed was twenty-five on the straightaway. She was more of an adventurer than I. Larry, Rhonda and Andrea had backpacked one hundred miles around the Wonderland Trail on Mount Rainier in Washington. At sixty-one years of age, she was in great shape and considerably more daring than I was at fifty-eight. Andrea was not only my sister-in-law and back door neighbor, but she was also my friend. I had admired Andrea since I was twelve years old when I first met her. She was the oldest of thirteen children and treated me with kindness like a younger sister.

We turned on the Young Road and slowed our pace to fifteen miles per hour, as it was a five-mile, gradual downhill ride with some mild curves. The left side of the road was a mountain, which caused a shadow where some snow and ice remained. But the sun shone on the wooded side, which made it dry and clear. We felt refreshed when the cold wind hit our faces. We continued to glance at the damaged terrain on our right. It was the result of the Rodeo-Chedesky fire, named after the mountain ranges that had burned a couple of years earlier. The damage spread for more than fifty miles. Many of the tallest trees were there, but were blackened on the trunks. The smaller ones had burned down to jagged stumps. Much of the prairie grass in between was charred. I was saddened to see all of that beauty wasted by a careless act of humans. I'm certain Andrea felt the same.

Larry led the way, I was in the middle and Andrea brought up the rear. As we reached the bottom of the hill, Larry was about five minutes ahead of me, but Andrea, who had stayed close to me, lagged behind by about a hundred yards. When the road turned to the left I rounded the corner and came to an intersection about a hundred feet past the curve. I looked back and didn't see Andrea. I stopped for a moment to look for fresh tracks to see if Larry went straight or had turned to the right. I spotted them so kept going. I figured she'd catch up soon enough to see the direction that I had taken. The road turned right again. When I got around the corner, I stopped to look for Andrea, again. I was concerned that I still couldn't see her. We were not going fast enough for her to be beyond my distance of sight. I continued on down the road and caught up with Larry, which only took me another ten minutes. He had stopped to wait on us.

"I haven't seen Andrea in fifteen minutes and I'm worried."

Larry got off his quad and walked over to mine and turned off the engine to listen for an approaching vehicle. Because the engine is uncovered, four wheelers are louder than a car.

"Why don't you wait here and I'll go back to find her. You know how Andrea is. She probably stopped to see an animal or go to the bathroom, but I don't want her to get lost. We've already missed the turn to the fish hatchery, but if we continue the direction we're headed, it'll probably be a shorter distance back to the main road."

He got on his ATV and turned around. He looked down to the ground and pointed.

"Oh look. That's fresh bear poop."

I jerked my head up. "And, you're leaving me here all alone?"

He smiled and laughed.

"You'll be fine. Remember how Andrea took a nap in the blackberry patch on Mt. Rainer? No bear ate her."

Then he took off. I waited another ten minutes, but felt anxious. I could hear no one in the distance. Every time I looked down at the bear poop, a shiver crept down my spine. I turned around and went back.

Ten minutes later, I was at the same intersection where I had lost track of Andrea. I stopped and turned my quad off to see if I could hear any noise. I recognized the hum of a motor as if it was idling. I could have gone right, down a new part of the road I hadn't traveled, but I went left, which is where I thought I heard the sound. I stopped again after I went a hundred feet and turned off my ATV to listen. I could still hear the engine sound so I got off my vehicle and looked around an embankment covered with scarred trees. I followed the sound and saw Andrea's camouflaged four-wheeler, but I didn't see her. I walked with careful steps down the side of the slope toward the quad and looked for Andrea. I called out, but received no reply. When I was about twenty feet away, I saw her on the ground hidden by the tall, desert grass and burned tree stumps.

I ran over to her and screamed her name as I went. "Andrea, Andrea."

I knelt down beside her. Her leg was bent backward away from her body, but her eyes and mouth were open. At first, I thought she had broken her leg because of the way it was twisted. Closer scrutiny revealed the right side of her face was distorted and flattened.

"Andrea, Andrea. Can you hear me?"

There was no response. My brain registered that she was dead, but my heart had no part of it. I tried to take her pulse on her neck and blood came out of her mouth. I tried her wrist, but could feel nothing.

"Oh my God. This can't be happening."

I ran back up the hill and blasted the horn on my quad until it broke and there was no more noise. I could only depend on my voice.

"Somebody help me. HELP!"

I stood on the deserted road and looked around at the forest with so many blackened trees damaged by the fire. I felt as if I was in the twilight zone or even a time warp like the world had come to an end and I was the only survivor. The air was getting colder, which caused me to shiver. I was lost and in despair.

I ran back down the hill and tried again to revive her hoping I made a mistake. I raked the blood out of her mouth with my fingers. I was prepared to give her mouth-to-mouth resuscitation, but she was gone. Then I heard a quad motor. I dashed up the hill and saw Larry far down the road where the fish hatchery must have been. I waved my arms and screamed. He saw me and sped up. My voice was shrill. I pointed my finger in the direction of the accident.

"Andrea's dead. Andrea's dead."

Larry jumped off his quad and ran down the hill. I followed him.

"NO, oh no."

He took off his jacket to cover Andrea's face as he couldn't abide to see her like that.

"I was scared waiting by myself so I came back this way and found her. I tried to help her, but she was already dead."

We heard the roar of engines coming our way and I ran back up the hill. It was Charlie and Rhonda. I held out my arm with my hand up to stop them. Rhonda saw my tear streaked face.

"What's the matter? Are you hurt?"

"No, it's not me, it's Andrea." I could think of no gentle way to put it. "She had an accident. She's dead."

Charlie practically flew off his quad and headed down the hill, but Rhonda was paralyzed.

"This can't be real."

She mustered all of the strength she could, climbed off her ATV and headed down the hill. She passed Charlie, who was on his way back up. He jumped on his quad, yelled to me.

"I'm going back to the fish hatchery to use their phone and get help."

It was a fifteen-minute ride to get there. When he returned to where we were about forty minutes later, a forest ranger came back with him. The rest of us simply sat on the ground near Andrea in stunned silence. The ranger had called 911 before he left the fish hatchery, but told us it would be at least an hour before the rescue team would be there. He explained we were under the jurisdiction of Gila County, which meant the sheriff, investigator and ambulance would come from Payson, which was forty miles west of our location.

"I'll stay with you until they get here. Is there anyone you need to call? I have my cell phone with me."

Charlie called his cabin neighbor, explained what had happened and asked him to tell Jason the bad news first.

Jason broke the news to his Uncle Jack. It was a big task for a thirty-two year old, who had never experienced a tragedy like this. Jason was apprehensive, but spoke to Jack in a soft, calm voice. Nonetheless, Jack's response was violent.

"Your father killed my wife."

Jason stepped backed a pace as he was shocked at Jack's reaction, but it was not the time to argue. He wasn't certain that Jack, in his grief, wouldn't lash out at him. The neighbor brought them both to the accident scene. By the time they arrived, there was a police car and paramedic truck at the scene. When Jack saw Andrea, he collapsed on the ground and sobbed. He put his arms around his legs and drew them toward his chest, which made his six foot one frame look small.

He rocked back and forth for a few moments and then splayed his arms out lying flat on the ground. He yelled at the emergency workers, who were next to Andrea.

"Cover her up. She's cold."

They obliged and placed a large sheet of plastic over her. The rest of us stood, helpless for his plight as he continued to scream at everyone around him. He was angry.

"Why are you leaving her on the ground?"

The lady paramedic from Forest Lakes, who had first responded to the call, walked over to Jack and put her arm around him in a gesture of comfort.

"I'm so sorry sir. We have to wait for the ambulance and accident scene investigator, who are coming from Payson before she can be moved. Why don't you go home? I'll stay here with her. I promise not to leave her alone."

Larry and Charlie helped Jack up off the ground. They each put an arm under Jack's arms and walked him back up the hill.

While all of this transpired, Jason shared Jack's initial reaction with me. I hugged Jason with both arms to soothe his hurt feelings. His body shook from sorrow and relief from pent up feelings.

"Uncle Jack didn't mean it. Your dad had nothing to do with what happened to Andrea. In fact, he was the only one who took time to give her safety pointers."

Jason said he understood that it was Jack's rage that spoke, but he was still unsettled.

"You didn't see his face, Mom. It was scary. I expected him to punch me he was so mad."

I hugged him again. "Give him time."

We had been there four hours. At six o'clock at night, it was dark and cold. The ranger had stayed with us so we could sit in his truck to warm up between interviews with the emergency service workers and the sheriff deputy. Charlie's neighbor drove Jack back to where we had parked our trucks. Charlie and Jason rode two quads back to load our trailer. Larry stayed with Rhonda and me. Because of his background with auto insurance claims and investigations at State Farm, he helped the county team to recreate a scenario of how the accident happened. Charlie came back with his trailer to pick up the last two four wheelers, while Jason drove Jack back to the cabin, where they called some of our family members. Jack wanted to leave and go home, but was in no shape to drive the two hours down the mountainous highway so Jason drove him back to Mesa.

Sometime during the post accident trauma, the deputy sheriff brought me some wet wipes.

"I thought you might want to use these."

He'd noticed the dried blood all over my fingers and hand from my feeble attempt to save Andrea.

"Thank you."

Tears blurred my vision. I was moved by his act of kindness. The action had slowed for a moment. I sat down on a rock and reality crept in. I cried and wiped the blood off my hands. I rubbed hard as if I was trying to rid myself of the awful memory. Now she was gone forever. Andrea was special to each of us in our own way. Larry and Rhonda had lost their hiking buddy. Rhonda and Andrea were flight attendants at the same airline and close friends. She was a pivotal person in all of our lives. Jack had retired three weeks earlier with big plans to travel with Andrea on some of her trips. My brother had experienced so much tragedy in his family.

With Andrea gone, Jack's life has become routine. Other than his one hobby of restoring hot rods, he watches TV in what Andrea used to call his man cave, which is a small room where his recliner is. There is a second chair in that room where Andrea used to join him. Now, it's like his cocoon; a place of safety. Larry has continued to mourn the loss of his good friend and hiking companion. It's a blessing to have people we love in both of our families, but it can also be a curse at times when a tragedy brings sheer heartache.

The most recent tragedy our family experienced was in November, 2007. Charlie and Rhonda lost their eighteen-year son in a traffic accident. Andy and several of his friends had gone to Forest Lakes to the family's cabin. One of the girls became ill and wanted to go home. Instead of everyone leaving as she had been one of the drivers, her parents agreed to meet them in Payson, which they did. Andy and his girlfriend, Hope, drove the girl the thirty-five miles down the road. The sick girl's parents allowed Hope and Andy to use their family vehicle for the rest of the weekend.

On the way back up to the rim, Hope, who was driving, overcorrected when one of the wheels of the car slipped onto the shoulder of the narrow road. When she turned the steering wheel to the left, she drove into the oncoming traffic lane and was immediately struck by a high profile, four-wheel drive truck. She and Andy were killed instantly.

Charlie and Rhonda called to check on the kids at their cabin around five o'clock. When they asked to speak to Andy, his friends fibbed and said he was outside. This only worked for the first hour. I guess his friends thought Andy would be in trouble for driving back and forth to Payson. Hours passed and there was no word. Like Charlie and Rhonda, the kids at the cabin feared the worse. Charlie and Rhonda decided they were going to drive up to the cabin if they didn't hear from Andy by midnight. The reason for the delay was that Andy and Hope had dated for two years when they were freshman and sophomores. Hope's father had put a stop to their romance by forbidding Hope to date Andy. He considered Andy to be a fine young man, but thought they were too young to be so serious. Since they hung around with the same group of friends, they still saw each other, but on a casual basis.

Before they left for this trip, Hope had shared with her mother that she still loved Andy and wanted to marry him. Since they had both graduated from high school the young lovers were allowed to date once more. Both sets of parents prayed they were spending those hours talking about taking their relationship to the next level as they checked in with one another to see if either had heard from one of the children.

At fifteen minutes past midnight, the doorbell rang. Charlie and Rhonda held onto one another and then opened the door. Two policemen stood on the other side of the threshold. One of them extended his hand to shake Charlie's and introduce himself.

"I'm sorry I have bad news."

As we had done before, Charlie called me and I called my brothers to tell them about Andy. Larry and I got out of bed, dressed and drove to Charlie's house to be with him. Jack showed up a few minutes later. Jim was in Oklahoma, where he lived. We decided not to call my mother until in the morning.

Rhonda's family also gathered at their house. We all sat around and mourned the loss of this gentle soul. I accompanied Charlie and Rhonda to make funeral arrangements at the church. They asked me to read the First Reading at the ceremony. I was honored. They chose First Corinthians 13.4. It was the same passage I had included in the eulogy I gave for my sister.

When folks were invited to say a few words about Andy, my mother rose and told an upbeat story about Andy and the two imaginary friends he had when he was little. It was what we all needed to lighten our heavy hearts. It gave me inspiration to tell a story too. When Andy was little, his imaginary friends' names were Jason and Alex. He told many tales about them. On one of his birthdays, Jack and Andrea decided to play a trick on Andy. They sneaked a card on the table and signed it from the two boys. When Andy opened the card, a dollar bill fell out. Rhonda read him the words and when she told him whom it was from, his eyes got real big. Then a grin flashed on his face.

"Yeah, well how come two kids only gave me one dollar?"

He couldn't be outdone. After I told that story and the people laughed, I walked over and picked up a vase with two rosebuds and posed the question.

"If Jason and Alex weren't real, how come they sent these roses?"

While I hadn't really planned to say anything at the funeral, I did send the roses. I wanted Andy's spirit to know that everyone loved him.

Larry has been my rock throughout all of these tragedies. It's not that he is stoic; rather, he's empathetic. It has been comforting to be able to share feelings between one another.

Chapter Twenty-Eight

In the course of writing this book, I wanted to include the picture Larry tore out of the *Playboy* magazine when he was in Viet Nam. I thought the visual would be more powerful. I knew I would need permission so I searched online for Gahan Wilson, the cartoonist. I succeeded in finding his website and was excited when I discovered a place to contact him.

I sent an email with my request and received an immediate response from the website administrator. He was equally enthused that Larry still had an original cartoon from the March, 1969 magazine. When I explained the circumstances surrounding why Larry still had the cartoon, he asked if I could scan it and send him a copy. It was fragile, but I placed it in a cellophane sleeve, which did the trick. He posted it on his website along with an original draft of paragraphs from my book. He also advised me that *Playboy* owned the rights and he couldn't give me permission to reprint it.

Throughout this book, I have explained that Larry is no ordinary fellow. No matter how small an incident might be to one person, it becomes an escapade, adventure or embellishment if my husband is involved. This event was no different. In an email thanking me for my contribution to Mr. Wilson's website, the administrator asked if Larry would be interested in being interviewed for a documentary on the life and works of Gahan Wilson. It took me two seconds to know the response, but I asked Larry anyway.

"So, Dahling, would you like to be in the movies?"

Larry stopped whatever he was doing and looked at me as though I was nuts.

"What are you talking about?"

I explained what had transpired and watched Larry's face transform from a furrowed brow quizzical look to a full-face grin.

"Does a bear shit in the woods?"

Larry was never one to mince words.

"Okay, I'll tell them yes."

I went back to my computer and sent his agreement. I received instructions back on who would be contacting us for filming. Steven-Charles Jaffe was the producer from Hollywood who called. He was a most down to earth gentleman. Steven and his cameraman flew from Los Angeles to Phoenix to film Larry. When Larry greeted them at our front door, he looked over their shoulders and behind them as if expecting something more. Steven looked back over his shoulder to see what else was back there.

"What are you looking at?"

Larry, quick wit that he is, replied.

"I'm looking for the paparazzi."

The two gentlemen laughed and the ice was broken. They immediately went to the business of shooting a scene. So as not to make Larry nervous, I went back to work in my home office. After an hour-long conference call, I crept back into the dining room in time to see the film crew packing up their cameras.

"Well, how did Larry do?"

Steven looked up from his job at hand.

"He was great."

Larry's excitement elevated at the compliment.

"My wife is writing a book about me. If you want to produce it, I'd like Brad Pitt to play me and Angelina Jolie to play my wife."

Steven looked at me dressed in my sweats and tee shirt and smiled. I returned his kindness with a grin.

"She and I look so much alike."

He laughed and told me he'd check in with them to see their availability. To ensure he knew we were joking, I turned the conversation to a more serious subject.

"Did Larry tell you he won a Bronze Star with a V for valor that same day he tore out the cartoon from the magazine?"

I had Steven's attention.

"No. He left that out."

"Well, that's the first time he's ever been humble."

Steven was intrigued.

"Do you still have it?"

"Sure. It's in a frame in his office. Want to see it?"

He immediately reopened his packed case and took out his movie camera.

"You bet I do."

He followed Larry into his office that looks like a shrine of his life with all of the memorabilia he has in there. Steven took shots of the medal and thanked us for sharing.

"Larry, you really did do a great job and I want to thank you for participating as does Mr. Wilson."

He gave Larry a folder and in it was a signed lithograph of the cartoon. He felt honored.

"Wow, this is great. I love it."

As we walked toward the door to say our farewells, Steven told us he'd let us know when the documentary was released. It is now finished and in the can as they say it. *Gahan Wilson, Born Dead and Still Weird* is on the market for release. You'll find Larry as the spokesman for the famous, "I Think I Won" cartoon that many Viet Nam vets identified with during the conflict; war as we called it.

Larry and I had spent a wonderful twelve days in Italy in May 2007, where we traveled with my cousin, Nancy and her husband, Bucky Sparks. We spent three days in Rome, four days in Siena, three days in the *Cinque Terre*, one day in Florence and two days in Venice. We returned to Rome and left from there for the United States.

My favorite city was Siena. Nancy had found a bed and breakfast online called *Fonte de Tufi*, which was a renovated farmhouse a mile out of the city. I think one reason for my fondness was that we stayed here four nights, which meant we didn't have to pack and unpack. Our proprietor was a delightful young woman named, Gabriella. She was studying English for an exam to earn credentials in her travel agent part time position and was thrilled to practice on us. Further, she was most helpful in arranging tours that suited our needs.

We were able to travel to Assisi from this location on a ninety minute bus trip each way. Our bus driver looked like Al Pacino, but spoke no English. He was able to communicate to us where he'd pick us up promptly at five in the evening to go back to Siena. We had also signed up for a Chianti tour before leaving the United States. Our guide was Roberto of Tours by Roberto. It was like taking a ride with a history professor. His English was excellent as he had lived in the US for five years and was married to an American. The Tuscany countryside looked like a patchwork quilt. It was spectacular.

The *Cinque Terre* was five colorful, quaint cities along the coast of the Mediterranean Sea. We had taken a train from Siena to Riomaggiaore, the first city where we had a hotel booked. Even though I thought I had thoroughly read Rick Steves' book recommendations for our itinerary in Italy, I missed the part where he warned the trains were so long that one might have to disembark in the dark tunnel. That's exactly where we were and missed the announcement. We road all the way to the fifth city and took another train back.

We were anxious to see each of the five villages even though we knew we couldn't spend much time in any of them. There were three modes of transportation; the train, a boat or walk on a foot path around and over the mountains. We walked from the first city to the second. The path to the third city was under construction so we opted for a boat ride to the fourth city where we wanted to attend the open market and have lunch. Nancy and Bucky, younger with more stamina than we, also walked from Vernazza, where we ate, to Monterosso, where the beach was. It was supposed to be the most difficult hike between the cities. Larry and I took the boat and went to the beach, where we rented lounge chairs. We had a bottle of wine, some cheese, the sun and the sea. We were at Italian coast heaven. However, after being separated from our travel companions for three hours, I began to worry.

"Do you think they have encountered some trouble?"

Larry was so content with his surroundings that he hadn't a care in the world.

"They're fine. If they don't catch up with us, we'll see them tonight at the hotel."

As we had this conversation, I watched the pedestrian path high above the beach and spotted Bucky. I called out and waved to him. He made his way to us. His face was beat red and he was sweating.

"Hot walk?"

I offered him a drink of our beverage, which he accepted and drank greedily.

"It was worse than that. We didn't have enough water and we didn't have any money with us to buy some."

I reminded him that our mutual fund pool that we used for dinners was in the lower pocket of his Bermudas. He felt in there and collapsed back on the lounge where he sat.

"What a bummer. I forgot I had this."

Larry suggested he go for a swim and cool off, but warned him first.

"The water is frigid."

He agreed to do that as soon as he located Nancy, who had stopped at a restroom near the beach.

The last leg of our itinerary was Venice. I had tried to study a city map given to me by a friend, but it looked overwhelming with its crowded blocks of buildings. I had the romantic notion of riding in a gondola and I knew from what I had read about the hand blown Murano glass that I wanted to go to that island. The first thing we did after our train arrived; was to call our hotel to get directions. She told us, it was a short walk from the station. That would have been a true statement had her English interpretation been correct.

"Go out the front door and turn left. You'll see a bridge over the canal. We're the first left across the bridge."

Nancy, Bucky, Larry and I hauled our roller bags and other baggage, which were becoming heavier from the gifts we'd purchased over the previous eleven days.

We saw the bridge right away and were pleased with its close proximity as it was a short block away. As we walked over the bridge, our bags clunked on each of the small steps up one side and down the other. I slowed my pace as I complained.

"I swear. Is everything in Italy *uppa*? It was a term Nancy and I adopted after the second set of stairs we climbed on one of our tours."

It was well into the eighty degrees temperature-wise that afternoon. Beads of sweat rolled down my face and stung my eyes. I noticed that Larry looked miserably hot as well. We were anxious to shed our baggage so that we could see Venice before nightfall as we only had one and a half days in this city. We took the first left after we crossed the bridge and no hotel. We tried the second left and the third. We had no luck. Each time was a dead end and the buildings appeared to be personal housing. A server from a restaurant stood in the lane leaning against the restaurant door, smoking a cigarette.

He was a pleasant looking Italian man with dark hair and dark eyes. He wore the uniform of black pants and white shirt with the sleeves rolled up and a black vest. I had noticed him the first time we passed him on our attempt at our final left turn. When we turned around and came back toward him, I stopped for more directions.

"*Buona Sera, Signore*, do you happen to know where the Hotel Swiss Alpena Edelweiss is located?"

He smiled as he stifled a chuckle; probably at my feeble attempt to speak Italian.

"*Si, signora*. It is just across the bridge and to your right."

The four of us stood there and stared at one another.

"*Grazie, signore*."

"Okay, you guys, let's go *uppa againa*."

Sure enough, he was correct. It was down a street so narrow that we could barely walk two by two and was past the bridge; not across the bridge. When we arrived, Nancy explained to the receptionist that across the bridge to Americans meant to walk over it.

"Perhaps the next time an American calls to ask you directions, you might want to use the word past the bridge."

I don't know if she appreciated Nancy's lesson in English, but the rest of us nodded our heads in agreement.

We took our luggage to our room, which we were all sharing. It was a huge room with big windows that were standing open. The white, insubstantial curtains fluttered in the small breeze. The wood floor was clean and cool. There was a small window air-conditioning unit that did not go unnoticed by Larry and Bucky, who were pleased for the respite from the heat. There were three beds; one double and two singles. We had shared a room for two nights in Rome. It was Larry's and my turn to share a bed. We deposited our suitcases and headed out for a walk.

We wanted to investigate where we should dine that evening, what we wanted to see the next day and how we were going to get there. We were relieved that our hotel was convenient to the boat taxis and the train station. After reading the outside menus of several restaurants, we determined nothing was going to be inexpensive and probably out of our budget range, but it was the end of our trip so didn't stress out about it. We went back over the bridge (*uppa* and *downa*) and ate at the place where we had received directions earlier. Besides, we had noticed it seemed to have plenty of patrons and deduced the food must be good.

Once inside, we realized the many patrons were just a reflection of the mirrored wall on one side of the dining room. It didn't matter, the food was good and we were hungry. Our server, not the one we originally met, tried to be clever in his communication, but failed miserably. Instead, he seemed like a smart aleck to us. We had learned to ignore the service in Italy because it was generally terrible. It was very slow and not too attentive. We grumbled to ourselves, but decided it was because Americans all ate too fast, us included and we caused our own disappointment in the service.

After dinner, we went back over the bridge, but took a break at the top. We stayed there a long time watching the boats and boat taxis and the people, but especially to see what we could of the sun setting. The reflections on the dirty canal water made it seem clean and enchanting.

The next morning, we rose early and took a boat taxi to Murano Island. As soon as we arrived, we were hustled away by a couple of men, who promised the best glass blowing demonstration on the island. We were ushered into a room with several other people from the boat. We stood so close to each other, our bodies touched. There were two rows; I was near the end of one. Between the heat of the three glass ovens and the body warmth from my neighbors, I became overheated. I stepped out of line to put my face near a vent from an air-conditioner. I spotted a door that led to a showroom, walked over to it and stepped inside. It was so much cooler in there. I was immediately joined by a sales person who rushed from one side of the demonstration room to follow me into the sales room.

"Excuse me, *signora*; this room is not yet available to visit."

I knew he must have thought I was there to steal something, but I was not going back into the hotter room. I stood my ground and confronted him.

"I'm too hot to watch the glass blowing. I've seen it before in the US and right now I need cool air. If you're concerned about my being in here alone, I'll gladly leave by the front door."

He was more interested in my spending money than my comfort, but offered an alternative.

"Perhaps you'd like to follow me to our other showroom where it is equally cool."

I followed him and perused the store while being closely watched by the sales staff. It wasn't long until Nancy, Bucky and Larry joined me. I bought some trinkets, but passed on the big pieces as they were too expensive.

The four of us sauntered down the walkway toward where the boat taxis were located. We marveled at the clever way goods were carried by boat and delivered to their recipients. For example, there was a building being demolished and a man pushing a wheelbarrow hauled all of the debris to a boat. Nancy, not one to mince words nudged me.

"Man, how would you like to have that job? Haven't they heard of trucks?"

"I'm sure they have, but they'd have to haul them over here on barges."

Bucky and Larry were much more impressed by the boat moving a family's belongings, which we nicknamed four men, and a boat. There was also a boat full of supplies for a restaurant. We were so intrigued by the unloading process for the supply boat, we stopped to watch them unload the whole boat. They'd move a stack of cases of beverages using a foot truck onto a small elevator inside the boat. The man on the dock would push a lever and raise the elevator to his level, scoop up the stack with his hand truck and take it to the restaurant. I suspect one has to be there to observe to fully appreciate the labor intensive methodology required when one has to transport everything by boat.

We shopped in a little store hidden under a covered walkway. The prices there were much closer to our budget. Not interested in spending any more time in Murano, we took the boat taxi to the marina by St. Mark's Square and went directly to a sidewalk café for lunch. Nancy opened a gift box to show me the earrings she had purchased and discovered one was broken.

"Some bargain. I'm going back to that store and get another pair. Bucky and I will do our site seeing from the boat."

We finished our lunch and went our separate ways. Our plan was to meet at the hotel later and go to dinner. Larry and I strolled down through the streets and did investigate some of the stores to ogle the pretty glass and other goods, but soon tired of that. It was like walking through an outdoor mall with so many stores. We stopped on a small footbridge and watched the gondolas lined up in the canal beneath us. It must have been rush hour as there were several of them waiting their turn to enter the large canal. There was a hairpin turn, which the gondoliers had to maneuver to get around. During our research mission the night before, we had learned the cost for a ride was sixty dollars per hour. I pointed to a long line of boats and elbowed Larry.

"Wouldn't you hate to waste twenty minutes of your hour in line? It doesn't seem so romantic after all."

We moved on.

"I need to use a bathroom. Let's find a McDonalds."

Our experience using restroom facilities in Italy had not been pleasant. Typically, there was no toilet seat or they were not clean or they wanted money and we wouldn't have the right change. One time, I found a clean bathroom and entered the stall to do my business. While I was in there, a male janitor came in to clean. In Florence, we were craving a hamburger and went to McDonalds. While there, we used their bathroom. True to their reputation in the United States, the bathroom was clean, had real seats on the stool, toilet paper and towels to dry our hands.

We found a McDonalds back near St. Mark's Square. The romantic atmosphere of Venice vanished when I reached the line for the bathroom. I tapped the shoulder of the gentleman in front of me.

"Excuse me. Where is the line for the women?"

The man turned around, leaned his head toward me with his chin jutting out. He squinted his eyes at me and tightened his jaw as if the question had annoyed him. He pointed his index finger to the ground where I was standing.

"There's only one line."

I waited a long time in the unisex line to use the toilet. I was worried my bladder would burst. As I approached the actual open door to the entire restroom, I noticed the liquid on the floor. When it was my turn, I had to wade through the water or whatever it was to get to a stall. I was grossed out thinking what could be lapping over my shoes. This horrible experience was exacerbated by the fact the toilets had no seats on them.

I had my backpack on with personal toiletry supplies, but the space was so cramped I couldn't get it off. Even if I could, there was no place to hang it and I certainly wasn't going to put it on the floor. Embarrassed by sharing a rest room with men and disgusted by the strong smell of urine, I pulled down my jeans and underpants and squatted over the toilet the best I could. At first, it was okay, but then all of a sudden, my stream took a left turn and I soaked my jeans. I had to go so badly that I couldn't stop. I had already done the damage and hoped it wouldn't be too noticeable. I finished, pulled up my pants and headed to the sink to wash my hands.

I kept my head down so that I couldn't get eye contact with anyone. I walked out to the restaurant and grabbed Larry by the arm.

"Let's go . . . now. And, stay close behind me."

He followed me out as I had demanded.

"What's your hurry?"

"I peed all over the left side of my jeans. Can you tell?"

Never one to hold back emotion; especially, if it's at the expense of others, he erupted with laughter. That's when the insults began.

"Oh wow, you are drawing flies."

I walked on with purpose in my step. I couldn't get the stench of the bathroom out of my nose. I stared at the ground as I walked and realized that there were times when the sidewalks were covered in water from the canals. In spite of my misery, I noticed this was not one of those days. Larry continued his taunts.

"Don't look now, but there's a whole line of dogs following us."

I began to cry from humiliation. "Please be nice and don't make fun of me. I'm miserable enough."

He made a feeble attempt at accommodating my request, but his wise cracking remarks continued on a smaller scale. He couldn't help himself. I suspect he was trying to cheer me up, but it wasn't working. We walked through St. Mark's square and only glanced at the beautiful cathedral we'd planned to visit. I was still avoiding eye contact with other people. Larry stopped me and pointed out a man who was covered in pigeons.

"I bet you could do that without offering feed to the birds."

I glared at him and punched his arm. He was having too much fun at my expense. We headed back to the sidewalk cafés. When we reached the café where we had eaten lunch, I quickly sat down.

"I'll have a bottle of white wine, please."

Larry ordered a beer. I drank the entire bottle of wine myself. By the time we were finished, my pants had dried. We took a boat taxi back to our hotel and took in the sites from the boat. Once back at the hotel, I showered, washed out my jeans and rested until Nancy and Bucky showed up. Larry was glad for the rest too so he stayed with me.

We went out to dinner at a lovely restaurant that bordered the canal. The prices were high, but the service was fantastic. Even though the gratuity was included in the price of the meal, we tipped our waiter even more. He had been courteous, attentive and charming the entire evening. We also ate slower, enjoyed our meal and shared our stories from our separate journey of the day. The next morning, we boarded the train for Rome, our final stop before flying home.

Chapter Twenty-Nine

Technology has passed Larry by. At sixty-two years of age, his opinion of the Internet is that it will be the downfall of the world. Second to that would be cell phones. He refuses to carry the latter, which is of particular annoyance to me. He does try to peruse the Internet and even uses email, but not without regular shouting for help from his office down the hall from mine.

We had shared space in our last house, but when we were looking at a new home to purchase, I insisted on having my own office. The work I perform includes conference calls; a phenomenon lost on Larry evidenced by his asking me questions while I'm on a call. His space is, well, just his space. Unlike my cluttered stacks of papers and books, his work environment is neat and orderly. Further, his walls are covered with framed pictures of different facets of his life such as football, motorcycle memorabilia, and an

Larry sky dives on his 60th birthday

Olympic pin collection from the 1996 Atlanta games, which takes up an entire wall and his parachute jump pictures from his sixtieth birthday. I also have a few framed pictures on the walls of my office, but the clear difference is that there is a story behind all of Larry's. Two rooms have worked out well with the exception of my having to traipse down the hall to help him.

We are also fortunate to have the cabin in Forest Lakes, AZ which we purchased in October 2007. The plan was to make this second home our primary residence after I retired. In the meantime, its location at eight thousand feet elevation is a welcomed respite from the summer heat of the Valley of the Sun where our current home is located. Larry would stay full time if I would agree. Since I'm still working and we have somewhat of a social life, I have insisted on keeping both homes. Our wooded acre acts as a sound barrier from traffic. On occasion, it's difficult to discern the difference between the breeze and the cars on the highway. The only convenience it doesn't have is a dishwasher; something I thought I'd never live without. I've acquiesced to washing dishes for Larry and me. When we have company, I usually get volunteers; sometimes, it's Larry.

The front of the cabin has three rows of windows. Larry built stained glass windows with the help and artistic counsel of our dear Andrea's daughter, Meri, who concedes that Larry was the major creator of the project. I take great enjoyment sitting in my recliner and staring up at his breath-taking artwork. At some point in time, we plan to spend May through October here to beat the heat and simply enjoy the pleasantry of a simple life.

Once Larry went up to the cabin for a few days with our long time friend, John Lowe. They were up there mowing the lawn and doing odd jobs in the mornings. In the afternoon and evening, they enjoyed the nice weather. However, when it was time to watch the news, Larry called me.

"I can't get the television to work. It's all snowy."

Slowly and methodically, I tried to explain to him, which remote to use first to get the television back to a viewing mode. He was getting testy with me.

"I already tried that remote. It didn't fix it. I've been pushing buttons and nothing works."

I cringed at the thought of trying to figure out how to undo what he had done without being there in person. "Stop pushing buttons. That's the reason it doesn't work. Now, listen to me and quit arguing with me."

I stepped him through the process, which of course, made the television work correctly. Then he began grousing about it. I didn't want to listen to his complaints. I'd had a long day at work and I was tired.

"Go watch the news with John. I'll talk to you later."

Two days after that incident, he called me at seven in the morning. He sounded contrite.

"Uh, John and I want to watch *Good Morning America*, but the television doesn't work. Do you have time to help or are you on a business call?"

I closed my eyes, shook my head and prepared myself for teaching another remote lesson.

"I can help. Did you watch a movie last night?"

"Yes, we did."

I exhaled a sigh of relief as I expected this explanation to be much simpler. Calmly, I asked him to get the remote for the DVD/VCR player, which, of course required describing what it looked like.

"Now, there are two buttons labeled DVD and VCR. They are blue and red respectively. Do you see them?"

He was quiet for a few moments.

"Yes."

He was sounding enthusiastic like he'd had an epiphany.

"Push on the red button."

"Wow, that worked. Thanks."

"You're welcome."

Later that day, I called to give him an update on the permit we were trying to get to build a garage at the cabin. He didn't answer the phone so I proceeded to leave him a message. Unfortunately, it was too long and the answering machine cut me off. I called back to finish what I needed to say and was immediately forwarded to our telephone service provided remote voice mail. I was certain he must have been outside, raced to the phone when he heard my voice and picked up the phone as that would be the only reason to be forwarded to the secondary voicemail.

The third time I called, he answered shouting at the phone.

"Can you hear me?"

I began chuckling to myself because I could picture him bent over with his face right next to the phone base, which sits on our kitchen counter.

"Of course, I can hear you. Are you shouting in the speaker phone?"

He was amazed I knew what he was doing.

"Yes, I can't find the damned handset."

He went on to explain to me what he had been through, which had me snickering, but I had my phone on mute as it would probably have hurt his feelings to actually laugh at him.

"I heard your voice on the answering machine and started looking for the handset, but I forgot where I put it. Then I ran upstairs to your desk to use that phone, but couldn't hear you. When you called again, I ran back downstairs and pushed this speaker button on the phone."

The reason he couldn't hear me on my desk phone was because there's a headset attached to it. Rather than putting on the headset, he put the phone to his ear. I explained how to use the page button on the phone to find the handset.

"Yeah, John told me about that the other day, but I didn't have time to try that when the phone rang."

We finished our conversation and hung up. I was talking to our son, Jake an hour later and relayed what happened to his dad.

"Maybe it's a good thing he doesn't have a cell phone, Mom. He called me the other day on my cell phone and when he got my voice mail, he began hollering . . . Jake pick up the phone. It's Dad. He thought it was like an answering machine."

❦ ❦ ❦

I don't know why I'm so surprised that he doesn't catch on quickly to anything of a mechanical nature. The first time I witnessed his lack of experience in fixing things or his understanding of how things operate was right after he returned home from Viet Nam. The light burned out in our bathroom. While I went to fetch a new light bulb, Larry was going to remove the small glass globe covering the old one. When I returned to the bathroom, I watched as he tried to rotate the globe as though he was unscrewing it. Small particles of glass were falling into the sink.

"Stop. You're doing it wrong."

I handed him the new bulb, gently pushed him aside and proceeded to unscrew the screws holding the globe in place. Larry stood there with his mouth open slightly and nodding his head up and down.

"Oh, is that how you do it."

Another significant blunder was the time he was jump-starting the battery in my car. It was dark, but instead of taking the time to walk into the house to get a flashlight, he hooked up the jumper cables to the battery, had my son get in my car to start the engine while he revved up the engine in his truck. The result was the entire computer system in my car melted. The wires were charred and my car was nearly toasted. He had put the cables on backwards. That stunt cost us about two thousand dollars.

The incidents in between have kept us laughing and crying for forty years.

೮ ೮ ೮

In May 2008, Jim and Francene Adcock, Cindy Walker and her beau had been spending a relaxing weekend at our cabin with us. The most strenuous thing we did was going for a walk to my brother's cabin, which was a mile away, to have cocktails. We watched for shell fossils on the way as this area had been under water eons before. After an afternoon of swapping stories and drinking bloody Mary's, we walked back home to fix dinner. With our meal close to completion and the table set, the three of us ladies, ages fifty-seven to sixty-two, decided one more short walk before supper would be pleasant. The only sound we heard was a slight breeze that swept through the treetops of the tall pines. Compared to the Valley where we all lived, the air was cool enough to require a light jacket. As we walked down the gravel road, Francene perused the quiet surroundings.

"When do all your neighbors show up? It's like a ghost town."

"It's never noisy, but I have to admit it seems eerie with no one around. Things will liven up in a couple of weeks on Memorial Day weekend when the summer occupants move back in."

I had no sooner said that when we saw someone off in the distance sitting at a small campfire. Francene and Cindy both chimed in at the same time.

"There's someone."

"Let's go meet your neighbor."

We headed in his direction and discovered a twenty-something year old man sitting there by himself.

"Hello. I'm Louise, your neighbor from down the street. What's your name?"

He blushed and bowed his head in a bashful manner before he looked around to see if anyone was watching him.

"Clint, but I don't live here. I'm just in town for a bachelor party."

He pointed toward the cabin as he said it. When the three of us turned to look at the dwelling, we discovered eleven pairs of eyes staring back at us as they peeked through the curtains in the front window. All of a sudden, the boys ran out the front door and screamed in unison.

"GIRLS."

I hate to point out the obvious, but I haven't been called a girl in a long time. My friends and I think we're old ladies but had to laugh when we heard the word that described our younger personas. All of these young men were in the twenty-one to twenty-three year old range with a twenty-six year old chaperone, who led the charge. Mr. Big Shot, who played the role of host toward us, took off his hat and gestured in a bow.

"Hey, want a Yagerbomb shot?

I had no clue what it was, so, of course asked. He explained that it was a shot of Red Bull with Yagermeister.

"I think I'll pass."

I turned to look at Francene and Cindy for their opinion. They both were shaking their heads no.

"Before you decide, hang on."

He disappeared into the house and returned right away with three shots. We squealed as if we were girls when we saw the glasses. They were round lime green plastic containers that had a second shot glass molded into the center. Francene took one and held it up.

"Isn't this cute?"

Cindy remarked about the nice presentation as the shot was in the separate depression in the middle surrounded by Red Bull. I looked at my watch.

"I don't think I can have that much caffeine this late in the day. I won't be able to sleep tonight."

The boys egged us on.

"Come on . . . one won't hurt you."

The three of us looked at each other and shrugged our shoulders. Francene winked at me and grinned that big smile of hers as if she looked to me to see how I'd respond.

"Okay, why not. It seems harmless enough."

We each took a glass, toasted one another and drank our shots. The boys all cheered. Mr. Big Shot surprised all of us then . . . girls and boys.

"Show us your tits."

At first, we were speechless. Then we howled with laughter. When we were finally able to calm ourselves down, we shook our heads no. Cindy didn't think that was convincing enough so she underscored our meaning.

"Not only no, but hell no. "

I cleared my throat to soothe the burn from the liquor. "Are you nuts? It would be totally gross."

I could tell by the looks on their faces that some of the boys were relieved we didn't accommodate them. Their spokesman offered us another shot anyway, which we respectfully declined. We turned back in the direction of our cabin and waived as we went.

"Goodbye."

When we reached the road, we burst out in hysterical laughter. The best part is that we knew the boys were being genuine and frankly, we were a bit flattered. Nonetheless, we headed home and were still giddy when we arrived there. We, of course, had to share our experience with our husbands, who got a big chuckle out of it too. I suspect that had we not been laughing so uncontrollably at the situation, they probably wouldn't have believed that it actually happened to us. What astounded Larry the most was the reason for the boys to come to Forest Lakes.

"Why in the world would you come up here for a bachelor party?"

I laughed. "I don't know, but doesn't it seem weird?"

None of us could figure it out. We all sat at the table to dine. Half way through our meal, we thought we heard an elk bugle. Larry jumped up from the table to investigate. What he discovered were the boys from down the street. They were lined up against our fence and one of them was doing his best imitation of an elk bugle. Larry called out to them.

"Okay boys, we know all about you. Come on in and have a beer."

We shared some beer and introduced them. We broke into clusters of four or five people, who joined in conversation. It was noisy in our small cabin with everyone talking at once, but we all seemed to be having a good time; even the non-drinkers, who stood in the living room and observed the silliness. A few minutes later, Francene came up to me.

"I can't believe this. At first all these boys wanted to do was see my tits and now all they're interested in is Jim. They found out he builds hot rods."

She and I shared a giggle and I told her I had discovered the groom had requested a quiet, innocent party. The best man's grandmother owned the cabin where they stayed.

The boys invited us all to come down to share their campfire so we finished our supper and went down the street. Larry and I arrived on our quad as we had lagged behind the others in order to put the food away before we left. Some of the boys were shooting a potato gun, which was homemade from two pieces of PVC pipe about five feet in length, a barbeque starter and an accelerant is used to ignite it. Larry's attention was drawn immediately to that action. The boys were shooting limes wrapped in paper towels from it as they had no potatoes. Larry was all excited as he had heard how much fun potato guns could be from his older brother, Tom. The boys let him take a turn or two. He was in macho man heaven.

He came around to the other side of the campfire where I was sitting and whispered privately to me.

"Hey. Show them your tits and they'll give me the potato gun."

I yelled him. "I will not. AND, do you realize your pimping me?"

He had a sheepish grin on his face.

"No, but will you do it?"

I told him he would NOT be going home with a potato gun that night . . . and he didn't. The next day, he and Jim went to the hardware store for supplies and made one of their own.

Chapter Thirty

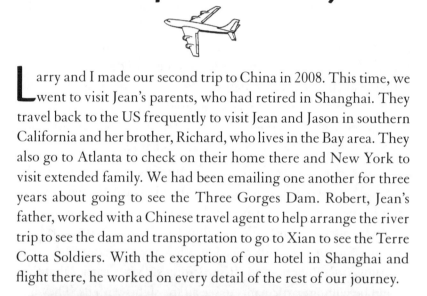

Larry and I made our second trip to China in 2008. This time, we went to visit Jean's parents, who had retired in Shanghai. They travel back to the US frequently to visit Jean and Jason in southern California and her brother, Richard, who lives in the Bay area. They also go to Atlanta to check on their home there and New York to visit extended family. We had been emailing one another for three years about going to see the Three Gorges Dam. Robert, Jean's father, worked with a Chinese travel agent to help arrange the river trip to see the dam and transportation to go to Xian to see the Terre Cotta Soldiers. With the exception of our hotel in Shanghai and flight there, he worked on every detail of the rest of our journey.

China 2008

Larry and I had watched a report on the bullet train earlier in the month as we watched the Olympics on TV and wanted to experience the fast as lightening ride. We snaked our way through the terminal building as we followed signs with pictures for transportation. Proud of ourselves for finding it and purchasing our tickets with no interpreters, we schlepped our bags onto the platform. Once on the train, we watched the LED display that clocked the train's speed. I took several pictures, but stopped when the display read four hundred and nine kilometers. We took a cab to the hotel from the train station like we were old pros. The Renaissance was a beautiful hotel and I was pleased when they upgraded our free room, which I had earned with hotel points, to the club level. This perk provided evening snacks, wine and cocktails at no charge.

Jean's parents kicked off our adventure by hosting a dinner the first night we arrived. Jean's brother, David, who had been residing with his parents temporarily, and her cousin, Jackie, a New Jersey girl, who also lives in Shanghai, dined with us. We discussed the itinerary for our two-week vacation. We knew from our experience traveling with Robert and Lily in Beijing six years earlier that they would be willing participants to see all the sights with us. They had even recruited some of their friends to join us on our cruise. We met them at the airport for our flight to Chongqing a few days later.

When we disembarked the airplane at our destination, Amy, one of Lily's friends tried to help Larry and I pronounce the name of the city.

"Do you remember eating Chung King Chinese food?"

In fact, we both did.

"Sure, we used to buy that when we were first married. It had a big can of chow mein on the bottom and the attached upper can those dry, crunchy noodles in it."

"That's right. This is the place where it was made; Chongqing."

This incredible city housed thirty-three million people. Larry practiced how to say it over and over and still spits out a Chung

Queen or something like that. It's like his tongue gets tangled. We went on a tour to see a shopping center, which was constructed in a similar style of that area. The Chinese would build several houses on top of one another that looked as if they would topple over in a strong wind. There were several stone statues around that depicted scenes and occupations of the people in the era. The rest of day was spent shopping as all good tourists should.

Our Chinese-American traveling companions raved about the type of restaurant where we were going to eat dinner that evening. In addition to a buffet, each table had a hot pot in the middle of it. Similar to fondue, but on a much larger scale, it included two cooking pots. The center pot contained hot spicy broth and the outer pot had a mild broth. There were too many in our party so we split up into two groups. We ate with Bao and Amy and left the ordering to them. At least twenty small plates of food were delivered to our table and scattered about. Using our chopsticks, we'd select an item and put it into the hot pot to cook. I was overwhelmed at the cuisine selection. I leaned in close to Larry to whisper my concerns as I didn't want to insult our friends.

"Look at all this food. I don't think I can eat any of it."

We searched the table for what we considered edible. We selected some greens and added a few shrimp to the hot pot. The shrimp were served whole; complete with eyes, antennae and shell. Once cooked, the locals bit the head off and ate the rest. We yanked the heads off with our fingers, peeled off the shell and then ate what was left. It took us much longer, but the time spent made us feel like we were eating more. Larry pointed to the fat noodles.

"Let's try that."

I was in agreement so we added the noodles to the mild boiling broth. We knew the spicy concoction in the center pot was beyond our palate tolerance. When the noodles seemed sufficiently cooked, we put them on our small plate. Larry tasted his first.

"They're not too bad. Try it."

So I did. They didn't seem too bad, but certainly didn't taste like anything I'd eaten before. Larry felt the same so asked Bao what kind of noodles they were. Bao smiled.

"They're duck intestines."

That's when I got up from the table and headed to the buffet. I stocked up on fried rice. At least it was familiar to me. I felt a bit embarrassed that my sense of experimentation in eating was so limited, but not having been raised on tripe and pig liver lessened my appetite. All I could think of is these folks would be great contestants in the TV show, *Amazing Race* if eating local food in a foreign country was the challenge of the day. Larry, on the other hand, similar to his first trip to China ate several, unusual to us, snippets of the food.

Amy even had her limits as one night, she warned me against trying the soup placed on the table.

"What is it?"

"Don't ask. You don't want to know."

After we left the restaurant, I inquired again of the contents as my curiosity was getting the best of me.

"It was pig's blood soup."

"Ah. Thanks for the warning. I doubt I would have tried anyway as whatever was floating in it didn't appeal to me."

Since all of these kind folks had raised children in America, they were tolerant of my lack of interest in their native country's food. I was grateful for breakfasts on the riverboat and in our hotels as western cuisine was served as well as eastern. Often, this served as my main meal.

The cruise on the riverboat exceeded our expectations. Larry and I spent hours sitting on the balcony and marveling at the mountains

Louise and Larry on Sanpan boat in China 2008

as we passed them. There were small villages nestled in the valleys that we knew had either been evacuated or were in the process as they would soon be flooded because of the dam. There were signs on the hillsides that marked the elevation objective of the water. It was remarkable how centuries of habitation would be wiped away.

We were in awe of the beauty of the landscape. A mist of clouds that encircled the mountains, but left the top peaks exposed, swept into the valleys like a waltz. The farmland that had been planted on the slant of the hills with various crops was lush and green. Our silent participation in the breathtaking views relaxed our minds and bodies. It was a spiritual experience.

As we cruised along the river, the pleasant, balmy weather took a sudden turn and became frigid and blustery. In spite of the cold, the riverboat guests crowded out onto the outside decks to watch as we neared the locks of the dam late afternoon of our third day on the Yangtze River. It took the captain five hours to maneuver through the multiple decks of the lock system. It mesmerized us to watch this process of crowding our eight-deck riverboat in among other large boats and smaller fishing vessels.

The dam, itself, was remarkable. There were hundreds of spectators on different areas at the top of the dam, which can be seen from outer space. We were like ants crawling about as we were insignificant to the total scenery. Our tour bus took us back to the riverboat where we proceeded downstream to Yichang.

Once docked, the local residents of the city scrambled to carry our luggage to our next mode of transportation. The gentleman, who won our attention, was slightly built like most of his compatriots. He carried a long wooden pole across his shoulder blades as an ox would. His partner placed all four of our large rollers bags onto leather straps and the forty or fifty something old man carried all of it up the stairs and onto the road. His workmate had a much easier job. He hailed our cab and crammed our luggage into the hatchback of a compact car.

Robert, Lily, and I squeezed in the backseat with our smaller carry-on bags in our laps. We looked like sardines in a can. Larry took the front seat, but was equally squished as our driver piled on whatever was left over to bring with us. Robert carried on a conversation with the cabbie to explain we wanted to go to the train station. I was quite uncomfortable and hoped it wouldn't be a long ride.

"Robert, would you ask him how far and how long it will be to get there?"

The question was promptly asked in Chinese. The driver held up his hand to show us five fingers, which was unnecessary as Robert understood his reply.

"He said it would be five minutes."

It took more like thirty minutes. I guess the driver didn't have that many fingers to display. Similar to the antics of the movie, *Planes, Trains and Automobiles*, we could add boats and taxis to our journey. The drive from the boat to the railway station was as scary as an "E" ride at Disneyland. We dodged buses, pedestrians and people on motor scooters as we drove on both sides of the road ignoring directional suggestions. When we passed a truck as we drove uphill around it, I gasped and then whispered to Lily.

"If we get killed, do you think they'll ship our remains back to the US?"

She held my hand for a moment.

"Don't worry, we'll be okay."

The taxi driver blasted his horn to foreworn any oncoming traffic. Fortunately, there was none and we got around and in front of the truck. Each time we hit a significant bump in the road. I turned my head and looked over my shoulder as much as I could to see if our luggage was still in the back. I expected to see fewer bags each time. We were finally delivered to the train station and instructed by the driver to walk to the end of the building front. I thought we were going to have to be extracted from the vehicle by the Jaws of Life, but with some shoves and tugs from Larry and Robert, we managed on our own.

There were hordes of people waiting for the station doors to open at the public portion of train riders. We, however, had a reserved sleeping cabin on the train. Therefore, we rang a doorbell on the side of the building where we had been advised to enter. Our summons brought a young woman dressed in uniform, who granted us entry. Our bags were sent through an x-ray machine and we had to walk through an archway much like the screening at an airport.

The attendant escorted us to a large room with several leather sofas. There was also a television for our viewing pleasure. The four of us settled into two, overstuffed, yet uncomfortable couches. The way they were shaped forced me to slouch down to the point my back ached. Perhaps it's from the piano lesson days of my youth, but I like to sit upright with good posture. The air was filled with incense that burned from a small crockery container in the corner of the room. The odor caused my nostrils to sting and a headache to form. Robert, Lily and Larry managed to take this opportunity for a snooze, but my discomfort interfered with my ability to relax enough.

I needed to use the restroom, but refrained as I hoped the train would have western toilets. Using the facilities was an altogether new challenge. In places not frequented by foreigners, slots on the floor were the only available toilets. Being overweight and sixty-two years of age, I had to rely on my learned ability from my younger years to squat. It was great exercise, but awkward. Larry had suggested boots would be helpful, but I learned to roll up my pant legs and wipe away the splatter afterward. I forced my urges out of my thoughts and turned my attention to the music that blared from the television as it was in English. The movie that played was *Picture Perfect* with Jennifer Aniston. I was intrigued to watch her speak in dubbed Chinese. After a two-hour wait, our train arrived and we boarded.

I experienced my first disappointment at the impending seventeen-hour train ride from Yichang to Xian when I went to investigate the toilet facilities. Robert helped me search, but it was fruitless. There were only Eastern toilets and no entry was permitted while the train was stopped. Once we left the station, I went down the hall to use the slot in the floor. There was no way I would be able to refrain for the entire trip and I decided to get it over with. As the train rolled down the tracks, the cars swayed from side to side. It was tricky as I tried to squat down without losing my balance. There was a handle on the wall, which I used, but it grossed me out some when I wondered if the hands using it before me were clean. When I looked down to the open hole in the slot and saw the tracks, I was horrified to think that human waste was littering the beautiful countryside we were traveling through. I returned to our compartment where the others sat. Lily and Robert, who had been grand traveling companions, were concerned for my comfort. Lily was the first to acknowledge my entry.

"Did you manage okay? I'm so sorry there are no western facilities on this train. Robert has looked in every car."

When Robert booked the train as opposed to us traveling to a larger city by bus, spending the night and flying to Xian, he thought it was an express train like the one between Beijing and Shanghai. He felt troubled and disappointed that the description of express train meant only that it didn't stop in every single town between our origination and destination points.

"There's no need to apologize. It's an adventure and this is part of it."

Our sleeping cabin on the train had four, narrow sleeping bunks; the upper beds folded up in order to use the bottom two as couches. Lily and Robert, though older than we, were in better shape and volunteered for the top. The aisle way had enough room for us to stand single file; consequently, we took turns maneuvering around the room. There was a small square table that was attached to the wall under the window. Robert had purchased a miniature Mahjong game so that they could teach us to play. The four of us had to scrunch our bodies together on either side of the table to reach the game pieces. We taught them to play Euchre, which is a mid-west American card game. We had plenty of fun learning each other's pastimes and it helped the hours tick away. While we retired early for the night, none of us slept well. We had been staying in five star accommodations on the trip and this one might not have earned one star.

Once we reached Xian and visited the museums housing the terra cotta soldiers, I felt the long train ride and lack of home comforts had been worth every minute. The rows and rows of handmade soldiers that had been so carefully created, subsequently savagely destroyed and then painstakingly reconstructed by archeologists was a spectacular site to see. They were placed with precision according to their ranks and service tasks. The taller, upright soldiers had protected the archers, who knelt at the front, when the devastation occurred. Larry, who was as awestruck as I, told me of his prediction.

"I think I would have been a general."

"Really, why, because you're taller than most Chinese?"

Larry laughed.

"No, because I'm handsome and can stand up straight."

I don't know how I manage to fall into his verbal traps so often, but perhaps it's the reason he loves me. I'm a good straight man for his attempts at humor. I pointed to the corner of the building.

"I believe you can still be a general. Come with me to that photo shop over there."

He reluctantly followed, but without much effort agreed to have his picture taken. The photographer returned a five by seven photo of a soldier with a general's rank and Larry's face. It was a cute memento of the occasion.

While we waited at the airport in Xian for our return flight to Shanghai, Larry returned to our little group after having used the bathroom facilities. He was laughing so hard, he had tears streaming down his face. One of the things we learned in our travels was to carry toilet paper with us as it is often not provided. Once he regained his ability to speak, Larry shared the source of his laughter.

"This elderly European man, who spoke no English pointed to the toilets and tried to ask me where a western toilet was. I shrugged my shoulders and pointed to the slots on the floor. He went inside a stall, looked around and came right back out. The walls of each toilet facility were so short, that he had been able to peer over them to check the stalls on each side of him. He gestured he needed toilet paper by pantomiming tearing of some sheets from a roll and rubbing his backside. I pointed to the hall outside the rest room door where I knew a dispenser hung from the wall. He walked out, grabbed the end of paper and slowly walked backwards across the room and into the stall with the toilet paper still attached to the holder. Poor old guy. What must he be thinking."

It was obvious that traveling in a foreign country with customs very different from one's own is an adventure for everyone.

Chapter Thirty-One

A fter forty years of being married to Larry, I still treasure lying next to him at night. Perhaps it's because of all of my travels. I've been on the road more since 1985 than I've been at home. I've slept in so many hotels rooms while I've been on business trips that I've sometimes woken up at night startled because I didn't know what city I was in.

Larry and I have made tough decisions on our living arrangements. We did it primarily for financial reasons, but we would be kidding ourselves if we didn't admit it was also for my professional development. I spent two years in Michigan while my family lived one year in Arizona and the other in Georgia. I flew home every weekend to be with them. I spent three years in Los Angeles, California when Larry was in Peachtree City, Georgia. These were the toughest years away from my family as Larry and I were dedicated to being good parents. We were forced to focus on our quality of time; not our quantity of time. That was especially hurtful for me. I worried I wouldn't be able to find another job if I quit and stopped the commute. It would put all we had worked to earn at risk. We wanted our children to have more than we did in our childhood, but I was concerned it would be at too great a cost to them. To our and their credit, however, both boys grew up to be independent, but caring men.

I was able to find another job in Atlanta for a few years and both of my children were hired to work at the same airline. We didn't work side by side, but I did see them on occasion, which was always fun. I was proud of the way they handled themselves in their customer service delivery. The headquarters moved to Orlando, Florida in 1997. The boys had both moved on to other jobs. I left the airline business in an effort to be with Larry, but had to work in Tampa, Florida for several months before I would be transferred out west. I knew the commute to Georgia from Florida would be miserable, but we agreed it was a worthwhile investment of time. Our firm collaborated with the public and private sector in Dade County, Florida on a new technology that would allow people to work telephone sales jobs from their homes. I was placed in charge of managing the project. My own good work ethic and talent in expediting results was so successful, the call center I thought I was going to manage wasn't required.

Larry thrives on having people around him. He has a tendency to get depressed when home alone for long periods of time. I was lonesome without him; especially, since I could only afford to come home every other week. This separation didn't work well for either of us. I shared my concerns with a colleague with whom I had worked at a former airline. He passed along my comments to another mutual friend, who contacted me within the week.

"I heard you were commuting again and I have an idea for you."

I was all ears and welcomed a better solution.

"I'm managing a call center business consulting group at Lucent Technologies and I think you'd be a great fit. The beauty of this position is that you'd work from home when you weren't on site with a customer."

I was so excited that my pulse increased, which made thumping noises in my ears. I had to take a couple of deep breaths to calm down so that I could hear her.

"I'm ready for a change, but mostly I'm ready to be home. When do I start?"

She explained she'd have her operations manager call me for an interview. She needed to uphold their hiring process and didn't think it fair to hire me straightaway. I understood. The last thing

I wanted was to be employed under false pretenses. The very next day, I received a telephone call for an interview and passed.

I was euphoric . . . live and work at home. It seemed too good to be true. It was, sorta. My first assignment was in Washington DC for six months. I was only home on weekends . . . again. My next project was in Denver, Colorado for six months. Just before that gig, we had moved back to Arizona. At first, I flew home every other weekend, but since Larry was retired, he came to Denver to stay with me. While it was a valiant effort by him for us to be together, it didn't work out well. I came home from work after a particularly long day and when I walked into our hotel room, he was sitting in his usual spot in the recliner watching TV.

"I'm bored. There is nothing productive I can do while you are at work. I think I need to go back to Arizona. As much as I appreciate our evenings together, I keep thinking of the work I could be doing on our house."

I didn't want to show my disappointment too much as it was my job that kept us apart.

"I understand. A hotel room, no matter how comfortable, is a lonely place. Now you know how I feel when I'm here by myself."

He drove home the next day and took a truckload of things I had accumulated while I had been there with him. Shopping had been my release for loneliness. At the end of the obligation, I moved home. Several of my assignments required travel, but they were only for a few days per week. We settled into a comfortable routine. At first, I was concerned we wouldn't be able to spend twenty-fours a day together after all of the separations we had experienced. While I had longed for Larry's companionship, now he was underfoot too much. We shared office space where my work area was adjacent to the desk that housed our home computer. Larry had a tendency to come in to read and respond to emails, and he frequently struck up conversations that inhibited my ability to perform my tasks. We had to learn to compromise and adapt to our new environment as our accustomed independence from one another caused conflict.

I was assigned to a three-month internal consulting job in Redmond, Washington. This required Monday through Friday travel. At the end of the engagement, I learned the general manager of the office was returning to England as his work visa was expiring. Because of this, my director was in the process of reorganizing the department where I consulted. She planned to assign the technical group to a manager in California, who would split her time between California and Washington. I met with my director in Denver, while there at a meeting and questioned the value of that decision.

"My partner and I have spent three months investigating ways to improve the customer service in the Redmond office. You have our report. The return on the investment to the company would be realized much sooner if I stayed there to implement the changes as an interim general manager."

She was interested.

"How long do you think it would take?"

"No more than four months."

Her pale, blue eyes lit up.

"That's a good idea. You're on, but I must caution you. Be careful what you ask for."

I didn't really comprehend her warning until four months later when I was permanently assigned the general manager's position in Washington. I was on the road, again, for four years. Larry and I considered moving to Washington as we both liked it there, but our roots had grown too deep in Arizona; not to mention how much we'd miss our grandchildren. Larry had made good friends in our community that was comprised of more retired people than young families. Further, with my brother as my back door neighbor, he spent much less time alone. He was in a better position to handle my weekly travel.

There were reorganizations every year. I reported to a different person each time. On the last occasion, in spite of the glowing evaluation I received, I was advised that I either had to move to

Denver permanently or find another job. Seems the vice-president of our division wanted me to coexist on a full time basis with my subordinates. The fact that I had teams working in Washington, England, Argentina, India and Colorado had no bearing on my place of habitation.

Instead, I applied for another virtual office position, where I've worked for the past four years. I still spend time away from home on occasion. It's no wonder; I love to share a bed with Larry, even though I've never been one who likes to cuddle. Larry would have his arms and legs wrapped around me if I let him. I tend to feel claustrophobic in addition to downright hot. He radiates body heat like an oven. What I do like is to sneak my feet close to his to warm mine up. And, I love it when he holds my hand as he drifts off to sleep. It's rare when he doesn't fall asleep before I do. Once he does, I lie there and thank God for my many blessings; Larry, not the least of them. Once I've rolled from side to side enough times to find my niche for sleep, I retreat to sweet dreams.

My Family

Jake and Nikki

Jean and Jason

The grandchildren—Chloe, Madison and Dylan

Afterword

Though he appears to be strong and healthy, Larry is fragile. This once robust man, experiences days of weakness and pain. The extended hospital stay has had long lasting effects. One day he'll get up, lace up his shoes and head outdoors for a walk with a spring in his step. The next day, he'll drag himself out of bed to get a cup of coffee and watch the news while he sits in his recliner. On occasion his voice is so strained I can hardly hear him speak. When this happens, I know it's time to have his throat stretched combined with his annual endoscopy procedure.

He's developed a propensity for getting hurt. I haven't figured out if he pushes his luck on the days he feels well, or doesn't have the strength, stamina and balance he once had.

Louise and Larry 2009

On those days when he doesn't feel good, I know he thinks the end is near. Not I. On cool days when we sit next to each other on our porch at the cabin and watch the pine branches sway in the breeze, I know that all of our hard work and sacrifice have come to fruition. I believe God's plan is for us to grow old together and have time to stop and smell the roses. To ensure we can appreciate the aroma, I have determined it's time for me to retire and spend these last precious moments with the man I love.

About the Author

Louise Laughlin

A post war baby boomer, Louise grew up in the fifties and the other side of the sixties, far away from Woodstock and the flower children in San Francisco. She fell in love, married her soul mate and had two children. She attended Mesa Community College and Arizona State University, but graduated from Central Michigan University, while on the road for her career in the airline industry.

Together with her husband, Larry, she built a quality of life despite the years of periodic absence when she commuted cross-country from her job to their home. The partnership in their forty-one years of marriage, and still counting, has been challenged; especially by her husband's trials and illnesses, but her positive outlook on life and faith in God has brought courage to its success.